IMAGES
of America

GRAND ISLAND

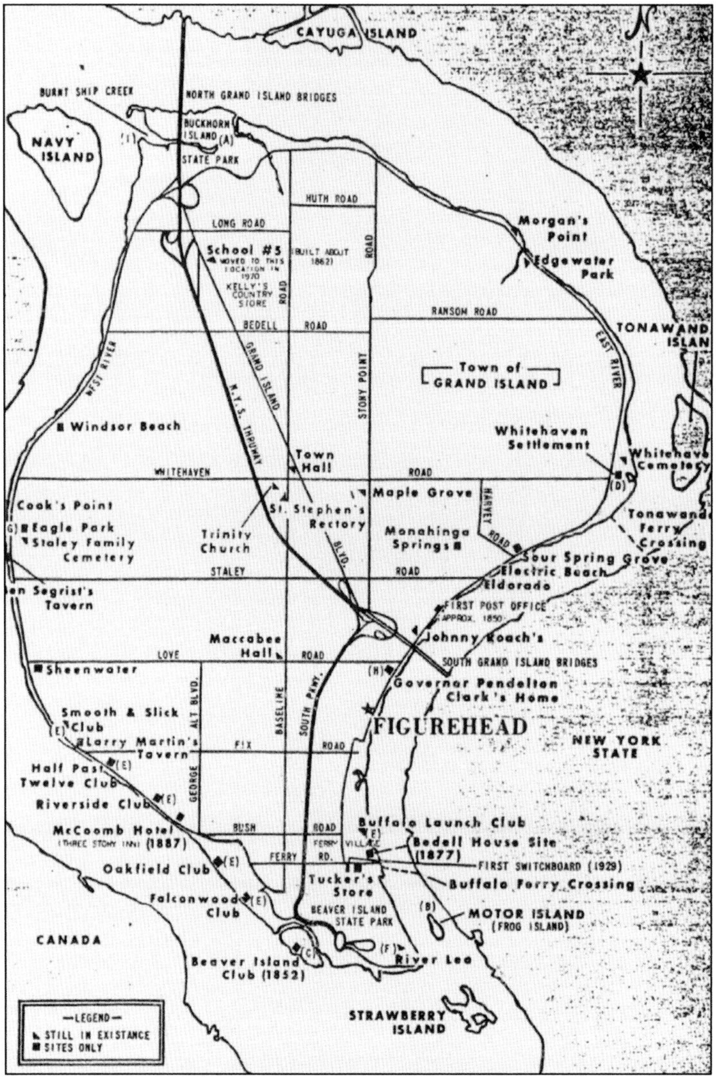

This map shows many of the historical sites on Grand Island, and the symbols indicate location and whether they still existed when the map was produced in 1957. (Courtesy of the Grand Island Historic Preservation Advisory Board.)

On the Cover: The 1935 opening of the first bridge that connected Grand Island to the mainland in Erie County on the south dramatically changed this isolated farming community. The addition of the bridges enhanced both local and tourist trade and enabled the connections between Buffalo, New York, and Niagara Falls and many of their suburbs. Four bridges now provide access to both Erie and Niagara Counties and the wonders of Niagara Falls via the Interstate 190, a part of the New York State Thruway system. An average of 80,000 cars now cross the island daily and make Grand Island a major access point for western New York and the falls. The New York State Parks provide beautiful, unspoiled vistas of the river, and recreational opportunities abound. Despite these modern changes, much of the island retains its rural flavor and provides a respite from city life for those who choose to make their home in the middle of the Niagara River. (Courtesy of the Grand Island Historic Preservation Advisory Board.)

IMAGES
of America

GRAND ISLAND

Gerald Carpenter and
June Justice Crawford

ARCADIA
PUBLISHING

ISBN 978-1-4671-2130-9

Published by Arcadia Publishing
Charleston, South Carolina

Printed in the United States of America

Library of Congress Control Number: 2013946822

For all general information, please contact Arcadia Publishing:
Telephone 843-853-2070
Fax 843-853-0044
E-mail sales@arcadiapublishing.com
For customer service and orders:
Toll-Free 1-888-313-2665

Visit us on the Internet at www.arcadiapublishing.com

Contents

Acknowledgments

Many residents of Grand Island deserve credit for assisting with this publication. The authors are not natives of Grand Island; our knowledge about the island was gained from reading historical documents and having that history come alive by talking to lifelong residents willing to share their memories, photographs, family albums, and stories they remember hearing from their parents and grandparents. The Grand Island Historical Society began the process of saving historical artifacts and information about the island, and everyone on the island is grateful to them for providing the foundation for this publication. The information from isledegrande.com, the official website about Grand Island, was also invaluable. Credit for much of this material goes to Teddy Linenfelser, former Grand Island town historian, who succeeded her mother, Marion Klingel. Between the two of them, the history of much of Grand Island has been protected and continues to be saved through their successor, Jodie Robinson, who gathered information and found old photographs. Credit also must be given to the Grand Island Historic Preservation Advisory Board (GIHPAB); they supported the creation of this publication from the beginning and provided invaluable advice.

We could not have completed this book without the amazing memory of Shirley Kreger Luther, who checked information and provided photographs, stories, and her personal scrapbooks. Patricia Frentzel and Liz Wilbert helped with old documents. Mary Cooke, town supervisor, believed in this project and helped us find missing documents and photographs. Island resident Wendy Duignan volunteered her photography expertise to salvage old photographs and prepare the images for publication.

Sharon Nichols and Barbara Zafuto not only shared the history of their family, but also spent many hours with us sifting through files. William Koch, preservationist and chair of the GIHPAB, Carolyn Doebert, and Joseph Macaluso shared their wealth of information, helped identify historical places, and provided much-needed support for this project.

Unless otherwise noted, all images are courtesy of the Grand Island Historic Preservation Advisory Board (GIHPAB) and the Grand Island official town website, isledegrande.com.

INTRODUCTION

Today, Grand Island is an idyllic suburban community located approximately halfway between Buffalo and Niagara Falls and surrounded by the mighty Niagara River. It enjoys all the amenities of such a place: shopping areas, parkland, ease of access to nearby cities and other opportunities, and the peace and quiet of settled neighborhoods. The island is approximately eight miles long and six miles across at its widest, totaling 17,381 acres. Despite development as a residential community, it maintains the natural beauty of a secluded island, with abundant trees and wildlife. The serene river flowing around the island seems a perfect metaphor for life there, but there have been times in its history when it was more like the roiling waters of the rapids downstream at Niagara Falls. Moving from its peaceful but isolated past to its current state was often difficult. Several factors affected the process, but by far the most important was that Grand Island was, in fact, an island. The island remained uninhabited until the 19th century, only used by Native Americans for occasional hunting and fishing trips. Long before the Europeans arrived, the river served as an international boundary between the territories of the perpetually warring Huron and Iroquois Confederations. Grand Island was not a main goal of either, but its location put it in the middle of a larger fight. When colonial powers France and Great Britain faced off to determine who would control North America, they drew their Indian allies from the opposing confederations. The British won after several wars, but that victory helped set up the war for American independence. Settling the line between British Canada and the United States necessitated the War of 1812, which still did not finalize the ownership of Grand Island.

By the time the line was finally drawn in 1822, another crucial force affecting Grand Island was already starting to have its transformative impact. The Erie Canal, under construction since 1817, changed New York State as it progressed from Albany to a still undetermined terminus on the Niagara River somewhere between the falls of Niagara and the small village of Buffalo. The canal would make New York City the largest port in the United States and open the whole area around the Great Lakes to world markets. Its imminent arrival changed the perspective on every place in western New York, including Grand Island, potentially a port with access to both sides of the international boundary. That did not happen, but an island in such a critical location inspired a series of dreamers who dominated its development in the early 19th century. While British and American negotiators spent years determining just where to draw the border under the terms of the 1814 Treaty of Ghent, Grand Island remained no man's land. It is not surprising that it attracted settlers who could not wait, usually known as the squatters.

Described as lawless loafers by alarmed mainlanders, these families were considered to "threaten the peace and good order of society." Indeed, they refused to recognize the authority of either British Canada or New York State. By some accounts, they considered themselves "a free and independent state" and recognized one Pendleton Clark as head of their government. They had taken up residence around the edges of the island and were eking out a meager living farming and, on occasion, cutting down some of the great white oaks that covered almost its entire surface.

They worked those trees into barrel staves to be shipped to Montreal, Canada, and then to the British West Indies for use in the rum trade. That activity seems to have been what the critics meant when they complained of the "depredations" and the inflicting of "great injury on the public property." Pressed by angry Buffalo residents, Gov. DeWitt Clinton had a law passed ordering the county sheriff to remove the intruders by force if necessary and to destroy their homes. In December 1819, Niagara County sheriff James Cronk, backed by a company of militiamen, spent four days removing about 70 farm families. Cronk and his men met no resistance and handled the settlers humanely, transporting them to either Canada or New York. All except one family chose Canada. The lone exception was Clark, "the King of the Outlaws."

The squatters were not the last to see Grand Island as the perfect spot for the realization of a dream. Once the border commission completed its work in 1822, the State of New York, now recognized as its legal owner, ordered that the island be surveyed and divided for sale in lots of no more than 200 acres, ostensibly for farms. Instead, four men, all well-known land speculators, purchased the entire island. One of them was an associate of the next visionary, Mordecai Manuel Noah.

Noah was an American patriot and political activist who regularly published his views in his New York newspaper the *National Advocate*. Coupled with his strong American patriotism was his distress at the treatment of his fellow Jews in Europe and around the world. A proto-Zionist, he was fully committed to the ultimate return of the Jews to Palestine, but he believed he had a plan that would protect them in the meantime and help prepare them for the achievement of that goal. Convinced that the United States was the only country that would grant full citizenship and equal rights to Jews, Noah saw a perfect marriage: a shelter for the Jews and a ready supply of the kind of immigrants America needed to develop its vast resources. As a politically involved New Yorker, he could see what was about to happen in western New York. The unfinished canal, coupled with the recent determination that Grand Island was part of New York, seemed to point to a perfect solution. Noah would establish Ararat, a "City of Refuge for Jews," on one end of Grand Island.

Noah set about preparing to launch his plan. He ordered a cornerstone from a Cleveland, Ohio, quarry and had it inscribed in Buffalo. In the meantime, he publicized his plan far and wide. It received almost universal derision from leading rabbis in Europe and America. They also rejected his proposal to tax every Jew in the world annually to support the project. He was not discouraged. In September 1825, shortly after the opening of the canal, he arrived in Buffalo to find that not enough boats were available to carry the throng of spectators and the official party to Grand Island. At the last minute, the route was changed, and the parade of bands, militia companies, Masons, and officials followed by Noah, resplendent in his elaborate costume, marched through Buffalo to St. Paul's Episcopal Church where the cornerstone lay on the communion table. After the Reverend Addison Searle gave his blessing, Noah delivered a grandiose speech declaring the reestablishment of the Jewish nation under the protection of the laws of the United States. That was as far as it went. The Ararat cornerstone was laid against the back of the church, and Noah left western New York without setting foot on Grand Island.

The next dream was not entirely imaginary, but it failed to produce the wealth the dreamers hoped for. Almost all of those giant white oaks remained untouched, and with the completion of the canal, they could be moved to the shipyards of the East Coast at a reasonable cost. The East Boston Timber Company bought most of the island and set up a large mill and other facilities to support the project. Many trees were cleared, but the cost of moving the timber to market led to bankruptcy in a few years.

By 1840, the state had reacquired title to most of the island and proceeded to sell land for farms. Some farmers had worked for the timber company, but many new immigrants from the mainland, Europe, and Canada took advantage of the opportunity. Creating working farms from land filled with giant oak stumps was hard work, but these pioneers were up to the task. Gradually, the population grew. Farm communities formed at various places around the island's shores. Some of the more successful farmers opened stores to serve their neighbors. In addition to sustaining the families, these farms produced crops that could be sold to people on the mainland, where the cities, especially Buffalo, were booming. To get their produce to market, the farmers had to use the available ferries, and that took additional time and money. Still, they were turning the island into a functioning community. Educating the children required the provision of schools, and the available transportation meant that would take the form of about a dozen one-room schools placed near the clusters of population. Churches with services in English, German, and Latin gradually appeared, reflecting the religious and ethnic diversity of the population. In 1852, the farmers finally were able to establish their own town government. Grand Island was a place characterized by long days of hard work, but it was still a beautiful island set apart in the middle of a majestic river.

In the mid-19th century, as farmers were still clearing those oak stumps, wealthy Buffalo sportsmen decided to restore the island's role as a hunting and fishing resort. In 1852, Beaver Island Club became the first of what would be a series of exclusive private clubs for the leading citizens of the mainland cities. Large, elaborate structures with wide verandas set on expansive grounds grew up along the shores of the island, particularly on the end closest to Buffalo. The proprietor of Falconwood, the second private club on the island, Buffalo real estate tycoon Lewis F. Allen, soon published a call for a watering place for the rising city's elite citizens. He would not be disappointed. From his 600-acre Allenton Farm at the southern tip of the island, he began to sell large plots to members of that elite group. As more private clubs were being added, so were mansions in which wealthy Buffalonians could find refuge from the summer heat and urban pressures.

Grand Island had entered its golden era. Large hotels and smaller inns soon appeared to provide regular mainland citizens with a taste of the same benefits Allen had envisioned for the elite. Every summer, they drew thousands who wanted to escape their usual lives. The tourist traffic grew even greater when a number of the hotels began to add amusement parks. Islanders had always relied on large and small boats to connect to the mainland. Part of Allen's case for his proposed watering place was the convenience of ferry connections from downtown Buffalo. When the crowds began to grow, so did the ferry fleets serving Grand Island. In addition to individuals and families, groups of all kinds soon developed traditions of celebrating in the island's various amusement parks and picnic grounds.

Ironically, as the number of visitors grew, the resident population began a half-century-long decline, from a peak of 1,156 in 1880 to only 626 in 1930. By 1900, the volume of summer visitors was shrinking, and the golden era began to fade. Improved transportation options on the mainland and competing recreation destinations took their toll. Then, in 1912, Eagle Park, one of the most popular destinations on the island, was the site of a horrific accident that seemed to seal the doom of the golden era. A huge and loudly celebrating group crowded the dock, waiting for the last ferry of the night. Just as it approached, the dock collapsed, dropping almost everyone into the river. When the bodies were finally counted, the toll was 37 dead. The Eagle Park disaster cast a long, dark shadow.

Between the two world wars, Grand Island experienced what might be considered its lowest point and then what was certainly seen as the welcome beginning of its future. The key was achieving something it had been pursuing unsuccessfully for decades—a bridge to the mainland. In fact, it received two bridges, but acquiring those bridges took great persistence. The bridges appealed to and were rebuffed by every level of government from the county to the federal. The pattern of response became all too familiar. A proposal received support, promises were made, hopes were raised, and then they were dashed when the effort brought no action. As the automobile age matured in the 1920s, Grand Island seemed to be falling behind the mainland, and its youth continued to leave for other opportunities.

The Great Depression had terrible effects on Americans, including island farmers and small businessmen, but it also coincided with the nativity of Grand Island's resurgence. Just before the Great Crash of 1929, New York State took the first meaningful steps toward building those bridges. By the time the severity of the Depression became evident, land had been acquired. Early responses to the Depression included creation of the Reconstruction Finance Corporation, the source of loans that allowed the project to go ahead. Construction began in 1933, and the bridges were completed in 1935. The state built Grand Island Boulevard connecting the north and south bridges, and completion of the bridges occasioned a major celebration.

The bridges were not the only things to celebrate. The state's approval of the bridges was tied to a plan to restore Grand Island as a major recreation area. The former Allenton Farm and other private properties at the south end of the island became the new Beaver Island State Park, which also opened in 1935. Simultaneously, Buckhorn State Park was established on Burnt Ship Creek. A parkway along the West River connecting the parks was in the works as well as a parkway from Beaver Island Park to the south bridge.

The effect of the bridges was almost instantaneous. Despite the continuing Depression, Grand Island soon saw its first housing developments spring up, and the population began what would become decades of rapid growth. Between 1930 and 1940, the population lost since 1880 was almost entirely restored. There was no going back.

World War II temporarily slowed the process, but the island's new way of life seemed unstoppable. The postwar baby boom boosted the American population and magnified Grand Island's boom. Between 1940 and 1950, the population tripled, and local businesses responded to the new opportunities. Town government and the school system had to race to keep up. The Charlotte Sidway School, built in the 1930s to replace all of the one- and two-room schools across the island, went through repeated expansions, but a second school was soon necessary.

At the 1952 centennial celebration of the town government's founding, Grand Island had much to celebrate. "A Grand Place to Live" was the slogan of the day. The population was tripling again during the decade of the 1950s. That meant more residential development, new roads, new shopping plazas, and other signs of increasing local business activity. Mainland companies moved or expanded to the island to take advantage of its location and connections to the surrounding area. There were also many challenges associated with this continued transformation, but they were welcomed. The island finally received its own high school in the 1960s, the decade in which the second set of bridges was added, along with a new connecting thruway.

Today, Grand Island still has the distinction of its separation, without the disadvantages. The growth rate of its population is among the region's highest, and the island supplies that growing population with all that they expect in the way of services.

One

Contested Territory

Given the strategic importance of the Niagara River, it is no surprise that the territory through which it passes, the Niagara Frontier, has been fought over repeatedly. First, it separated the Huron Confederation, centered south of the Georgian Bay in Canada, and the Iroquois League in New York. A people the French called the Neutres lived on the Canadian side of the river in southern and central Ontario. They maintained strict neutrality, allowing the Huron and Iroquois to pass through freely on their way to attacking each other. The fight intensified in the Beaver Wars of the 17th century, when the European fur trade raised the stakes. The Dutch gave the Iroquois an unlimited supply of guns and ammunition, and the French tried to match that for the Huron. Spread around the Great Lakes, the fighting never actually touched Grand Island, but the outcome did have its effect. After defeating and dispersing the Huron in 1649, the Iroquois turned on the Neutres, who had sheltered some Huron refugees. The Neutres and Huron fled to Wisconsin. Grand Island fell to the Seneca of the Iroquois League, who, like the Neutres, used it for hunting and fishing.

The Niagara Frontier became part of the disputed boundary between the British and French empires in North America. Both European powers depended upon Native American allies to hold and extend their control. Loyalty was rewarded with continued use of the lands in dispute. Greatly outmanned, the French built a series of forts designed to resist any attempted westward assault by the English. In this area, Fort Niagara was the key prize. When the British took the fort in 1759, the French line was broken and ultimate defeat was assured.

Removal of the French set the stage for American independence and a long, slow drawdown by Britain, which occupied Fort Niagara until 1796. As for Grand Island, uncertainty about the exact location of the border line in the Niagara River left its ownership in question until some years after the War of 1812.

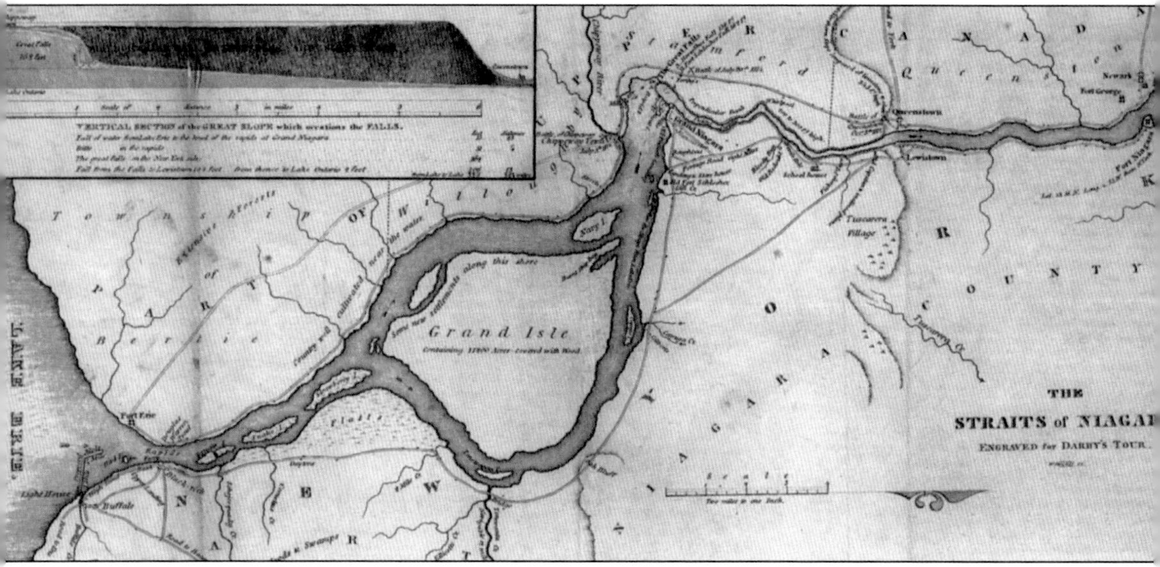

This map indicates why Grand Island was contested territory. The island itself was not the prize, but it lay in the middle of a wide, ambiguous frontier area. Today, the border between the United States and Canada is clearly delineated as a line in the main channel of the Niagara River. That clarity was not always present. The hunting grounds of the Native American groups overlapped considerably, and repeated wars failed to settle the matter. The projected limits of New France and Britain's North American colonies included a broad band of land that could control not only the source of beaver pelts, but also the water routes by which they could be delivered to markets.

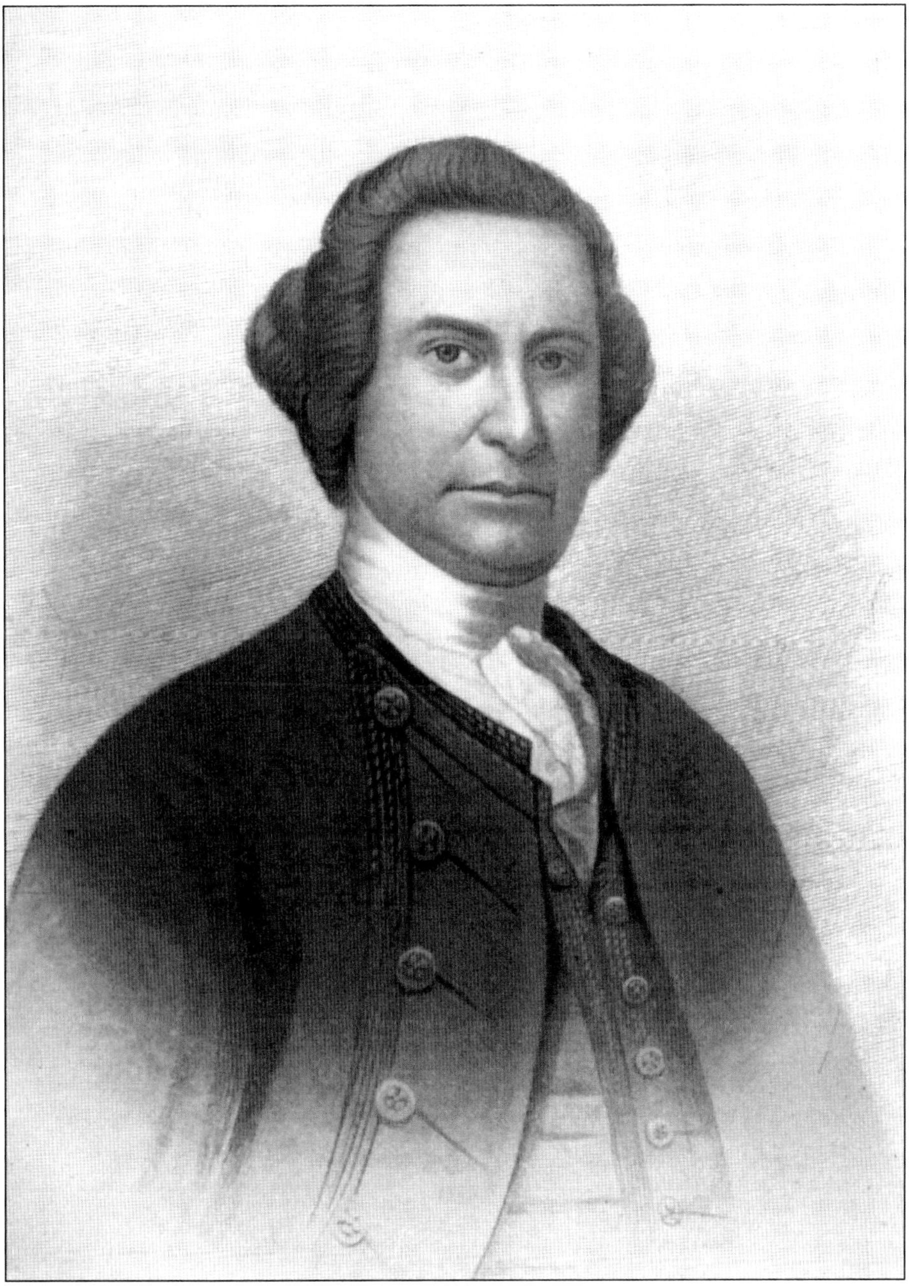

In 1738, Anglo-Irish immigrant William Johnson came to America to help develop land on the Mohawk River owned by his uncle. He began trading with Mohawk Indians, the easternmost tribe of the Iroquois Confederation, and they developed a close relationship. Johnson was adopted and made an honorary sachem. By the 1750s, he was the key to maintaining the Iroquois-British alliance in New York. During the French and Indian War, Johnson led combined forces of local militias and Iroquois warriors. He was credited with winning the Battle of La Belle Famille, considered the key to British victory over the French at Fort Niagara. After the war, the Seneca of the Iroquois Confederation granted Johnson ownership of all of the islands in the Niagara River, including Grand Island. Johnson passed ownership over to King George III.

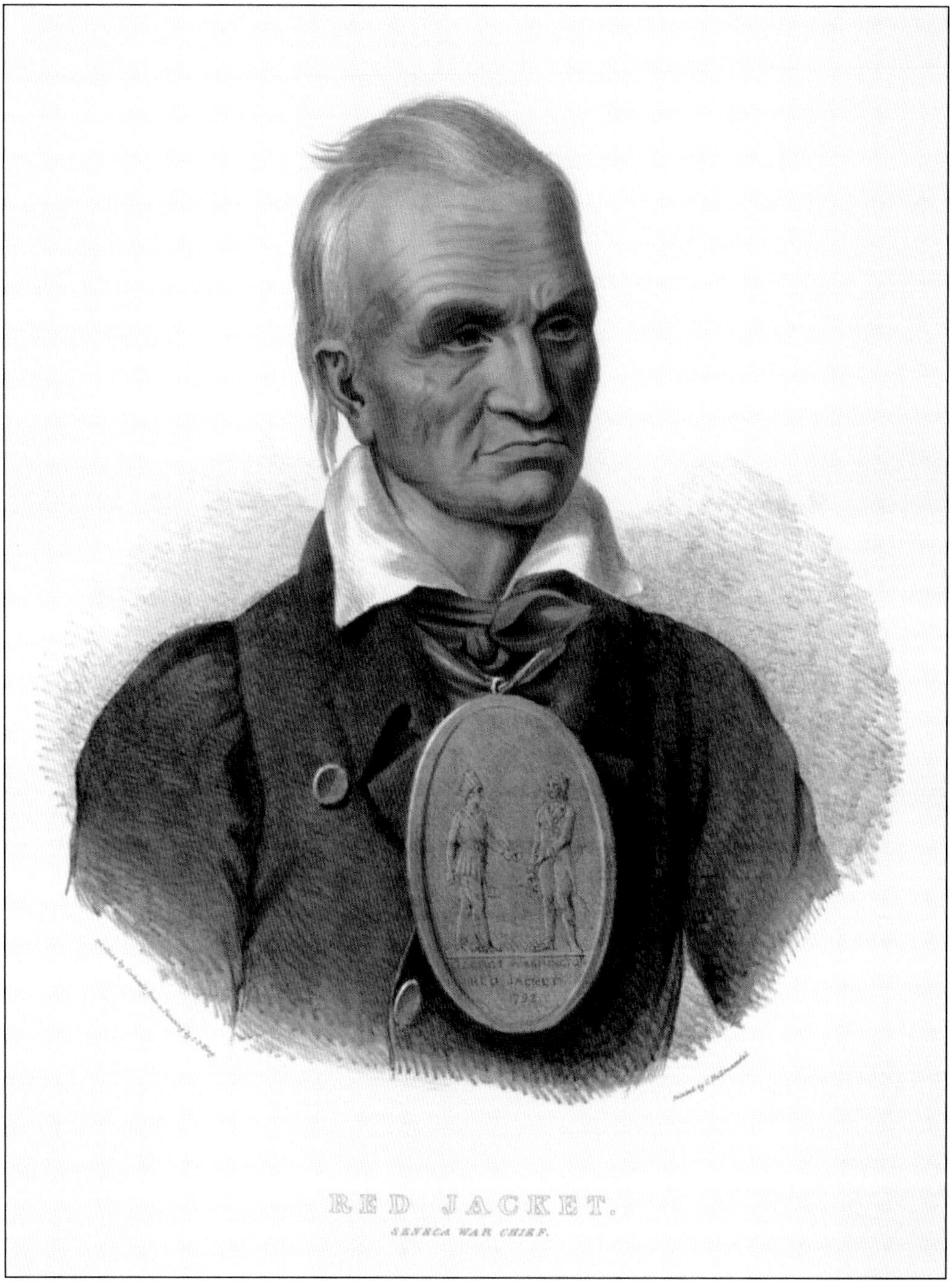

A skilled orator, Seneca chief Red Jacket often represented the Iroquois Confederation in dealings with the white man. He led negotiations with the United States after the American Revolution. As British allies, the Iroquois were due to lose most of their lands. Chief Red Jacket negotiated with George Washington and received the peace medal. In 1815, Chief Red Jacket negotiated with New York State to sell Grand Island and the surrounding islands for $1,000 plus an annuity of $500. The Iroquois had already given those islands to the British in 1764 and the boundary between the United States and Canada was still unsettled, so it was not anyone's to sell.

Two

Fantasy Island

From the end of the American Revolution until 1821, Grand Island was literally no man's land. Americans had won their independence, and the 1783 Treaty of Paris delineated a new international boundary, but whether all or only part of Grand Island lay inside the United States remained an unsettled question. That uncertainty intensified the air of mystery that surrounded the uninhabited island. One history called it "Cinderella Island." In a sense, it was like a fairy tale, especially in the early 19th century. It was a perfect blank canvas upon which a series of visionaries and entrepreneurs could and would project their dreams.

Despite New York's 1815 dubious purchase of the Niagara River islands from the Seneca, until the international boundary had been determined, ownership was also unsettled. In a sense, it was free land, or so claimed the settlers who moved onto the island and began eking out a living. Usually referred to as the squatters, they established farms around the island's shores and their own independent government, on the basis of which they refused to pay taxes to either New York or the British crown. With the Erie Canal making its way toward Buffalo, such an enterprise was doomed, and they were soon removed.

When the state finally received clear title, the way was opened for the most interesting vision of the period, Grand Island as the site of a "City of Refuge" for the persecuted Jews of the world until they could reclaim Palestine. That vision had even less success than the independent republic of Grand Island. Its failure opened the way to ambitious entrepreneurs who recognized the opportunity created by the combination of Grand Island's two most obvious assets, its thick forest of white oaks and its proximity to the Erie Canal. Although they had a brief success and harvested the trees, that effort, too, lacked a positive, lasting outcome.

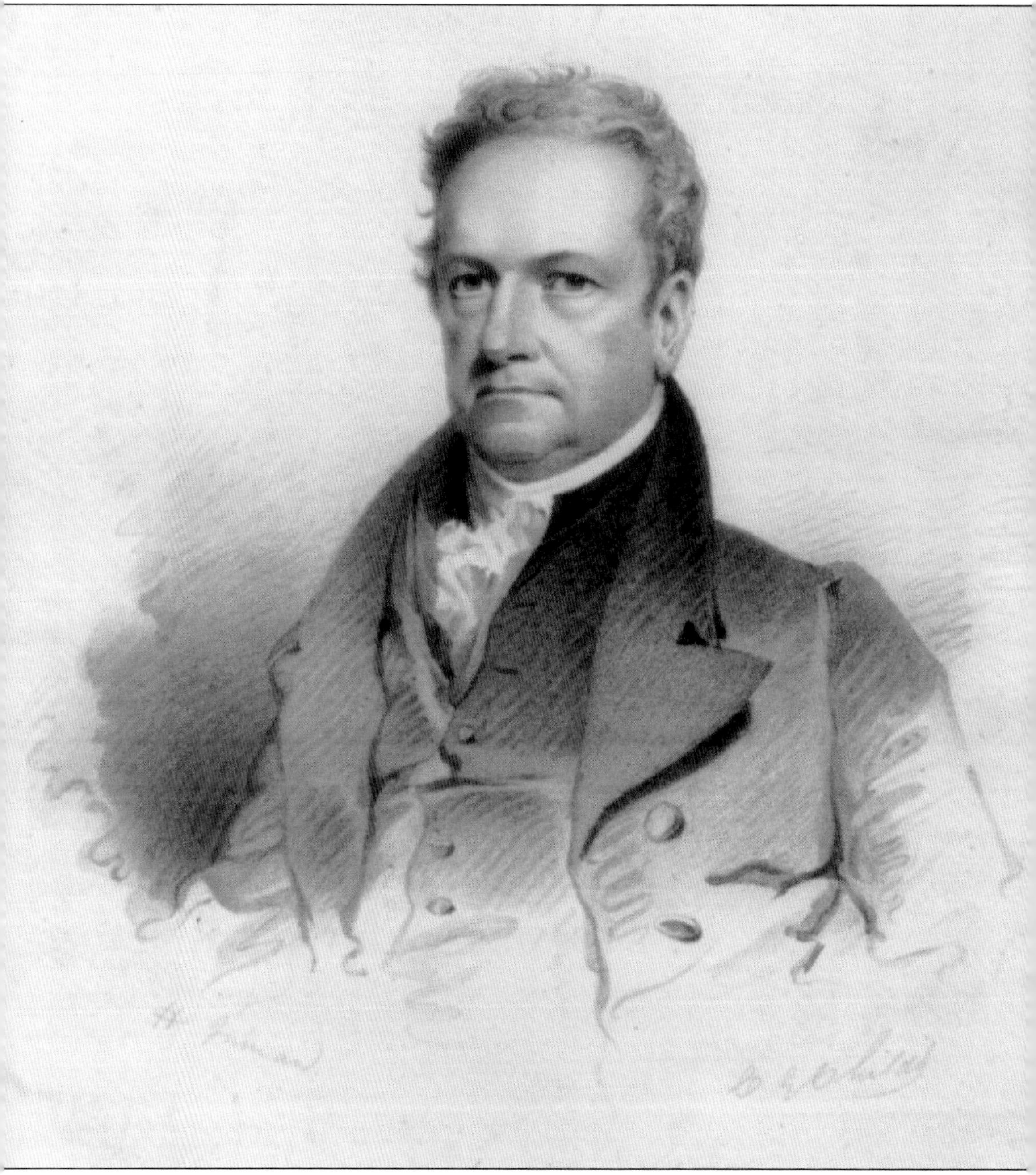

Gov. DeWitt Clinton launched the canal project that would change Grand Island's fate. He was also one of those responsible for the eviction of the squatters. Dr. Cyrenius Chapin of Buffalo raised the alarm in the spring of 1819, complaining about deforestation and the imminent threat to the whole area from the lawless habits and customs of this "collection of the refuse of society" who established their own internal regulatory body. Chapin bemoaned the settlers' rejection of either British or American rule, but his main complaint stemmed from the settler's use of the island's plentiful forests. The timber was about to become more exploitable and valuable. The legislature granted Governor Clinton's request for an order to remove the squatters.

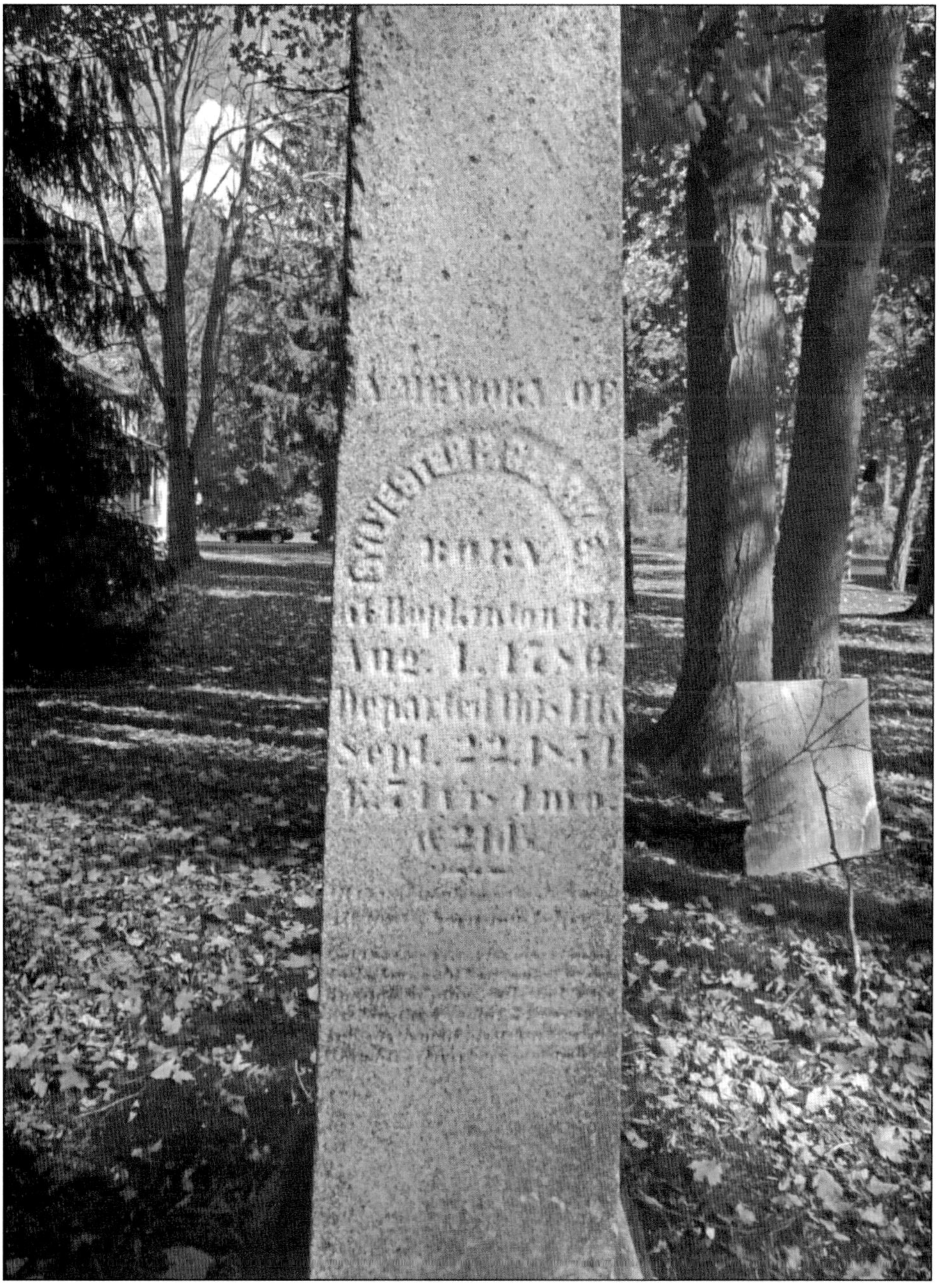

Sylvester Pendleton Clark was recognized as the leader of the squatters, the approximately 155 men, women, and children who resided on Grand Island between the War of 1812 and their expulsion at the end of 1819. Characterized as governor of their free and independent state in at least one proclamation, Clark was called the "King of the Outlaws" by Sheriff Cronk who, with 30 militiamen and two officers, rowed over to the island to execute the order of eviction. Cronk was authorized to use armed force if necessary. He met with each of the settlers, explained his mission, gave them time to pack their belongings, and transported them to either Canada or the mainland United States. Then he and his men burned the squatters' homes. Clark's was the only family that chose the United States. His grave is near his next home in Pendleton, New York.

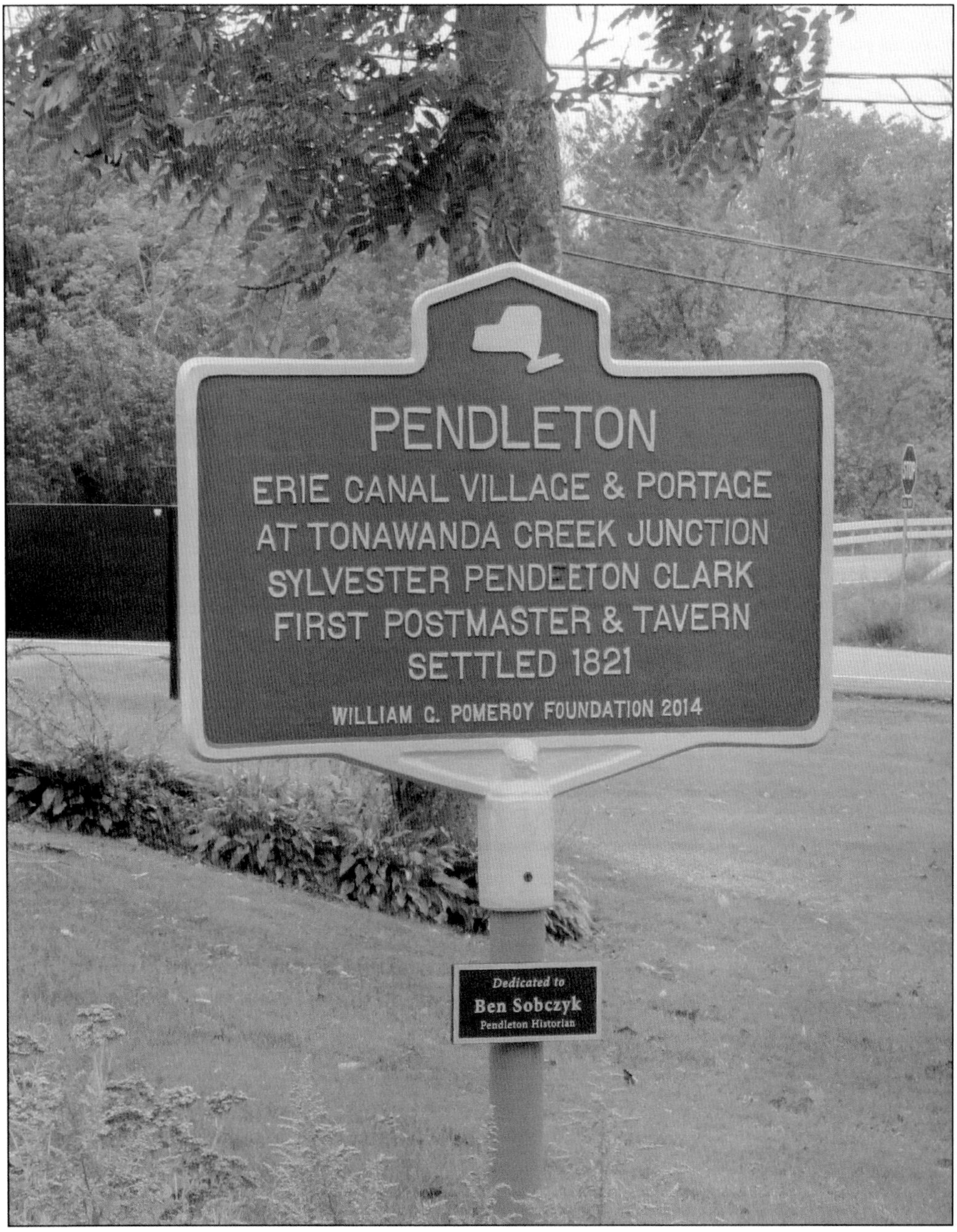

Pendleton Clark moved to Niagara County near the junction of Tonawanda Creek and the future path of the Erie Canal. There, in 1821, he opened a tavern and a store and that later gave the current town of Pendleton its name. Clark never returned to Grand Island, but a number of families did. When Sheriff Cronk came to order them off again, they argued that he had already fulfilled his orders and had no authority to evict them a second time and agreed to pay New York taxes. That was enough to satisfy the state assembly, which ignored Governor Clinton's request for a new removal order. In 1825, when the state conducted the first official survey in preparation for selling the land to private owners, the surveyor's report showed 13 buildings around the island designated with different family names, presumably white settlers.

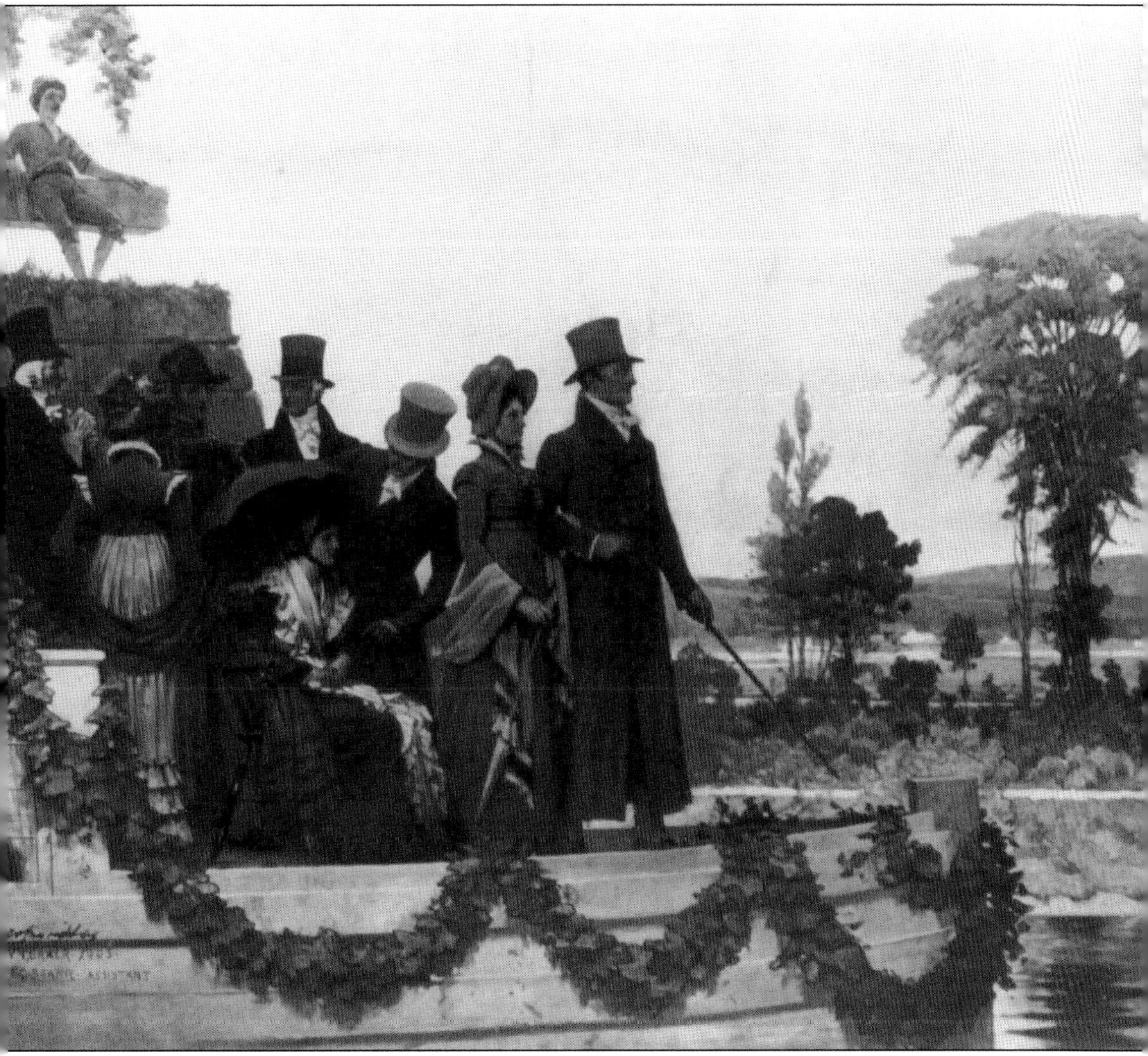

In October 1825, the packet *Seneca Chief* carried Gov. DeWitt Clinton from Lake Erie to New York City where "the wedding of the waters" would occur. Clinton poured water from the lake into the Atlantic Ocean, officially opening the Erie Canal. The canal was an immense success. Trade along its path intensified as it moved westward, and Buffalo quickly turned from a village into a booming metropolis. The canal's imminent arrival naturally enhanced the economic potential of every place in western New York, nowhere more than Grand Island. Although the focus of territorial disputes for centuries, it had never had permanent residents. Its location in the Niagara River, near the western terminus of the greatest infrastructure project of the early 19th century, made the island site invaluable.

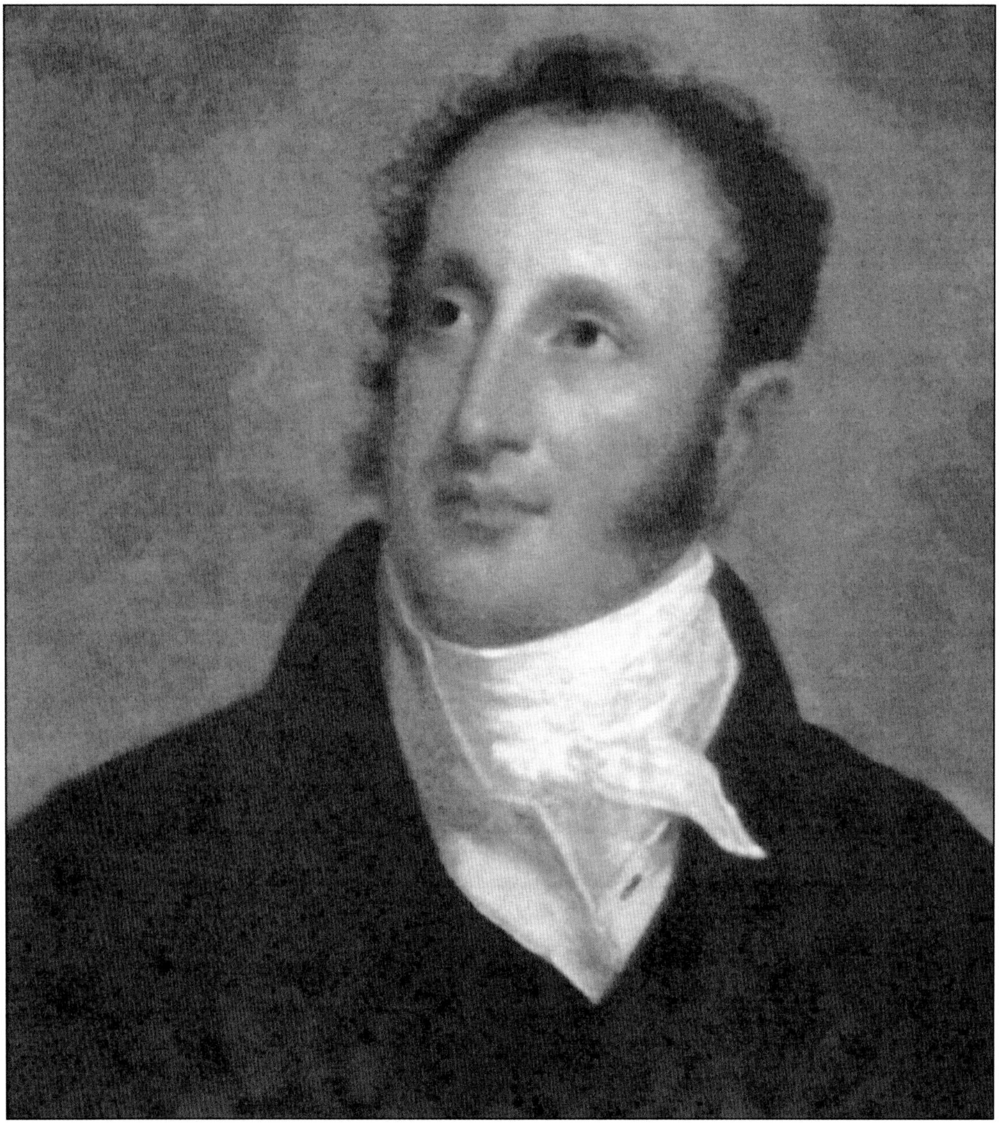

"Editor, journalist, playwright, politician, lawyer, court of appeals judge . . . major in the New York militia and, foremost, an ardent utopian Zionist" only begin the list of terms applied to Mordecai M. Noah, perhaps the best example of a visionary with a dream for Grand Island. Noah believed he had found a solution to two problems: America needed intelligent and hard-working immigrants and Europe's Jews needed shelter from growing persecution. The resolution of Grand Island's status as American territory and the imminent arrival of the Erie Canal seemed providential. When New York State failed to give him the island at his request, Noah had an associate, Samuel Leggett, buy 2,555 acres. There he planned to build Ararat, a refuge for Jewish people until a time they were able to reclaim Palestine.

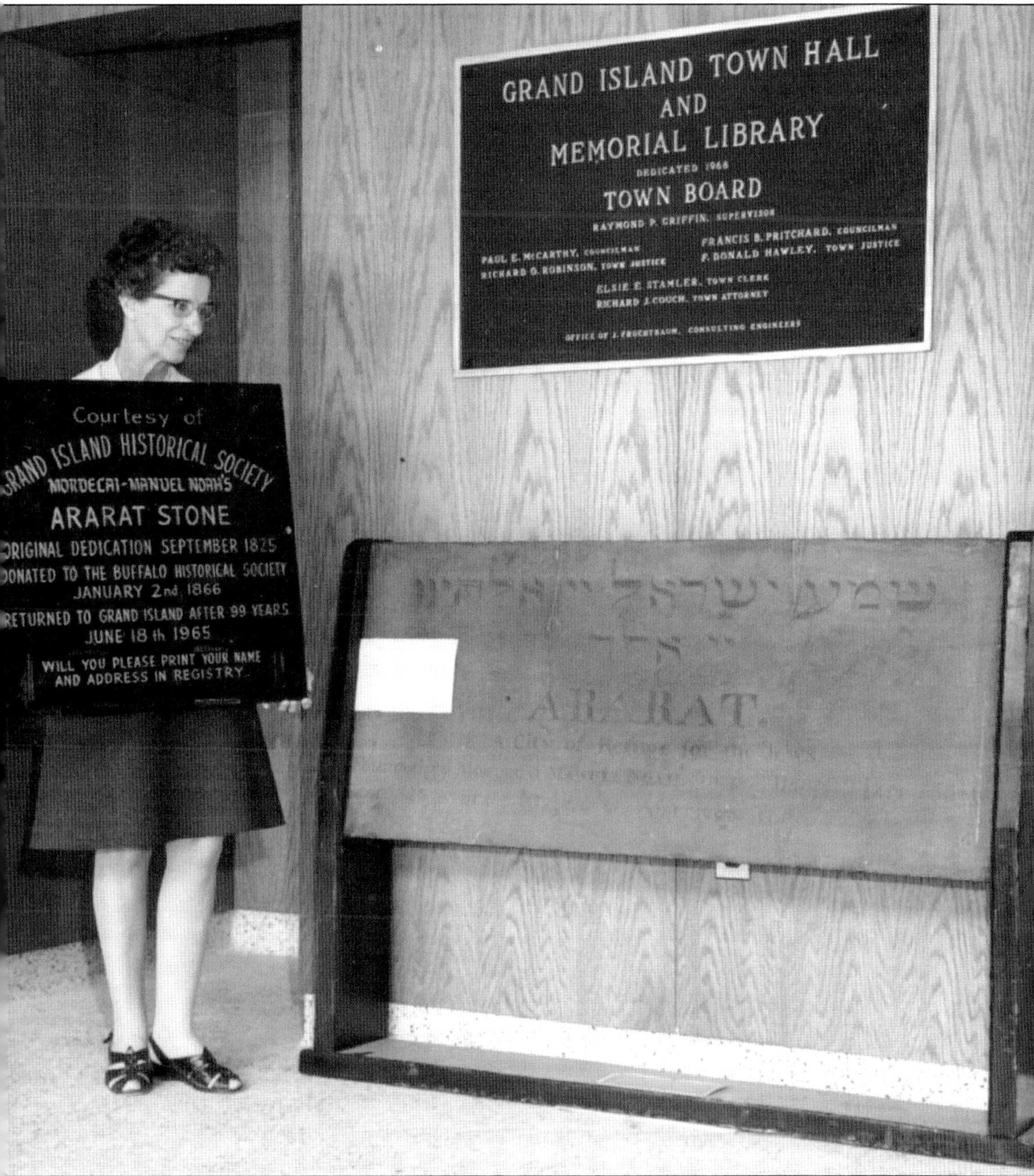

With his newspaper and political connections spreading the word, Noah planned an elaborate ceremony to launch his city. The cornerstone was inscribed with "Ararat, A City of Refuge for Jews, Founded by Mordecai Noah in the month Tizri 5586, September 1825 and in the 50th Year of American Independence" in both English and Hebrew. Finding too few boats to carry the expected crowd to Grand Island, Noah led the parade from Buffalo's courthouse to St. Paul's Episcopal Church where the cornerstone lay upon the altar. The self-appointed "Governor and Judge of Israel" proclaimed the restoration of Israel. The stone finally made it to Grand Island almost a decade later, but Noah left Buffalo without setting foot on the island. His vision evaporated.

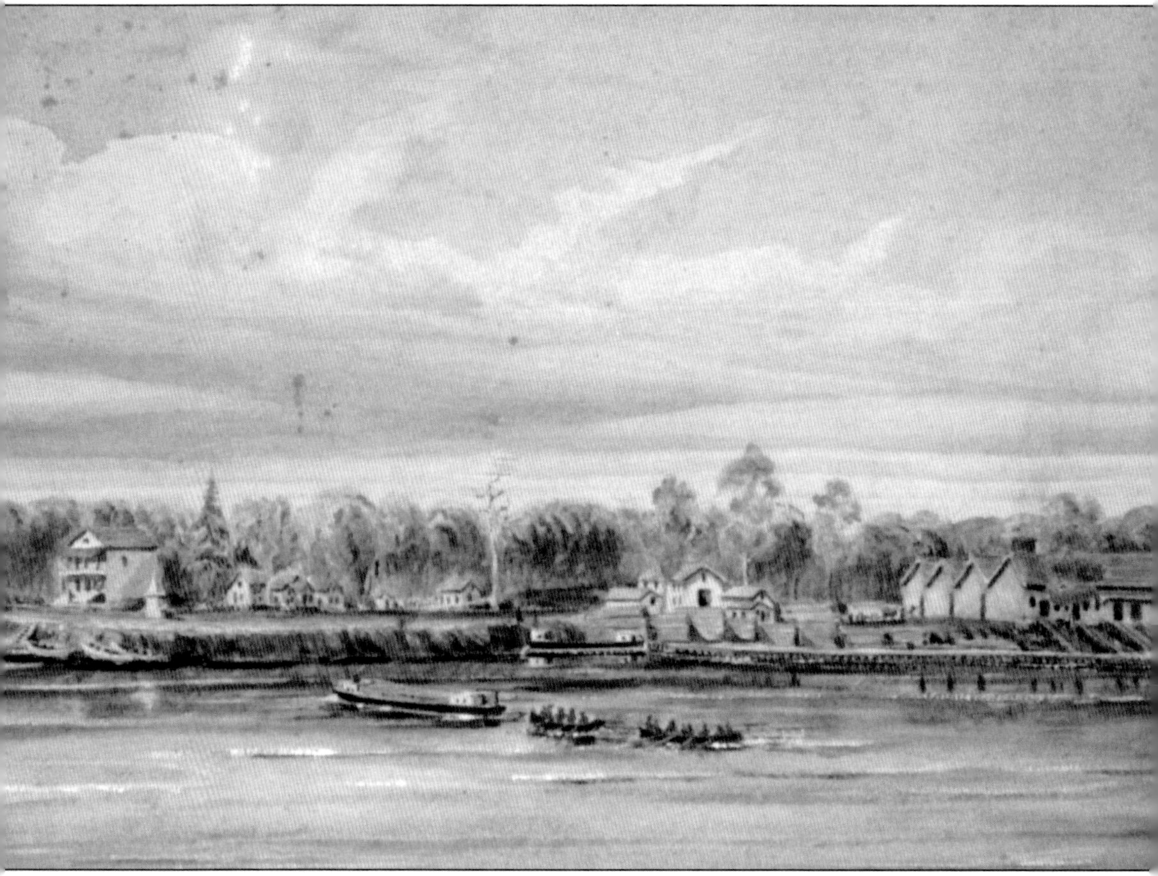

In a world where wooden ships were the key to political and economic power, Grand Island's abundant giant white oaks could hardly go unnoticed. The white oak needed for Yankee Clipper ships was becoming scarce on the East Coast as the number and size of the ships increased. The grand design of the East Boston Company, a Massachusetts corporation, was to harvest the island's timber, move it eastward on the new Erie Canal, and sell it. Grand Island's trees were especially valued because their inordinate size and unique quality were ideal for the giant structural elements of those ships. In 1834, a subsidiary company managed by Stephen White bought most of Grand Island and built a mill with the world's largest steam-powered saw to work the trees into marketable timber. Called Whitehaven, it is considered the first permanent settlement on the island.

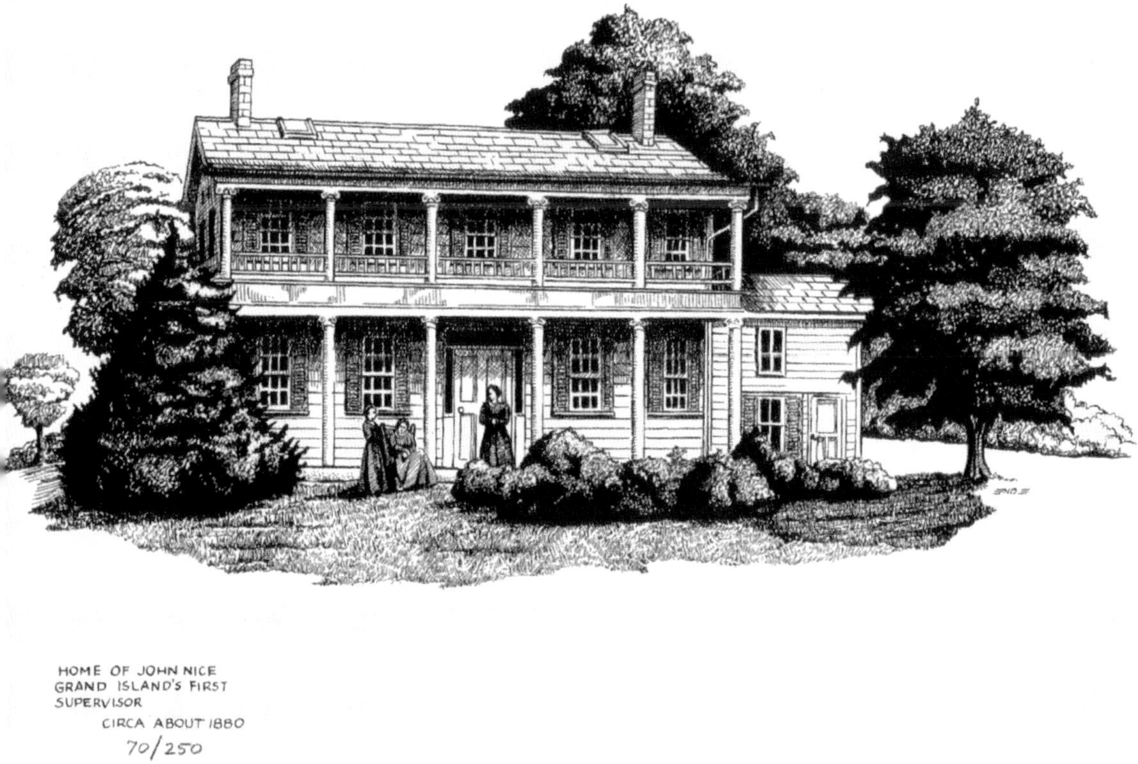

The Whitehaven compound included a large mansion, Riverhaven. It was the home of the company's resident general agent, Jedediah H. Lathrop, when he was not traveling on company business. Most of the time, his lieutenants lived there and ran the mill. Stephen White had his own larger mansion on White Island, now Tonawanda Island, directly across the river from Whitehaven. He could see the mill, but he almost never set foot on Grand Island. After the company failed, John Nice, first supervisor of the Town of Grand Island, bought Riverhaven. The meeting that set up the first town government took place there, and the house stayed in the Nice family until 1911.

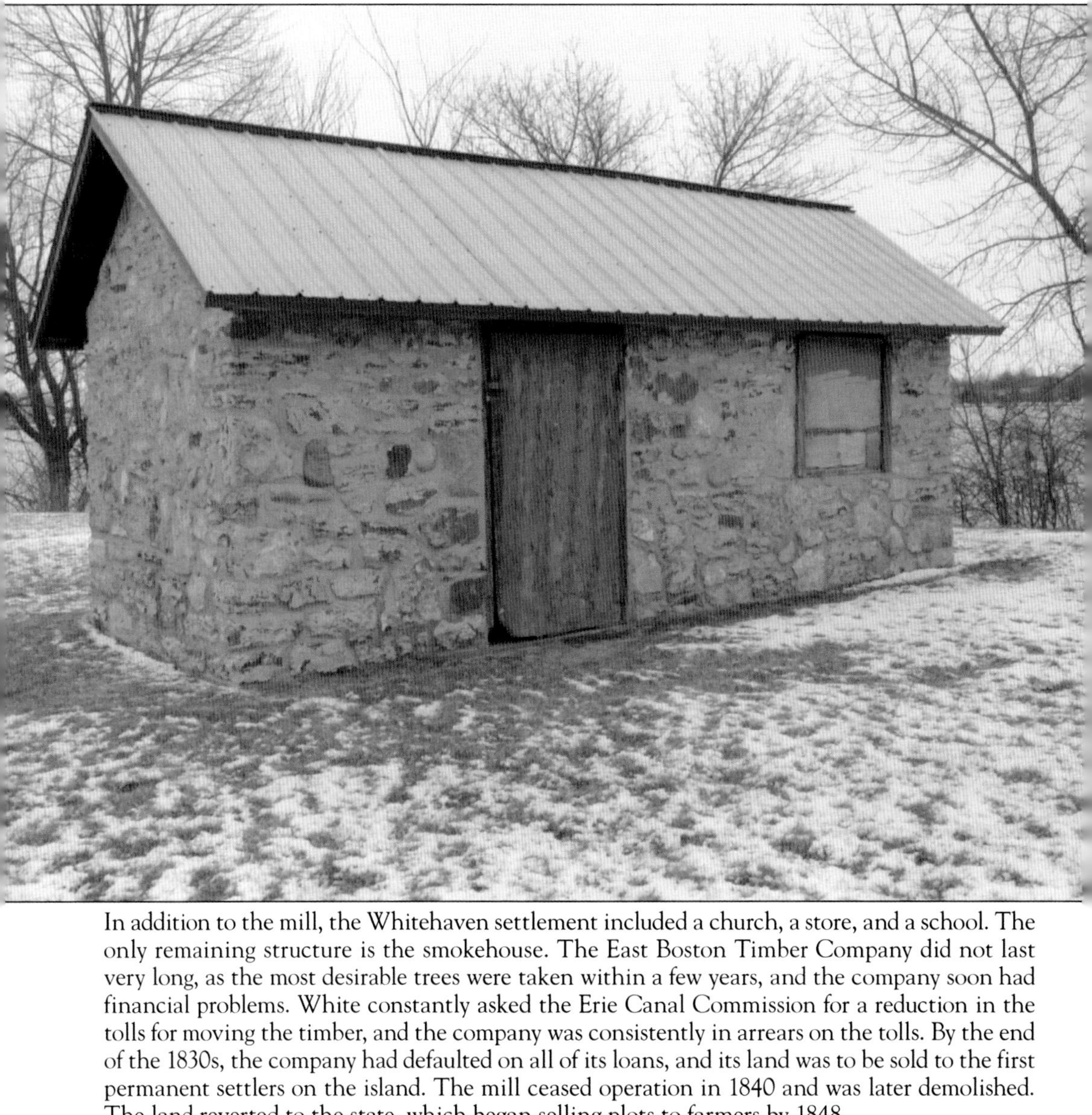

In addition to the mill, the Whitehaven settlement included a church, a store, and a school. The only remaining structure is the smokehouse. The East Boston Timber Company did not last very long, as the most desirable trees were taken within a few years, and the company soon had financial problems. White constantly asked the Erie Canal Commission for a reduction in the tolls for moving the timber, and the company was consistently in arrears on the tolls. By the end of the 1830s, the company had defaulted on all of its loans, and its land was to be sold to the first permanent settlers on the island. The mill ceased operation in 1840 and was later demolished. The land reverted to the state, which began selling plots to farmers by 1848.

Three

A Farming Community

The end of the East Boston Timber Company opened 16,000 acres to other uses. In some cases, it was the harvesting of some of the remaining timber other than white oak, but for most of the island, it meant the opportunity to establish family farms. With the rapid development of the surrounding area and its cities, as well as the continuing improvement in transportation, the opening of that acreage seemed overdue.

The soil was rich, and the markets were available, but farming on the island still faced a few handicaps. Despite the proximity of Buffalo, Niagara Falls, and the Tonawandas, there was still an additional shipping cost to get agricultural products to market. Before that hurdle, the land had to be cleared of the remaining trees and the stumps of the giant oaks. Dependent on horse, ox, and manpower, that was a major hurdle. Still, the island had a population of 954 by 1860, mostly farm families.

A variety of crops thrived on the island. Pear, peach, apple, and cherry orchards produced abundantly. Wheat, oats, and rye grew on other farms. Hay fed local beef cattle and was shipped to the mainland on a seasonal basis. Dairy products and eggs also found multiple markets on and off the island, but the agricultural economy had its limits. The island could not attract the same diversity of occupations as other communities in the area. Thus, the population grew relatively slowly to a peak of 1,156 in 1880. Unable to provide its youth with the same opportunities as the cities, the island's population saw a long, slow decline over the next half century. Between 1880 and 1930, the population of Buffalo increased by 371 percent while Grand Island's declined to its lowest point, 626 persons, or a little over half of its 1880 figure.

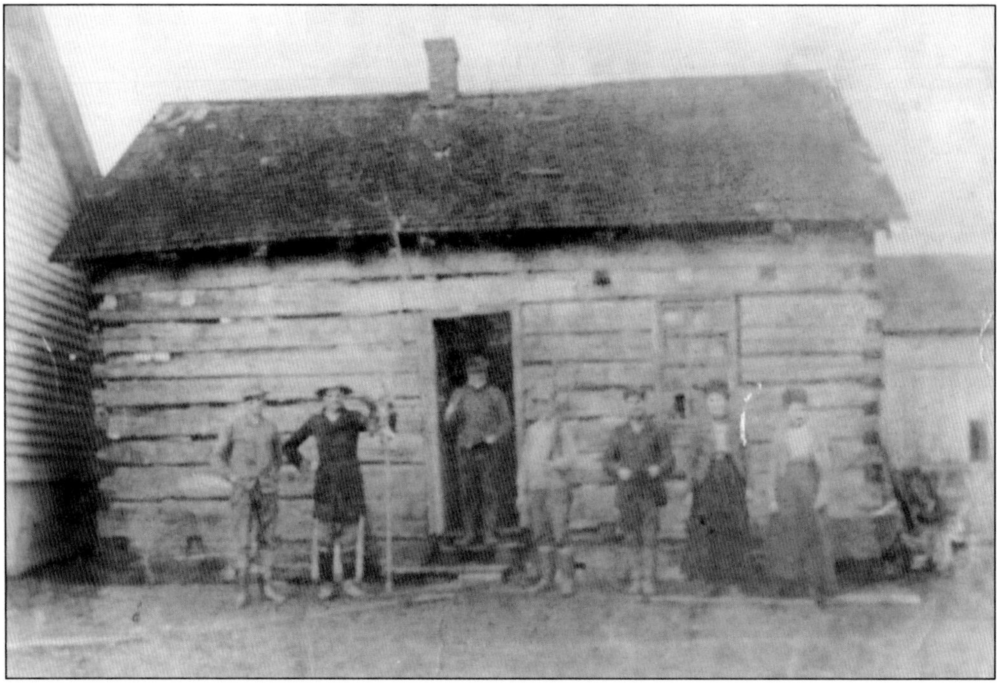

Like many of Grand Island's early settlers, Joachim Long was born in Germany. Three of his brothers were in western New York when Joachim; his parents, Johann and Sophia; and his other two brothers immigrated in 1858. After laboring on Grand Island and Tonawanda, the family bought 393 acres of farmland that was later divided evenly among the six brothers. Joachim's son Henry was born in this rough cabin in 1864. A "McKinley and Roosevelt" banner over the door dates the photograph to 1900. Pictured here are, from left to right, Charles Long, "Big George" Long, Henry Long, "Little George" Long, Albert Stoll, Laura Long Trautman, and Hattie Long. The house below is where Joachim and his wife, Katherine Spohr Long, later lived.

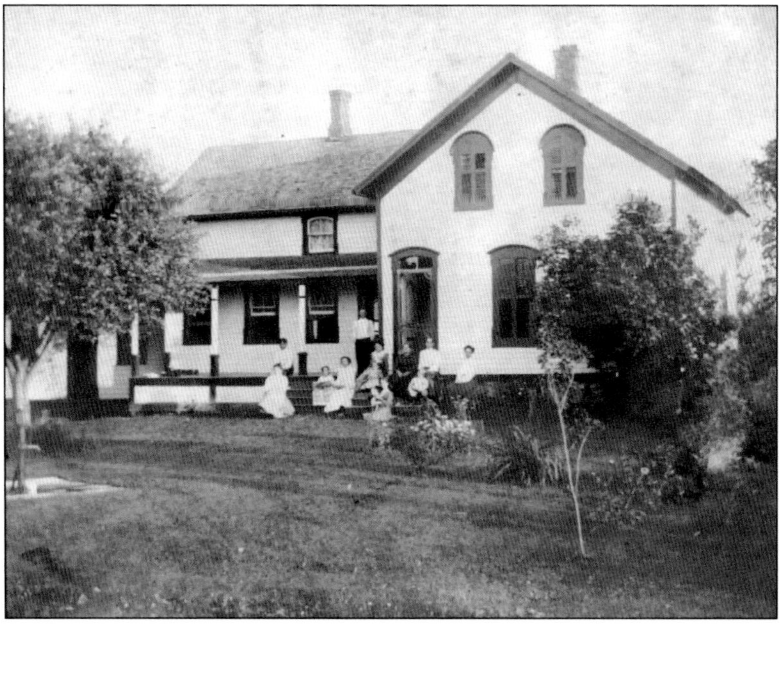

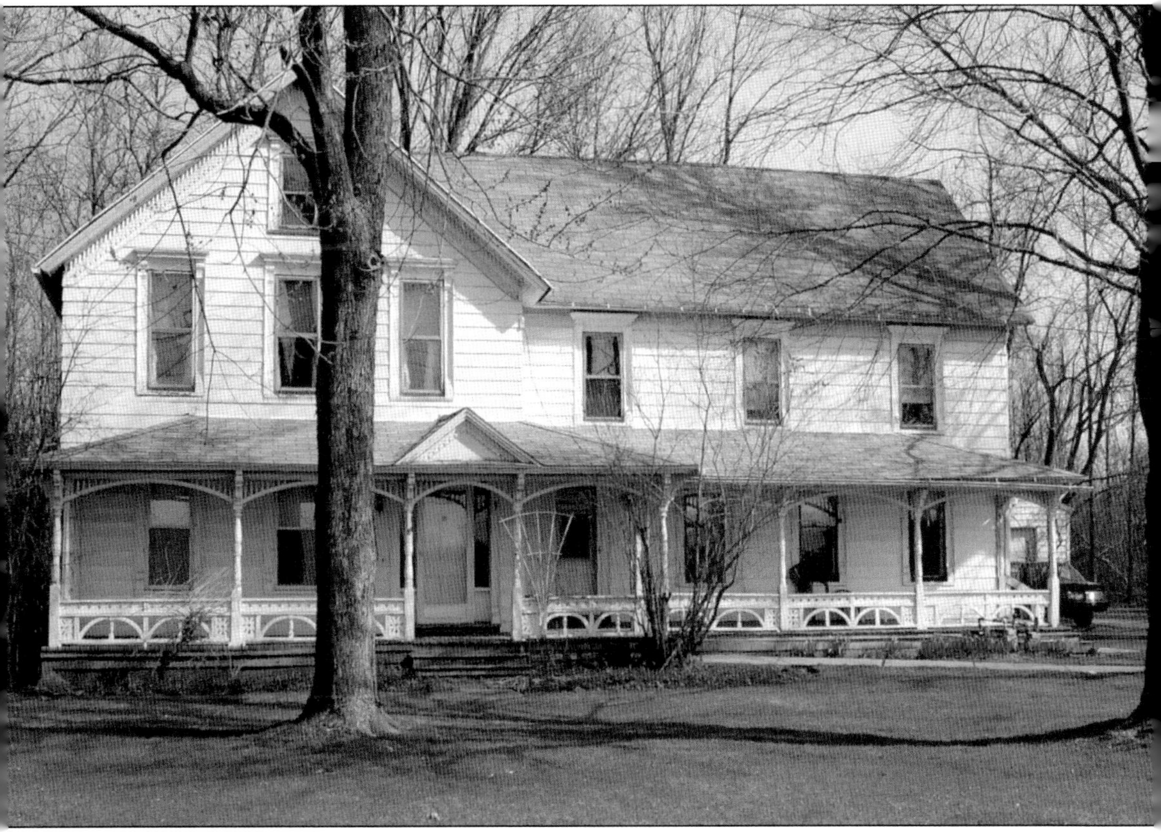

This house was among the first farmhouses on the island. To be more exact, the east end was originally built between 1840 and 1845 by a Mr. Delaplant. Patrick Conboy bought Delaplant's 100-acre farm, including the house, in 1850. The house remained in the Conboy family until 2014. Among those who lived there was William Conboy, who served as town supervisor and led several unsuccessful efforts to construct a bridge around 1900. The western half of the house was added in the 20th century.

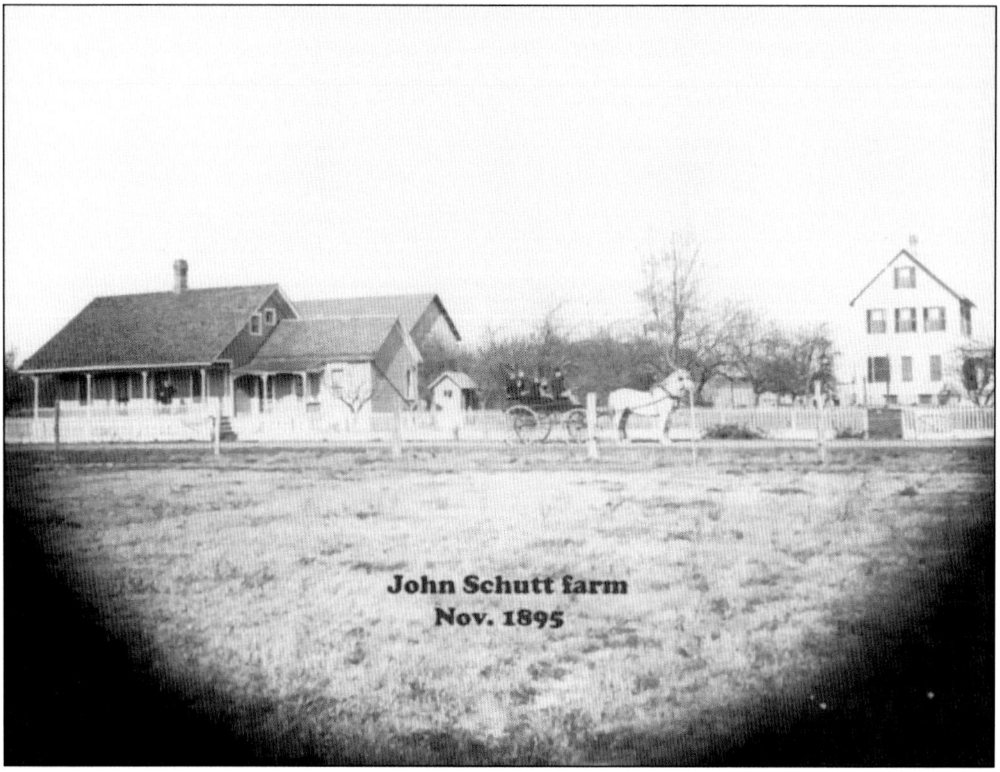

John Schutt was a prominent figure in Grand Island life at the start of the 20th century. A wagon maker and teamster, he came to Buffalo from Germany in 1873. His ambition, hard work, and natural way with horses helped him build a large business serving various Buffalo companies. The growth of his business led him into farming, and he sold his entire operation and moved to a 240-acre farm on Grand Island in 1888. One of his main crops was hay, which he baled to ship to Buffalo. He also had abundant orchards. Later, he opened Schutt's Store near the town hall. The Schutt house appears below.

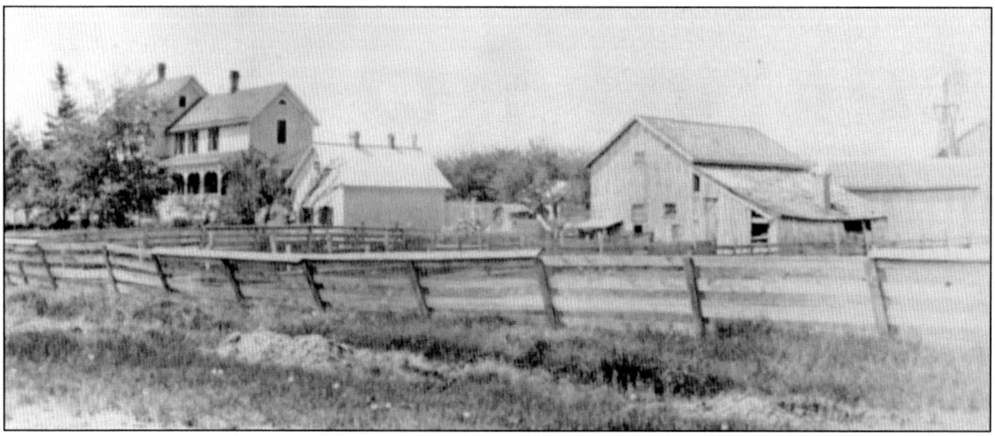

Grand Island farming was hard work, but some early families prospered, often combining farming with the sale of general merchandise. In addition to a successful farm, the Schutts operated what has been called the island's first five-and-dime store. Pictured here are Schutt's four sons, from left to right, (first row) John Schutt Jr. and Henry Schutt; (second row) Frank Schutt and William Schutt.

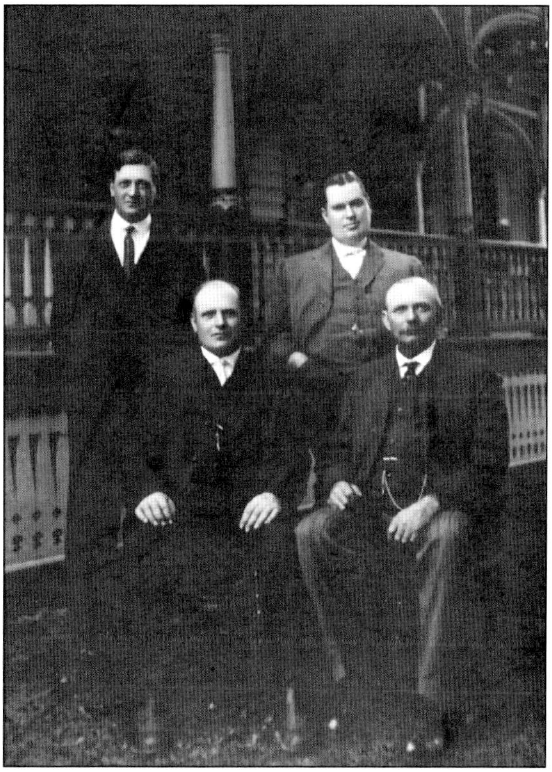

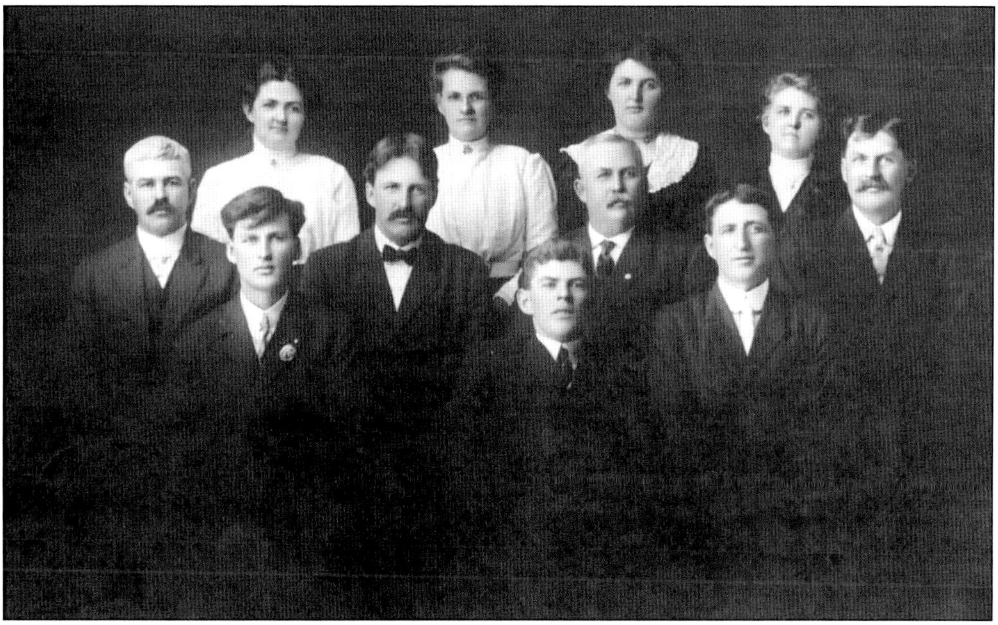

Pictured here in 1909 are the descendants of Joachim Long, who arrived on Grand Island in 1858 and became a successful farmer. From left to right are (first row) Samuel Long, Harry Long, and Charles F. Long; (second row) Edward F. Long, John C. Long, Henry W. Long, and William H. Long; (third row) Katherine Long Consier, Elizabeth Long Schulte, Laura Long Trautman, and Mary Long Lonsdale.

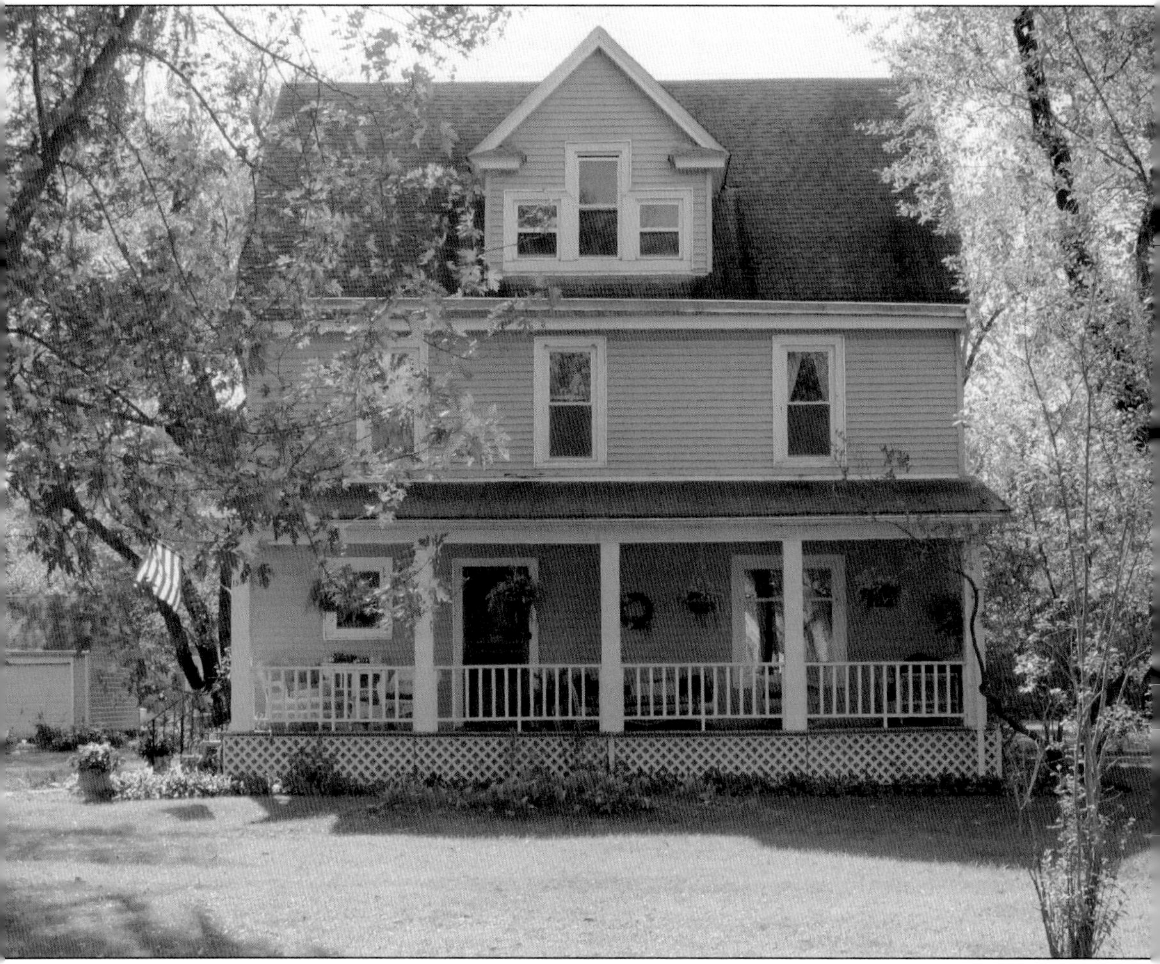

John Neilan was one of the two original mail carriers on the island in 1902. His son George Neilan, who had served on the town board, delivered mail in the 1950s. The Neilan home on the corner of Cox and Elmwood Roads in Ferry Village was built by the family in 1906. The house has a double parlor with pocket doors, a dining room, a large kitchen with a pantry, and a front and back stairway. Originally, there were seven bedrooms. The family had a large farm; 91 acres were sold to the state in 1931 for Beaver Island State Park, and the remainder of the farm was sold off for the Beaver Island Golf Course in 1958. The bunkhouse and barn were destroyed in 1958, marking the end of the farming years for the family.

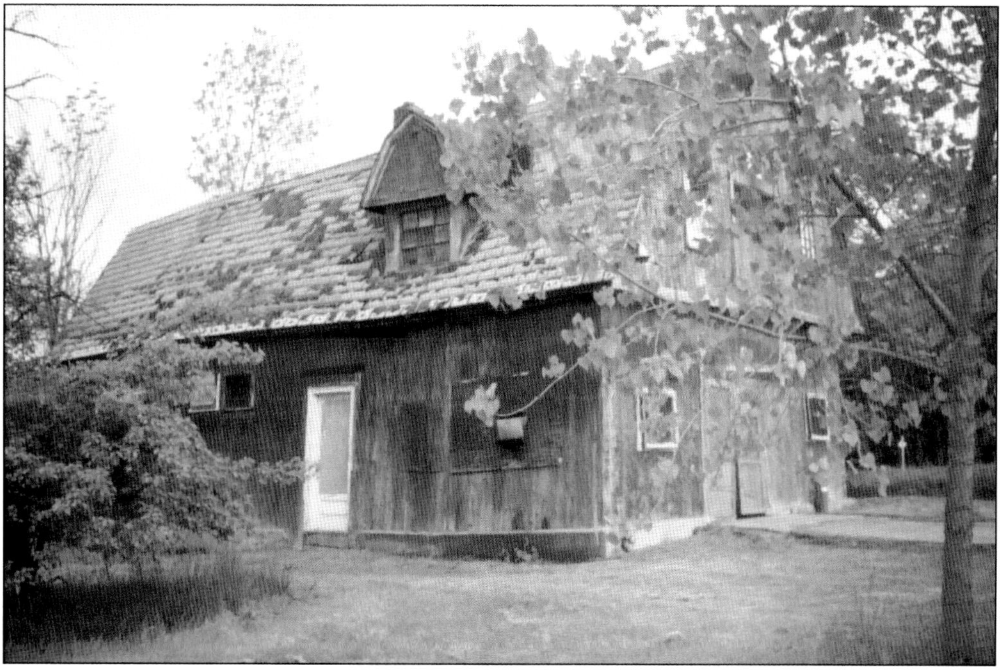

The barns that were so common and essential on Grand Island when the population was primarily dependent on agriculture have become rare. The one shown above was on the farm of Fremont Simonds on East River Road near the south bridge. Simonds came to Grand Island as a child. The original farmhouse was being used as a tavern and restaurant called the Idlehour Inn when it burned in 2000. This barn was finally torn down in 2010. The barn below is on the property of the Killian family, but it was originally part of the Troutman farm. The farmhouse burned to the ground in 2000.

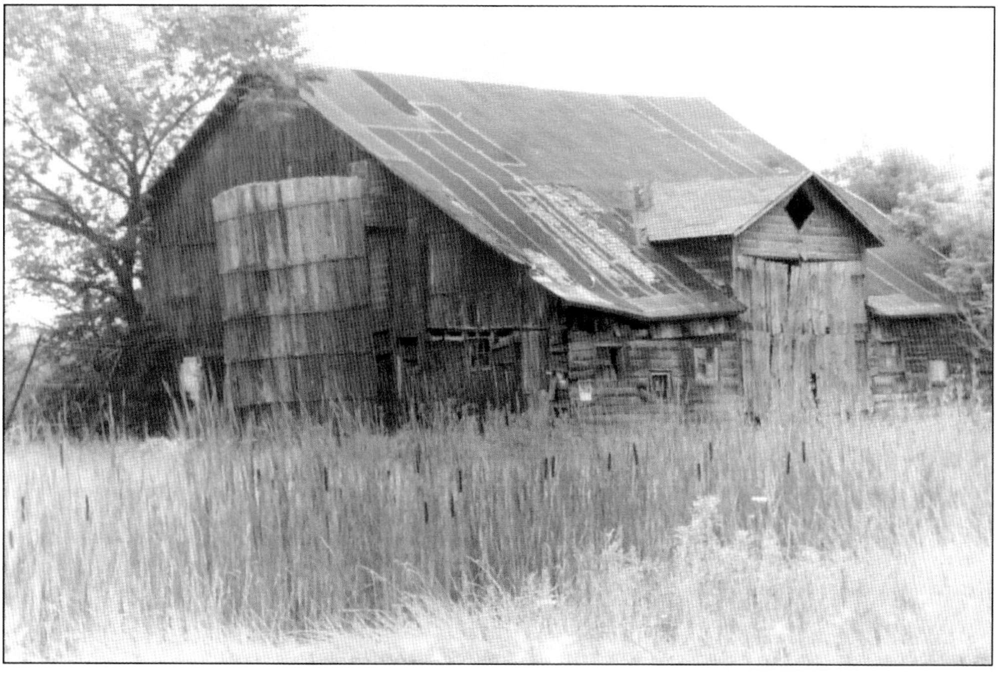

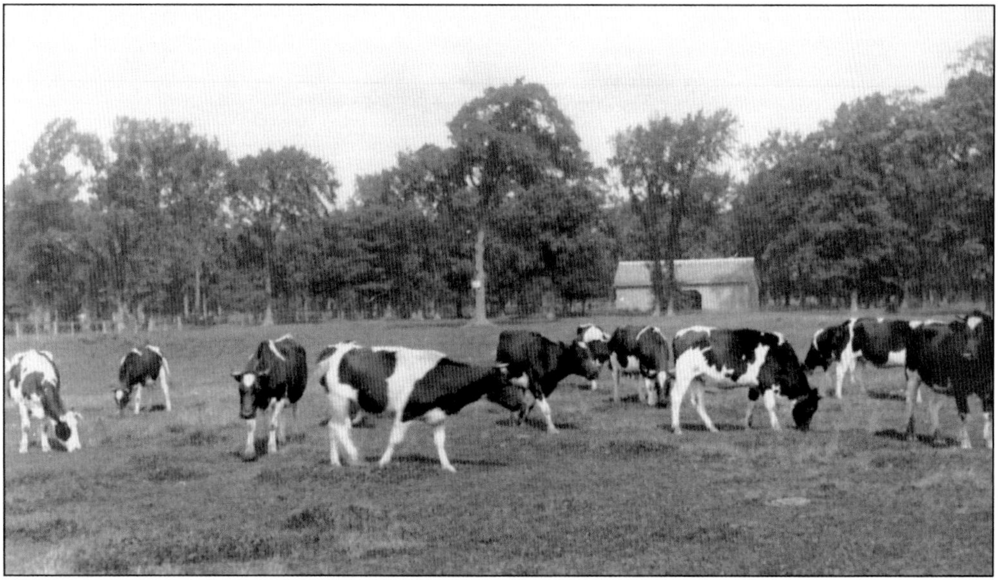

Not all of Grand Island's farms were small family affairs. Some of Buffalo's leading citizens found the island attractive as more than a summer retreat. Lewis Allen, a real estate and insurance magnate, took the lead. Shorthorn cattle became the early focus of his Grand Island life. Founding president of the Buffalo Horticultural Society, he used his Allenton Farm to become a national leader in developing the breed. He compiled 24 volumes of the *American Short Horn Herd Book*. Allen had other interests in scientific farming: peaches, pears, apples, and grapes. Allen was not the only member of the Buffalo elite to engage in stockbreeding on Grand Island. Elbridge G. Spaulding, a wealthy lawyer, banker, and political figure, shared that avocation. Riverlawn, Spaulding's estate, featured a large house overlooking the West River. The barns for his Holstein cattle were equally impressive.

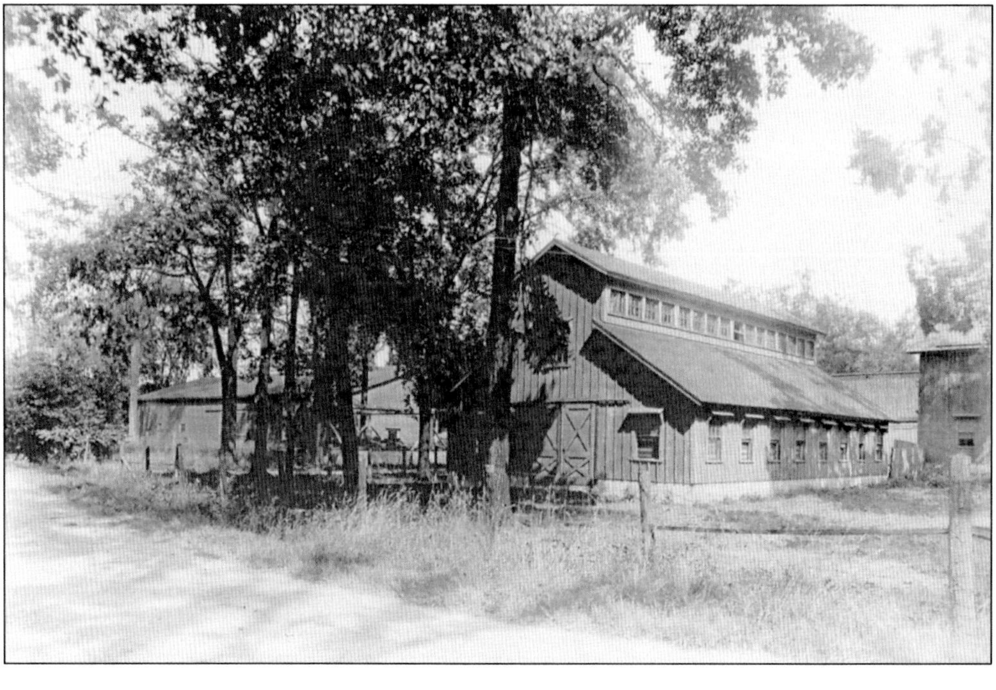

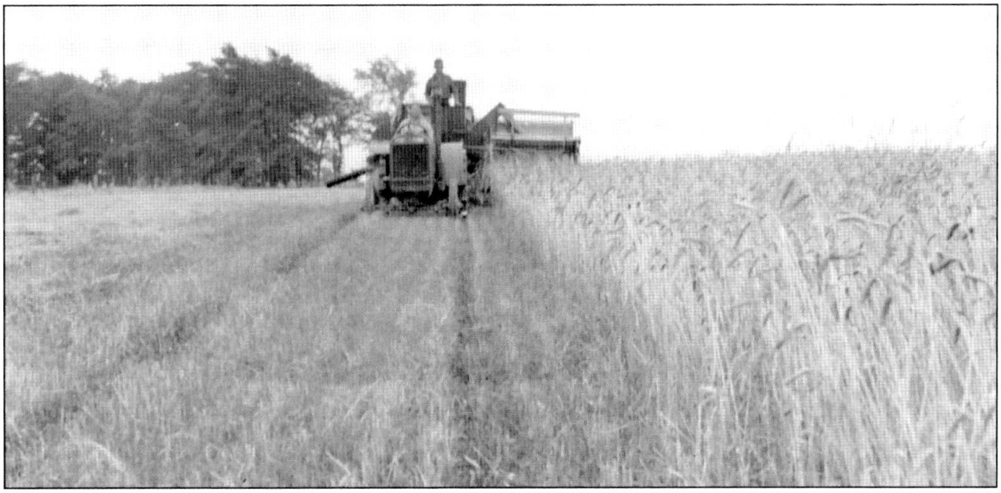

Farmers on Grand Island raised a variety of crops, from fruits and vegetables to grains and hay. For years, hay was a leading crop because it was well suited to the island's soil, and it was nonperishable, important for an island with limited connection to the mainland. This 1937 scene shows George W. Alt Jr. driving the tractor and Carlton W. Alt operating the harvester on Oakland Farm on Whitehaven Road.

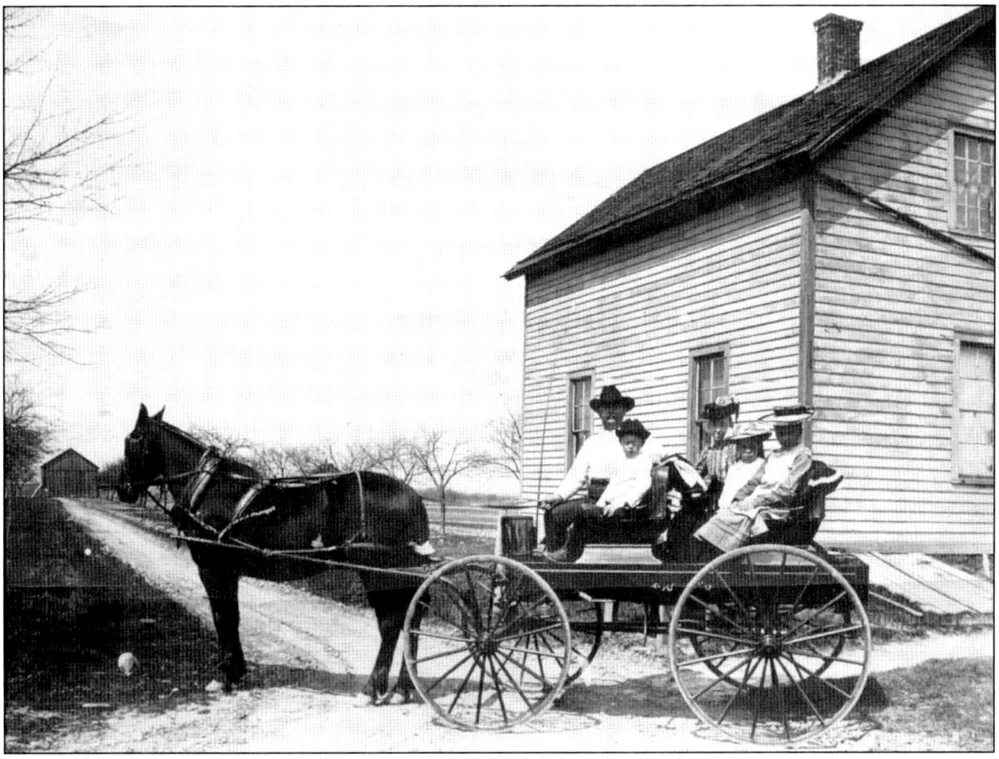

This photograph from the late 19th century shows the Long family in Sunday-best clothes in front of the signs of their success, probably with their best-looking horse. It also depicts the main means of private transportation on the island well into the 20h century. Pictured are, from left to right, Henry W. Long, Harold Long, Flora Seyler Long, Ethel Long (Rickerts), and Mabel Long (Kreger).

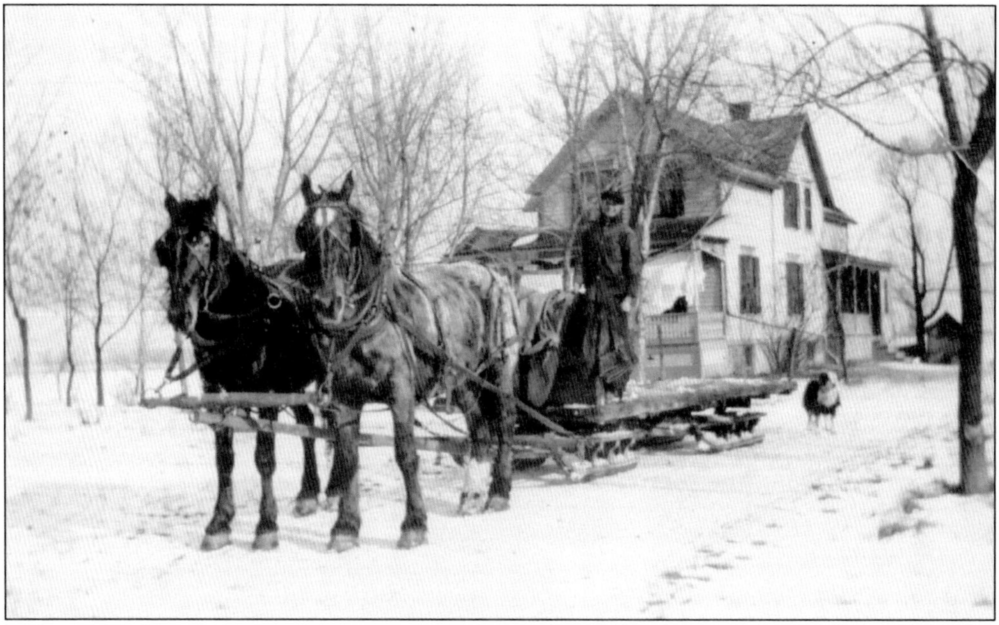

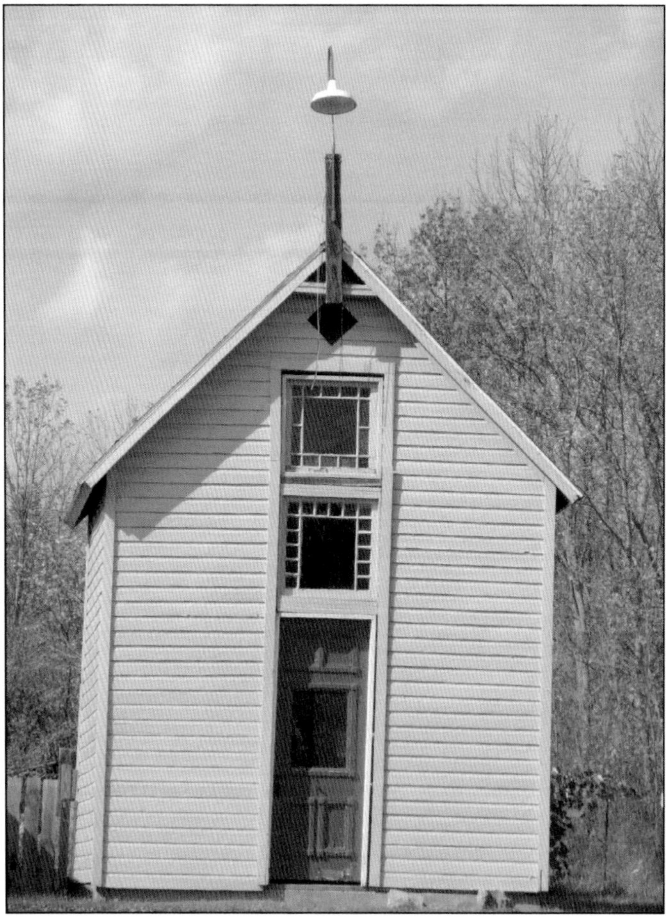

In the days before electricity, refrigeration was a challenge once winter ended. Great quantities of ice needed to be collected and stored for the warmer months. Grand Island had an advantage in this over many farm communities; it was surrounded by an abundant supply of ice just waiting to be taken. Moving that ice harvest in winter required sleds like the one shown above in front of the Henry W. Long house at Baseline and Bedell Roads. Then the problem was long-term storage. The solution in rural areas was often an icehouse, built with double walls that were filled with sawdust and cork. The last remaining icehouse on Grand Island has been maintained by its owner.

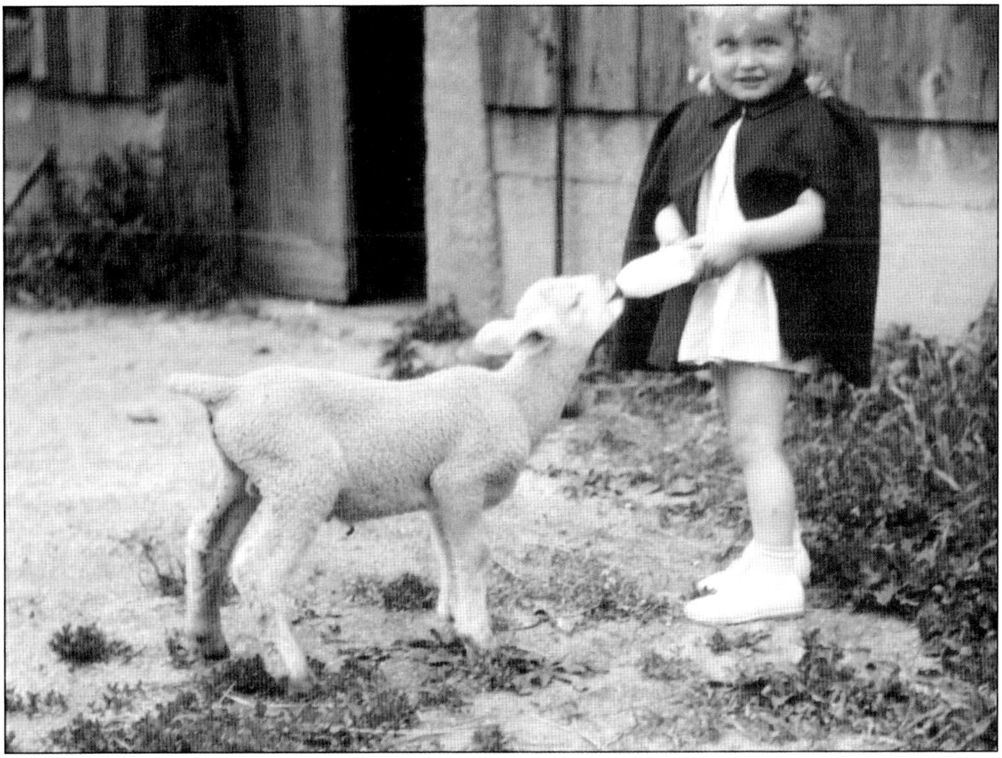

Nearly all of the children on Grand Island lived on farms like that of the Alt family's Oakland Farm. Life for these children included a mixture of chores and play when they were not in school. Five-year-old Carline Alt is shown here feeding one of the lambs on the family farm. The photograph below suggests that it was part of a bigger operation. Island farmers raised a variety of crops and animals in response to changes in the mainland markets, but it also reflected a need for self sufficiency.

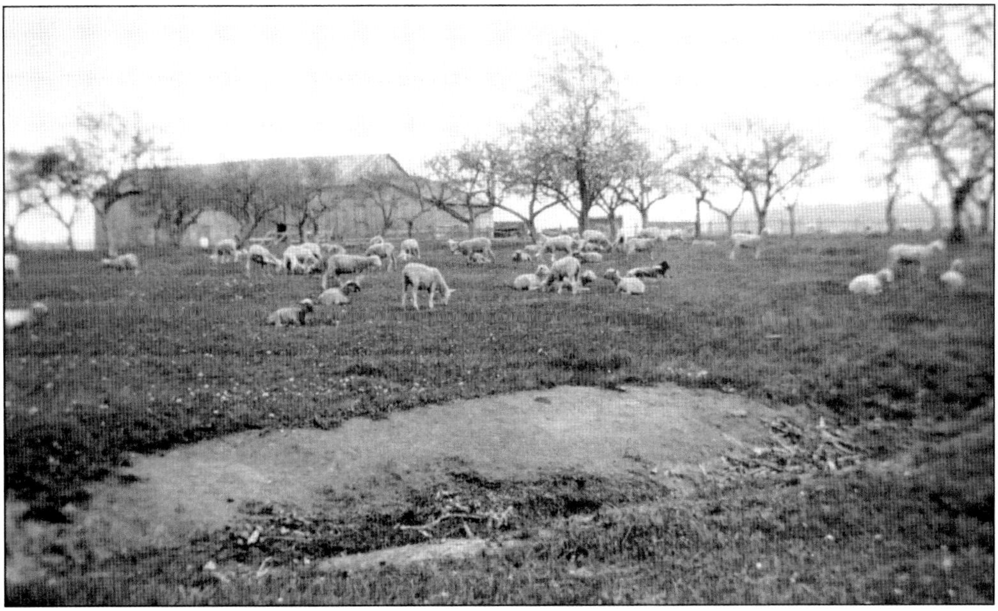

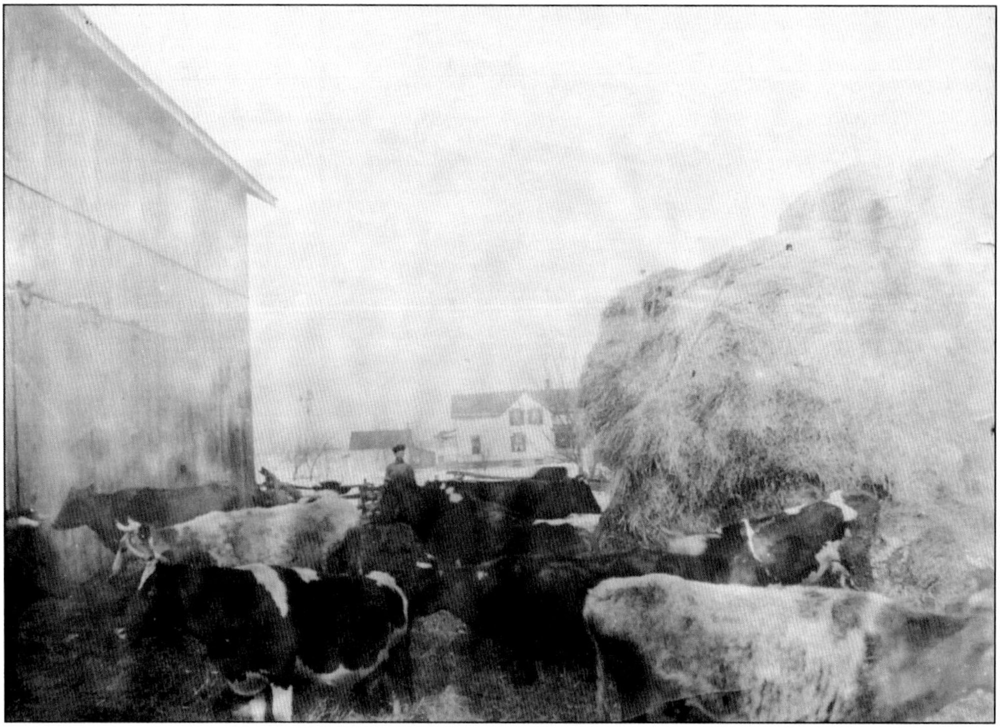

Like almost all of Grand Island's residents before the arrival of the bridges in the 1930s, town supervisor Henry W. Long was primarily a farmer. The scene above, with a view of his barn and cattle, was typical. As the Long family arrived on the island in 1858 with five sons, it is not surprising that there were several Long farms. The photograph below, of a different Long family farm with the buildings and other features labeled, shows how diversified many of the island's farms really were, with a variety of animals as well as field crops.

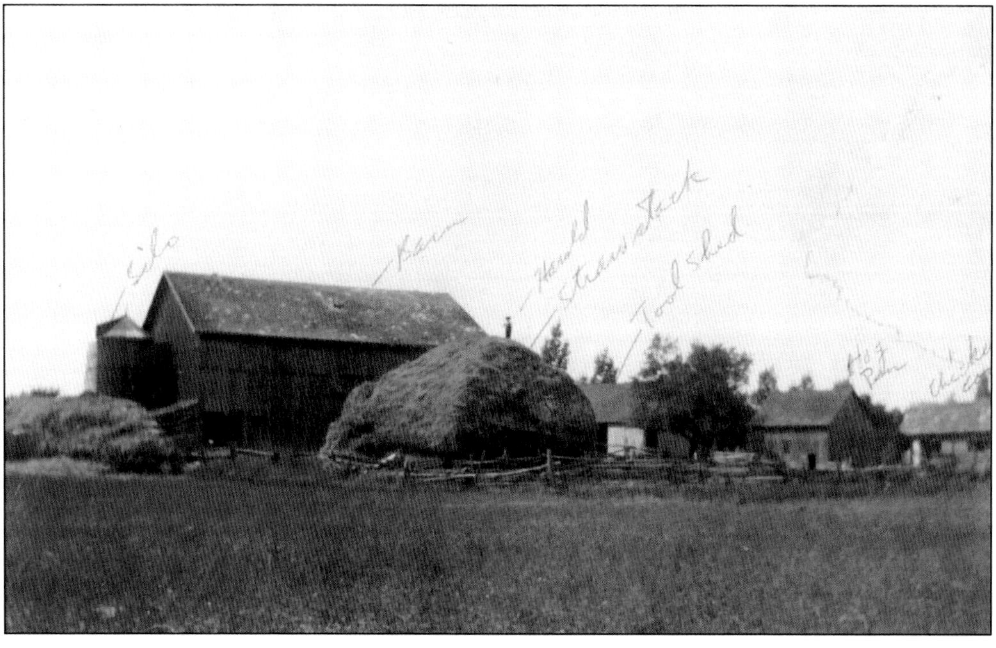

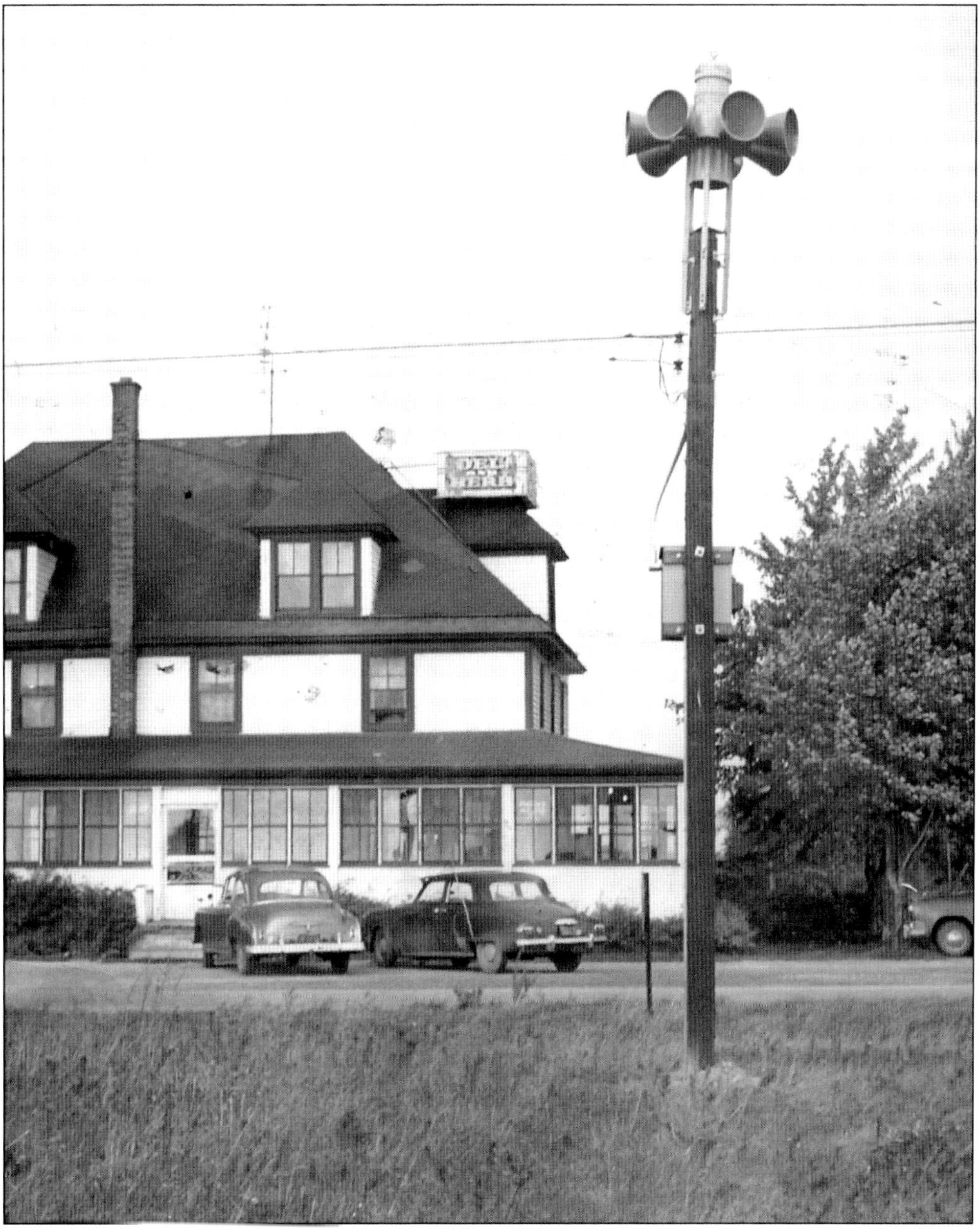

In the late 19th century, farmers across America responded to industrialization by joining in various cooperative ventures to increase their bargaining power and their efficiency. The idea took root on Grand Island first with the Maccabees, the Fraternal & Benevolent Policy Holders of the Maccabees Life Insurance of America, a farmer's cooperative, which began on the island around 1890. Later, a successful co-op creamery was formed, and dairy farming became the principal farm activity on the island. This building, originally known as Maccabee Hall, was built on Baseline Road midway between Staley and Love Roads. It was moved to the corner of Love and Baseline Roads to make way for a railroad that never materialized and later reopened as Scheurman's Restaurant in 1936. In 1954, when this photograph was taken, it was the popular Del and Herb's Grand Island Grill. Recently, it became Dick & Jenny's Bake and Brew.

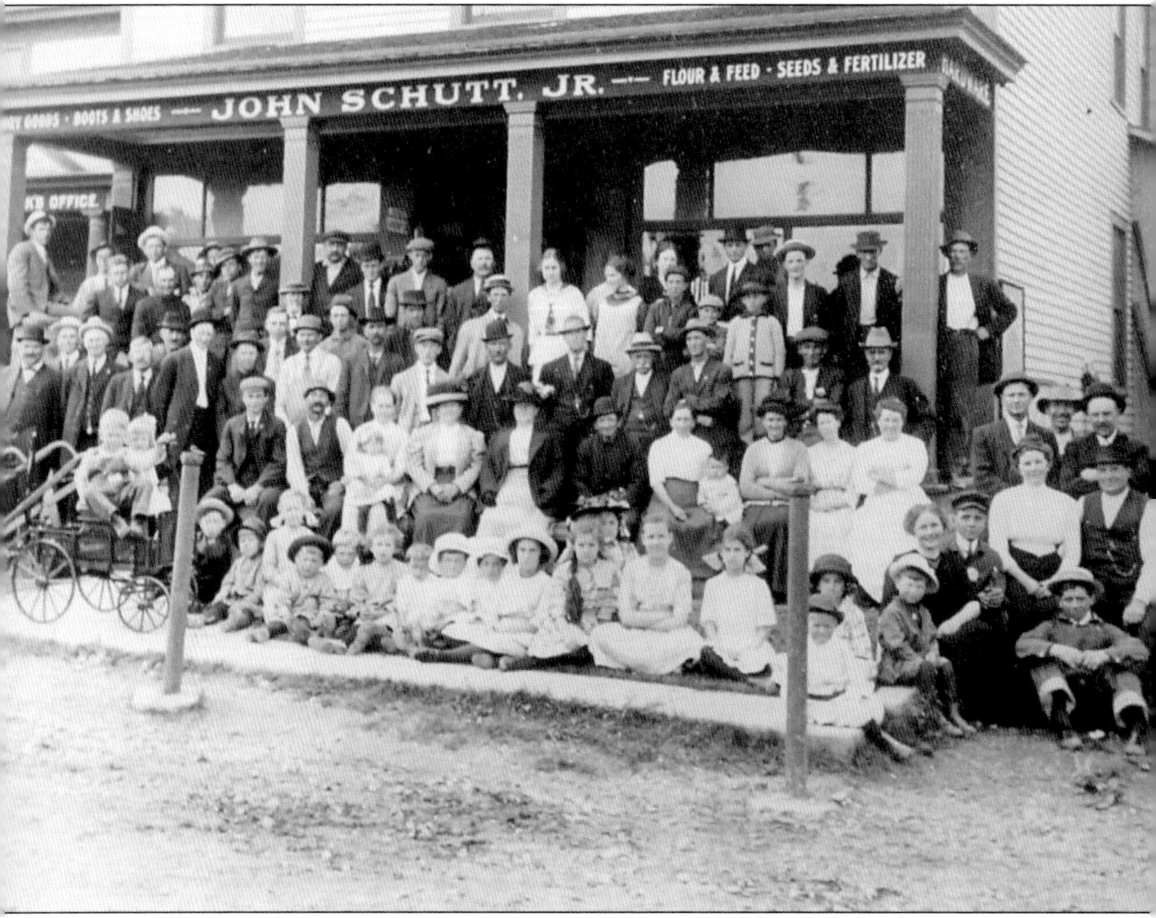

Despite enjoying its golden era as a summer retreat for western New Yorkers and its growing role as a supplier of farm products, Grand Island's population was beginning to shrink in the last part of the 19th century. Nevertheless, it supported a number of local businesses that often served multiple purposes. One of the best known was John Schutt's store near the town hall. For this photograph, a significant portion of Grand Island's residents gathered in their Sunday best. Barely visible to the left of the storefront is the office of the town clerk, John Schutt.

This advertisement for Capt. Richard Pettit's store gives a good picture of the range of services provided by rural stores in the horse-and-buggy days. Pettit's store eventually was sold to Harry Tucker, and the Ferry Road store turned private residence still bears the Tucker sign in the window. Charlotte Tucker was postmistress from 1902, when Rural Free Delivery began on Grand Island, until her death in 1937. The post office was housed in Pettit's General Store. Tucker stands on the porch with young Clarence Schutt and his father, Henry Schutt. The twin girls are Betty and Kitty Lutz, daughters of Capt. Matthew Lutz and his wife. The third man from the left is Capt. Richard Pettit.

Tea,
Coffee,
Groceries,
Candies,
Baked Goods,
Stationery,
Hardware,
Laundry Agent

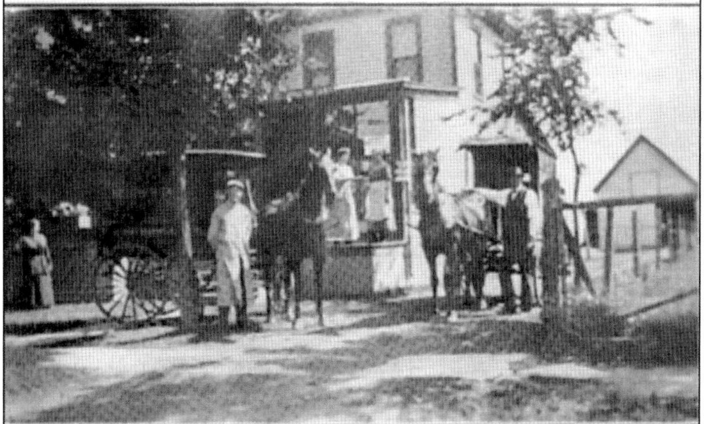

RICHARD PETTIT

Grand Island, N. Y.

Prepared Drugs, Gauze Bandages, Etc.

Subscriptions received for all Newspapers and Magazines.

Fresh Meats and Salt Meats Phone No. 20.

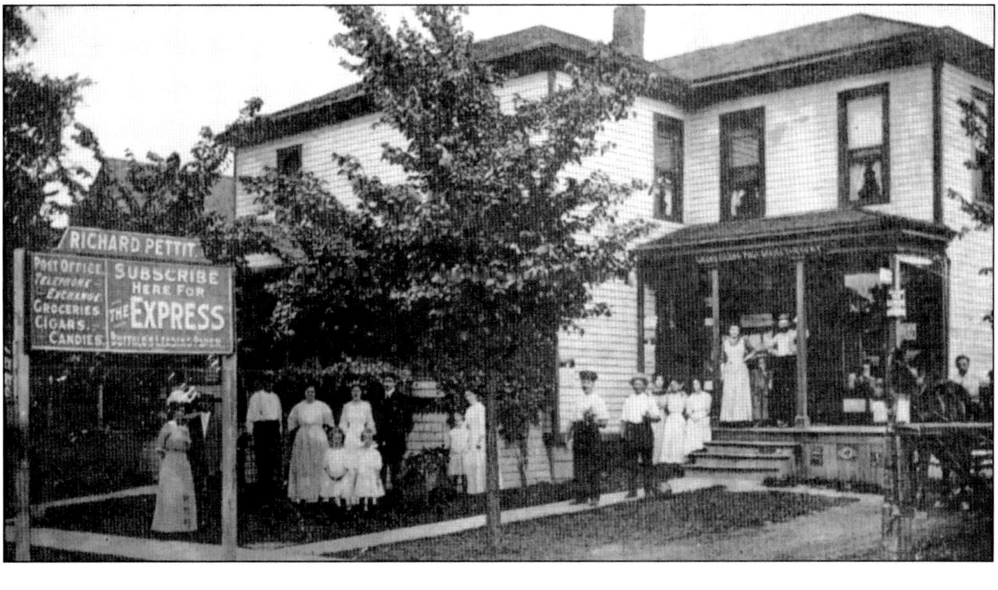

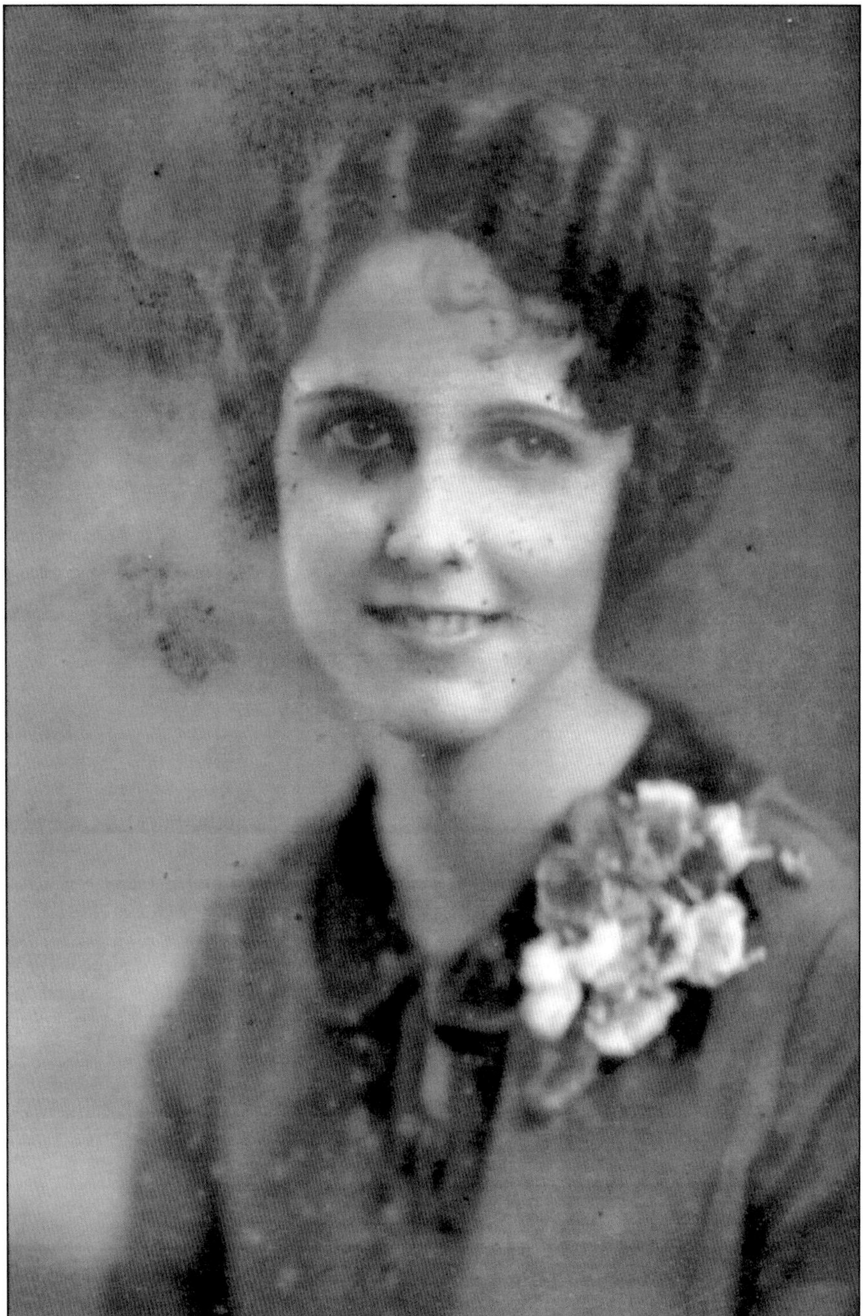

Pettit's store was also the original base for the Grand Island Telephone Company that, along with the Island Telephone Company, provided the island's limited service. Initially, the single line to Buffalo shut down at 9:00 p.m. each night. The switchboard first relocated to the home of Frank Fix. On April 1, 1923, it moved to the home of Marion Staley, where she began operating it, recruiting her mother to help. The New York Telephone Company took over both companies between 1930 and 1941. Soon after World War II, the number of telephones more than doubled from 300 to 625, finally requiring a two-operator switchboard.

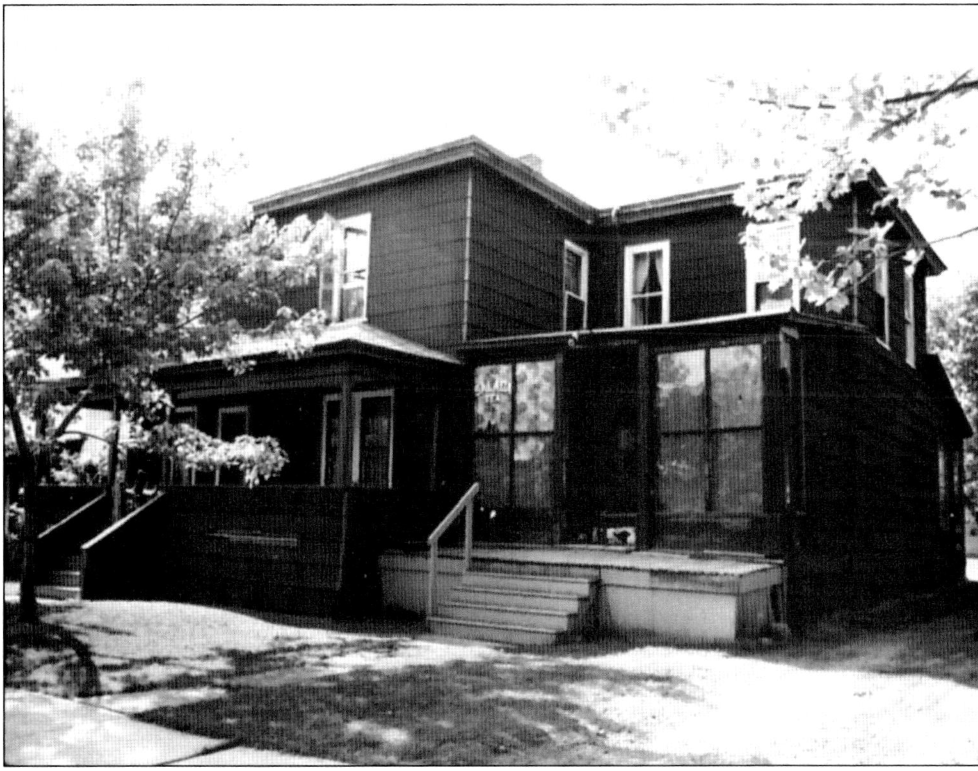

With limited transportation, farm families depended on a number of general stores in different parts of Grand Island to provide goods and services. Two of them are shown here: the Pettit Store on Ferry Road and Geschwender Bros. store, located at Baseline and Staley Roads. Captain Pettit was a well-known boat captain, so he was not always available to make deliveries. In 1922, Harry Tucker took over what had originally been the Pettit store and continued to operate it until the late 1960s.

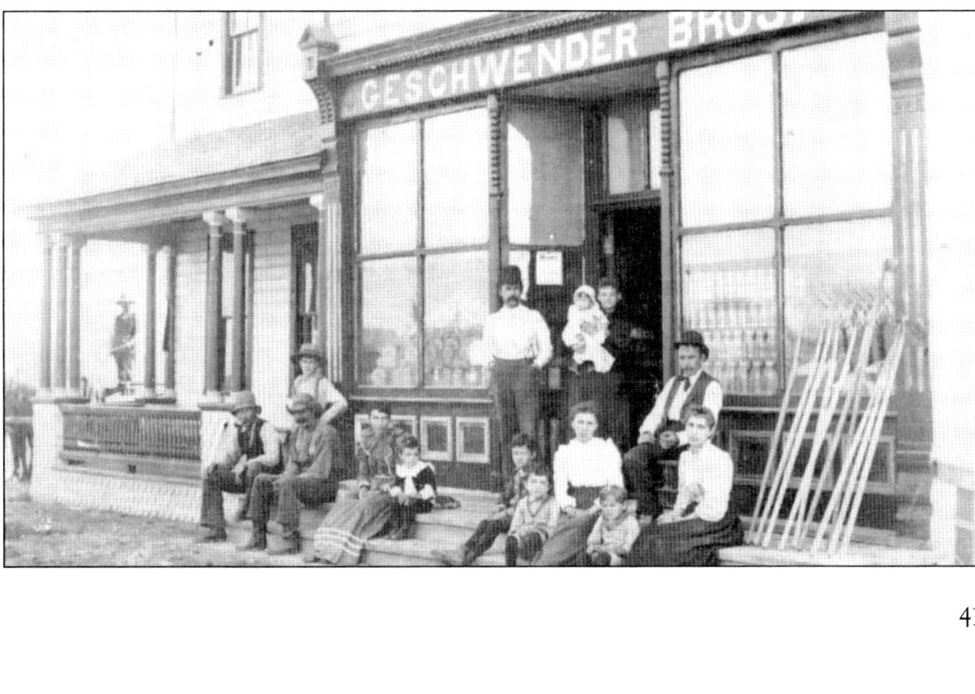

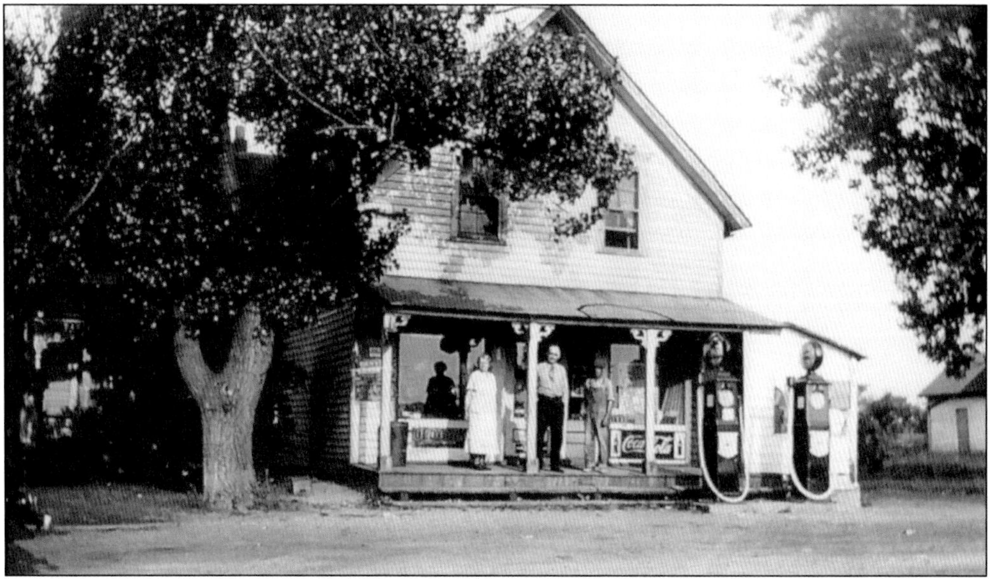

F.C. Stoll built this store sometime before 1900. Its location near the center of the island across from St. Stephen's Church made it convenient for many islanders. The store was subsequently operated by A.A. Stoll, Fred and Eva Long, Frank and Amelia Ehde, Erwin and Agnes Pinkel, and finally Ray Carline. Stores were often favorite gathering places. They served a social purpose much like that associated with churches. Sometimes the two came together, as in this photograph of Eva Long's Sunday school class on the roof of the Long store's porch in 1920. Note that the gas pumps had not yet been added. The store finally closed in 1965.

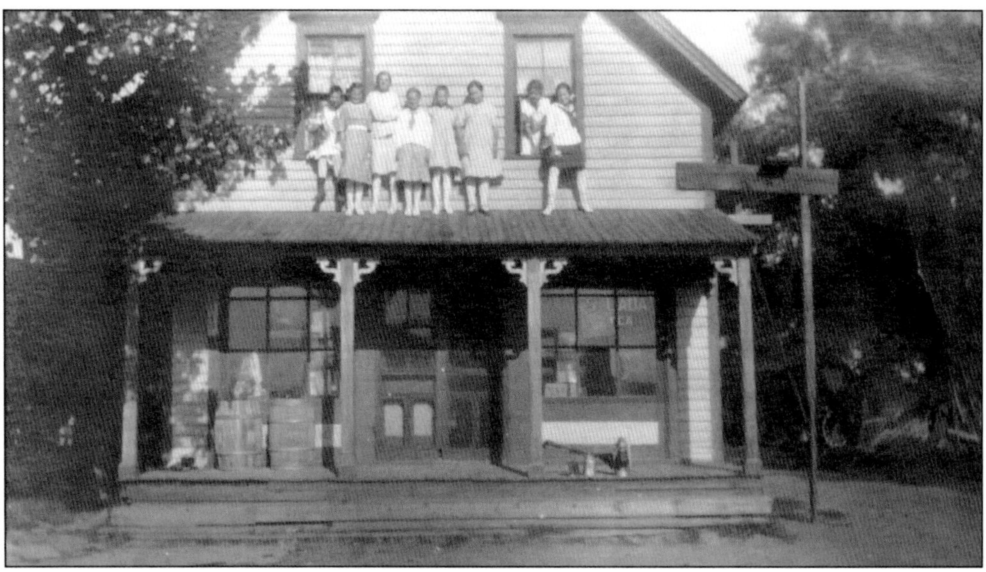

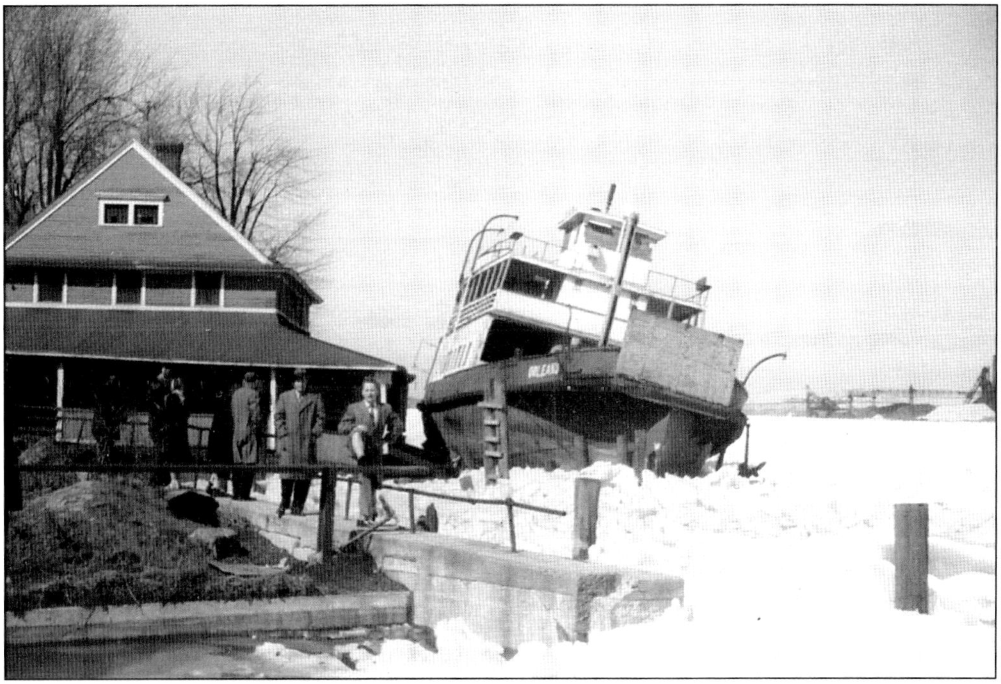

For an island totally dependent on boats for over a century, there were sometimes problems. With western New York's climate, the situation pictured here was hardly rare. Ice often clogged the river, making navigation difficult. Boatmen stayed on the river as much as possible in the winter, but sometimes they misjudged conditions. Currents and winds could turn a routine run into a nightmare.

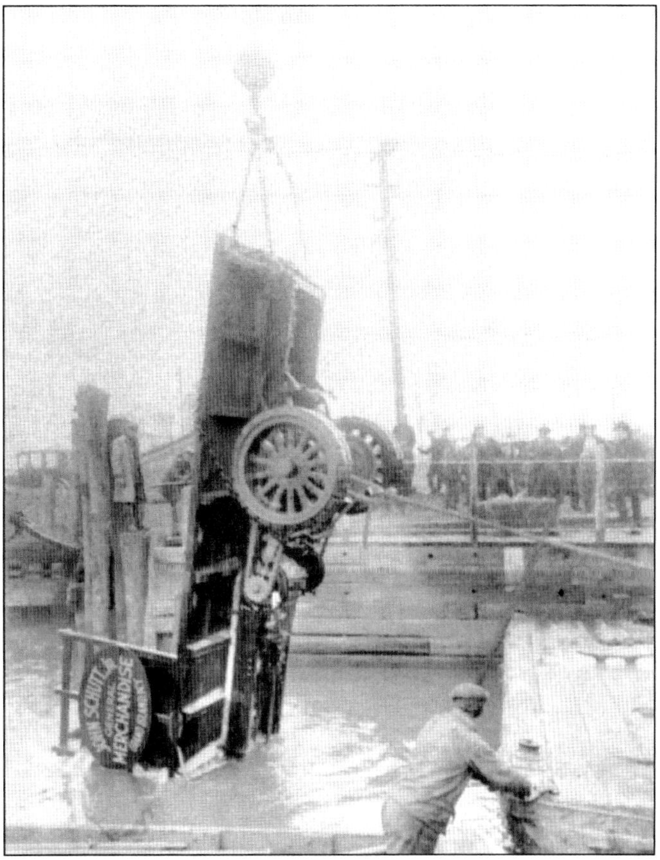

In addition to adding an extra cost to everything, reliance on the ferries to move people and goods to and from the mainland also carried a risk. This ferry mishap in the 1920s involved the truck from John Schutt's store. Having service halted because of weather was much more common and certainly did not draw a crowd.

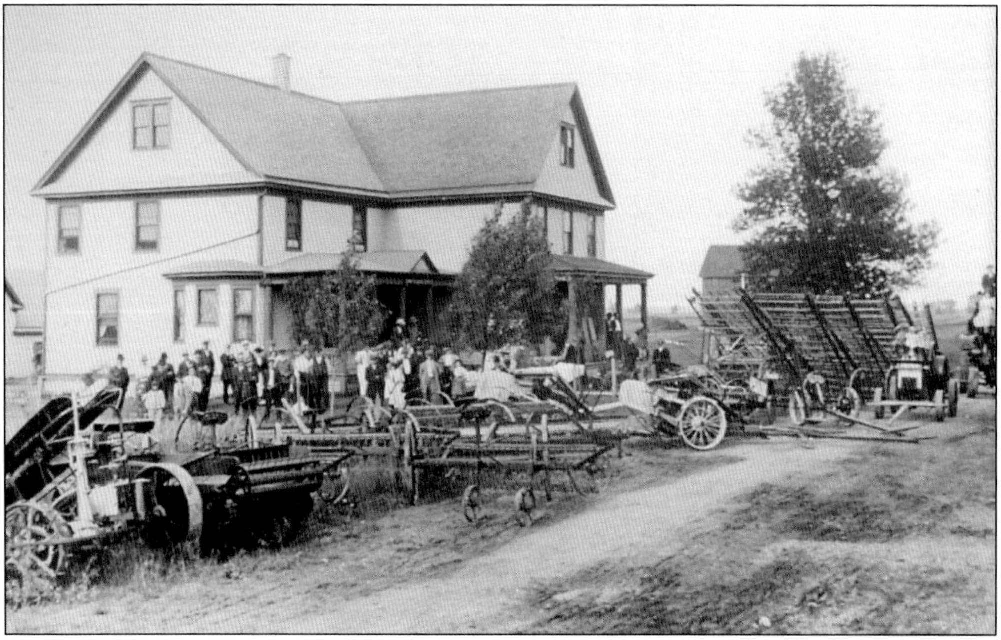

A large supply of farm equipment attracted a crowd to the Schutt store. Inside the store, owner John Schutt also had a huge elevator and hoist to take carriages and customers to his second floor buggy room. The Schutt operation continued to expand and change over the years. In the image below, the Schutt store and Schutt Lumber Company appear in the foreground. Behind it is the second town hall, constructed in 1938. The store remained in the family until 1945, when Ernie and Edith Godfrey took over. In 1950, they turned the second floor into a five-and-dime store.

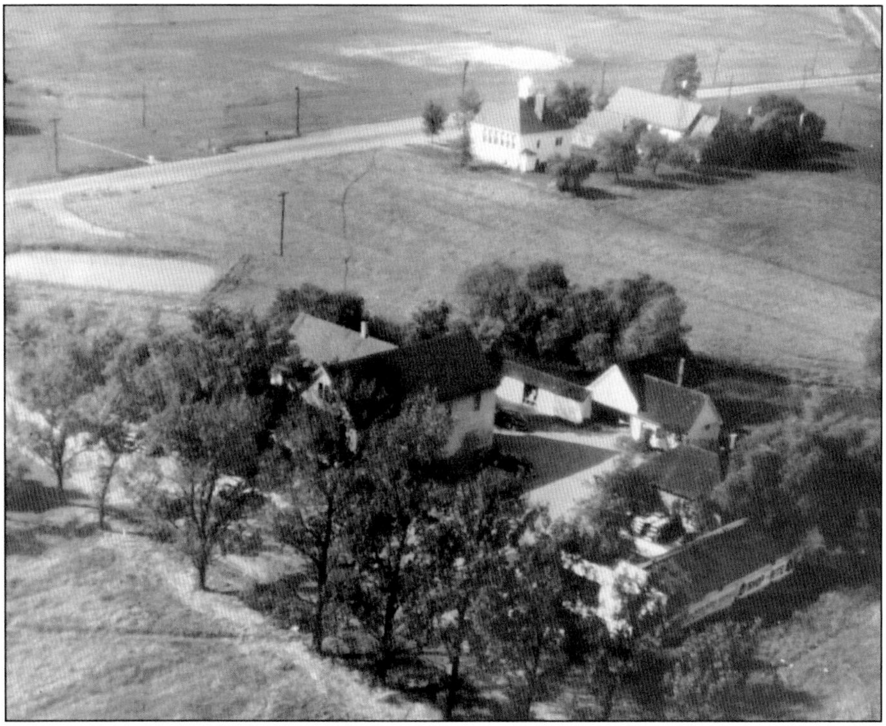

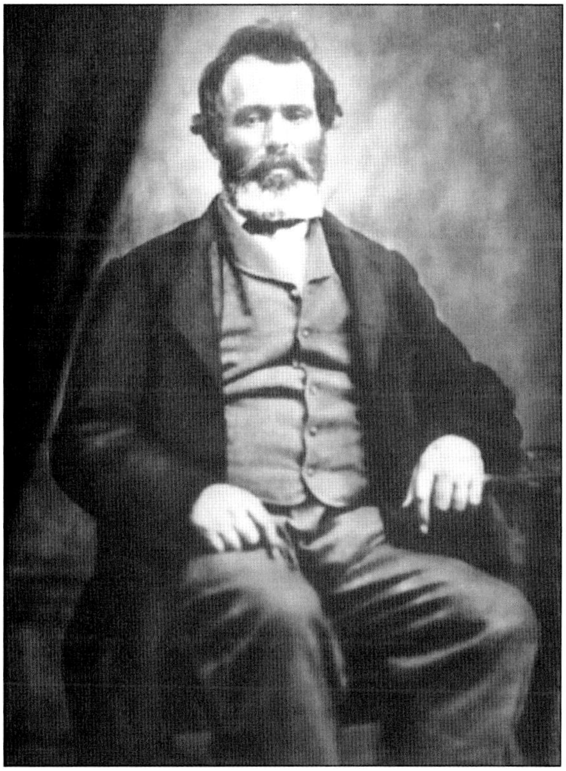

In 1822, the New York Legislature created Erie County out of the southern portion of Niagara County, and Grand Island became part of the town of Buffalo. In 1836, Grand Island was separated from Buffalo as part of the town of Tonawanda. In 1852, the Tonawanda Board of Supervisors created the town of Grand Island. The state legislature confirmed that move in 1853 and directed that the first town officers be elected at the home of John Nice, who farmed 600 acres on the East River. With Nice were Lyman Thompson and Asa Ransom. On March 1, 1853, John Nice was elected the first supervisor of the town of Grand Island. Nice headed Grand Island's government until moving on to the state assembly. Below are the minutes of the first meeting of the town board during which the first officers were elected.

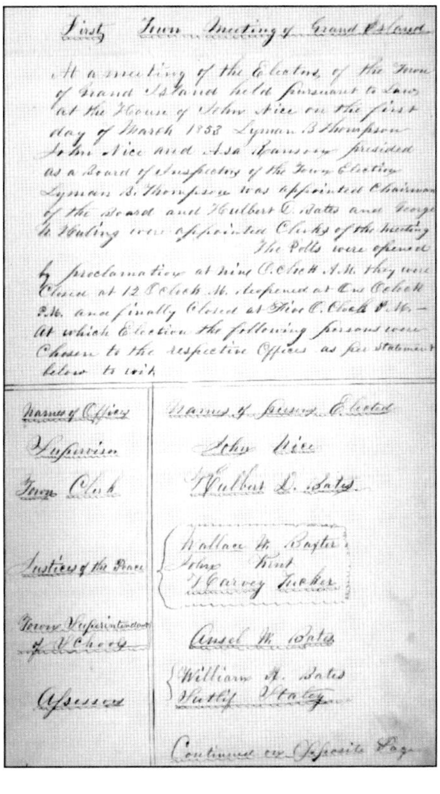

First Town Meeting of Grand Island

At a meeting of the Electors of the Town of Grand Island held pursuant to Law at the House of John Nice on the first day of March 1853 Lyman B Thompson John Nice and Asa Ransom presided as a Board of Inspectors of the Town Election Lyman B. Thompson was appointed Chairman of the Board and Hulbert L. Bates and George W. Huling were appointed Clerks of the meeting

The Polls were opened by proclamation at nine O.Clock A.M. they were Closed at 12 O'clock M. reopened at One O'clock P.M. and finally Closed at Five O.Clock P.M. — At which Election the following persons were Chosen to the respective Offices as per statement below to wit

Names of Offices	Names of persons Elected
Supervisor	John Nice
Town Clerk	Hulbert L. Bates
Justices of the Peace	Wallace W. Baxter John Kent Harvey Tucker
Town Superintendent of Schools	Ansel W. Bates
Assessors	William A. Bates Phillip Staley

Continued on Opposite Page

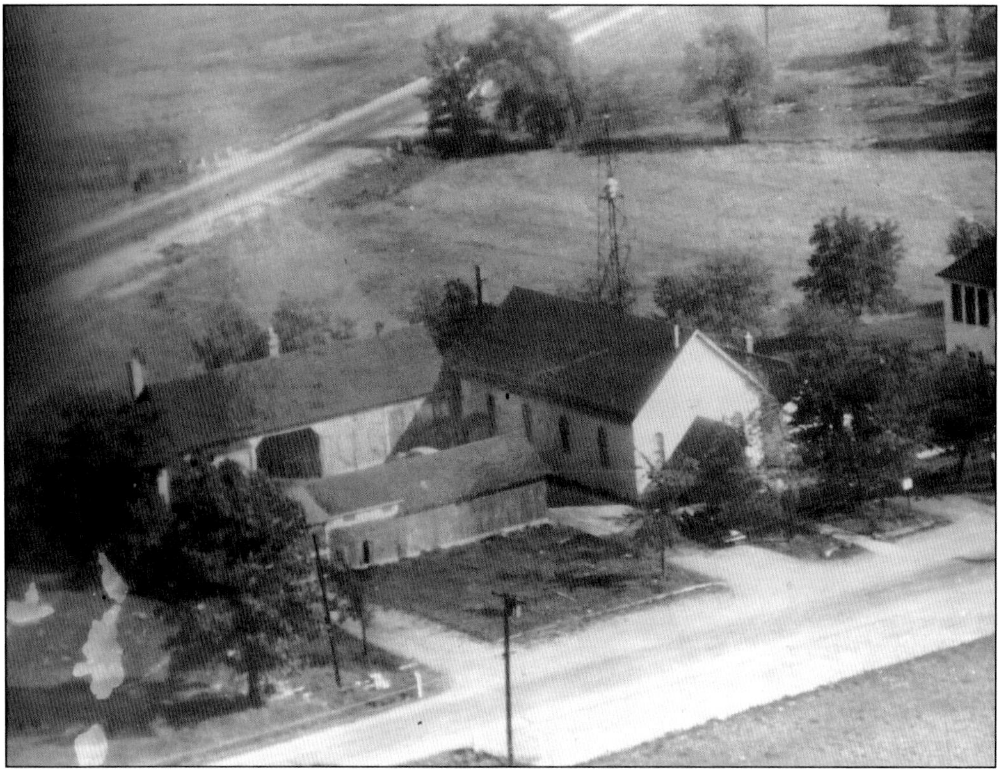

Grand Island became its own township in 1852, but it did not have a town hall until 1875, when the structure shown above was built. The town barn is in the background. Before 1875, town business was conducted in the homes of elected officials. The first building was lightly used by the town government, as it met infrequently. The building saw more use as a gathering place for dances, card parties, church and community meetings, rehearsals, and dinners. In 1938, the town government gave what had been School No. 9, pictured below, for the first home of the new Grand Island Fire Company.

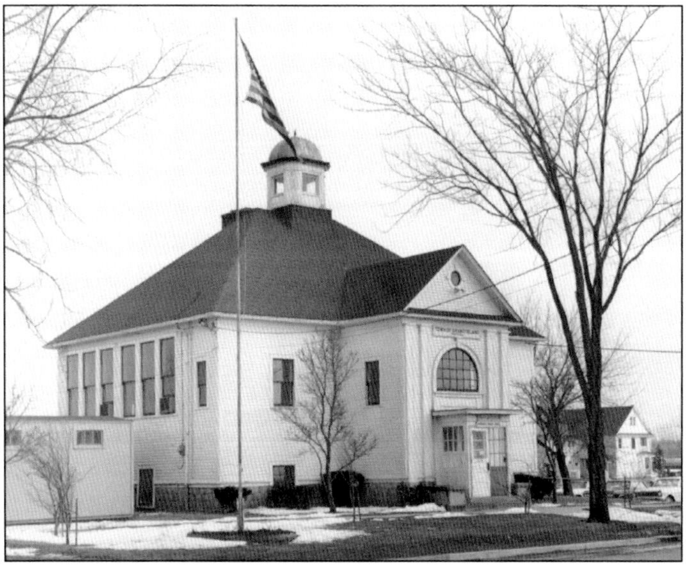

Four

Schools and Churches

The earliest schoolhouse on the island was built as part of the East Boston Timber Company's Whitehaven village in the 1830s. The building also served as a church for the community. It was necessary to supplement the workplace with support for the rest of the lives of the workers and their families. In the years that followed, a system of one-room schoolhouses served different parts of the island. Beyond the elementary grades, children had to be ferried to the mainland to complete their schooling.

Like the United States as a whole, Grand Island was a community built by immigrants, and from their varied points of origination, they brought their own religions. Originally, worshipers met in private homes or sometimes in temporary structures made of readily available natural materials. As the population of the island grew, more permanent arrangements appeared. By the end of the 19th century, there were three churches: St. Stephen's Roman Catholic Church, Trinity Evangelical United Brethren (EUB) Church, and the Congregational Church.

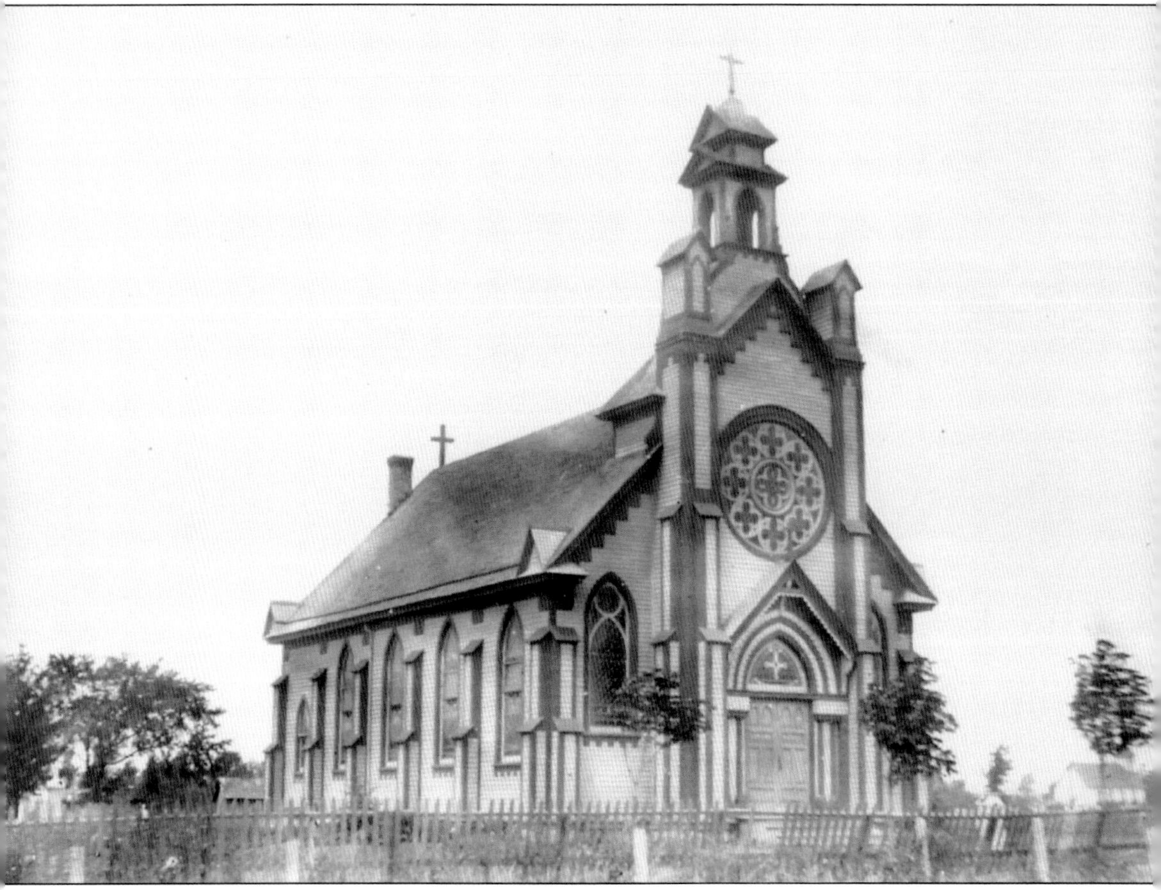

The first Catholic Mass on Grand Island took place in 1847, with a visiting priest serving communion to Irish and French Canadian families brought primarily for timber-cutting work. Masses were said in various homes but infrequently. Fr. Francis Stephen Ulrich began coming to the island in 1854 as the farm population grew, and he committed to building a church for the parishioners. In 1862, the new building was named for Father Ulrich's patron saint, Stephen. What became known as the Old Church replaced that structure as it was gradually completed between 1890 and 1895. The services were still held monthly—provided Father Ulrich could get to the island in winter. Finally, in 1906 the parish received its first resident priest, Fr. William J. Kuellertz. The congregation outgrew the building in 1957, and it was restored and rededicated in 1977.

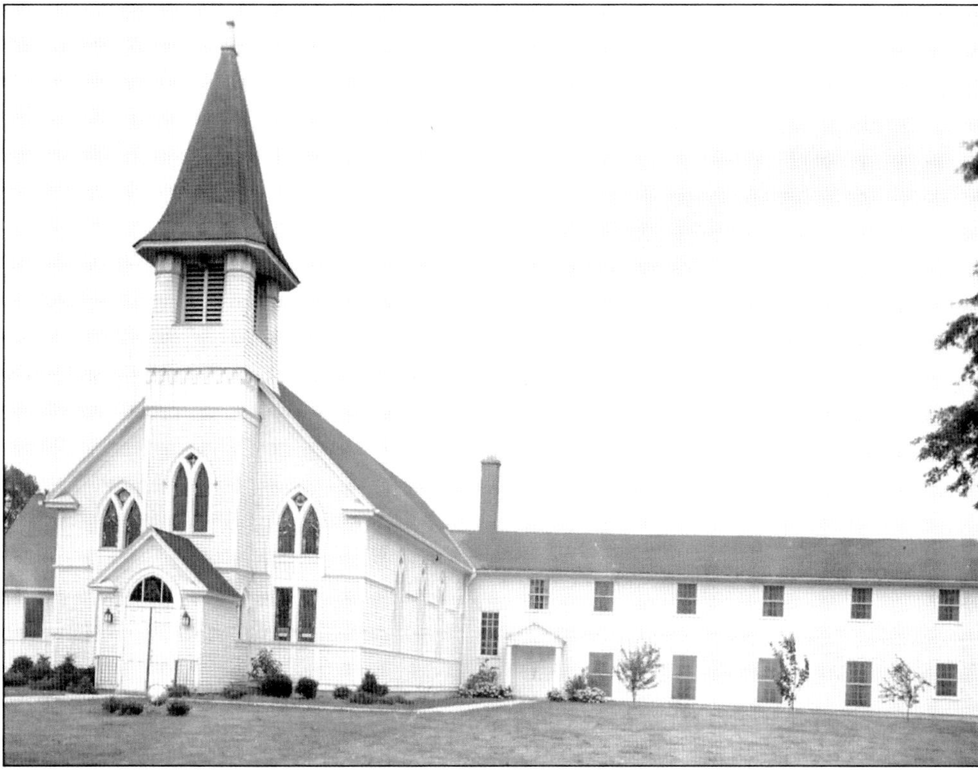

In 1907, the congregation of Trinity Evangelical, known to islanders as the German church, dedicated what is now called Historic Trinity (shown above). It was the third structure built to serve worshippers. The first and second, built in 1867 and 1886 respectively, were destroyed by fires. As first-generation immigrants and their children assimilated, pressure grew to switch services from German to English in order to better serve non-German speakers. That movement started in the early 1890s; World War I led to all services being in English. A fourth church, now known as Trinity United Methodist, was dedicated in 1965. In the early 1990s, determined preservationists saved Historic Trinity from the wrecking ball. The interior of the sanctuary is shown below.

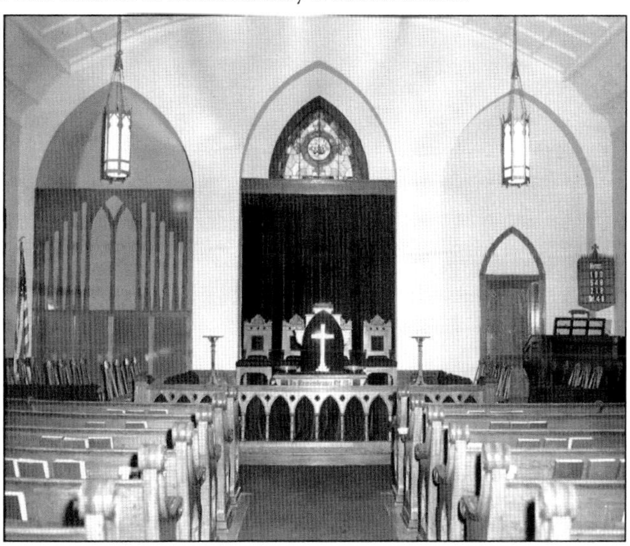

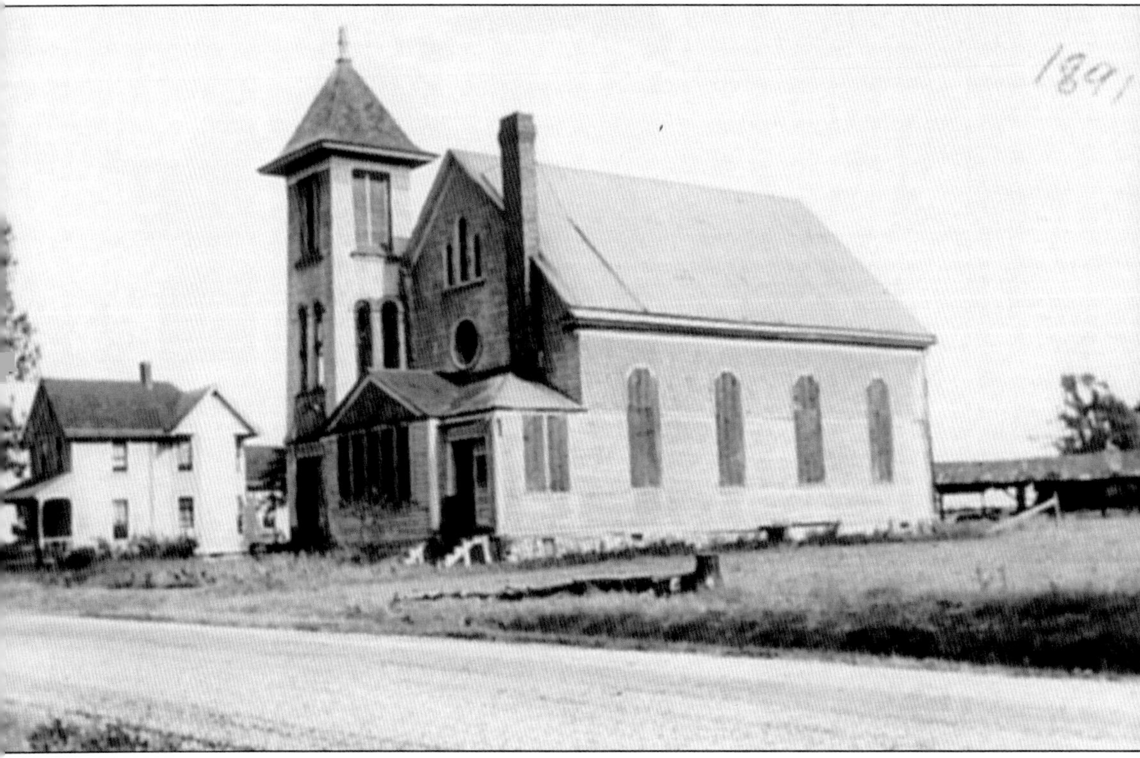

Before becoming the First Congregational Church in 1893, the Protestant congregation always referred to as the English church went by a variety of names. It started in 1864 with only 12 members and a pastor, Rev. A.M. Ball, who served without pay, relying instead on income from his sawmill and other business interests. The church grew slowly to 50 members—English, Scottish, and Irish, plus a few Dutch and German members. In the early 1890s, its original building on the West River burned, and the church in this picture was built near St. Stephen's and Trinity toward the center of the island. The church disbanded in 1914, a victim of the depletion of the Grand Island population.

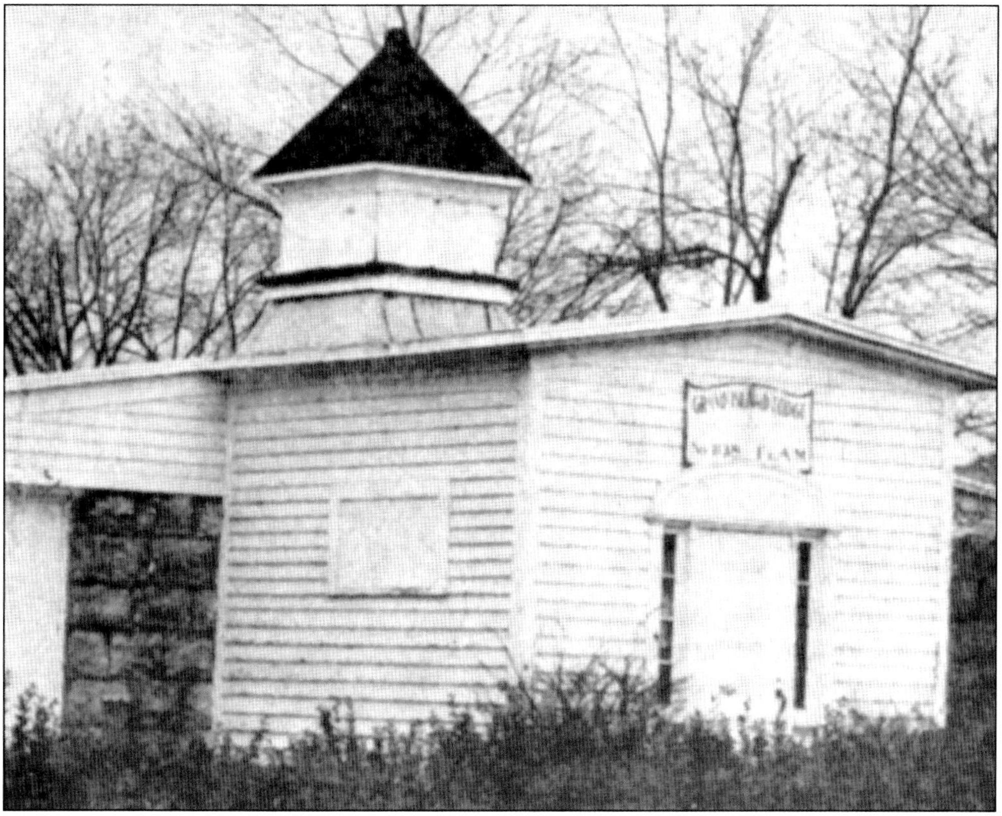

With large numbers of nonresidents still crowding onto the island in the early 20th century, the local churches responded. In 1913, both St. Stephen's Church and Trinity Evangelical Church decided separately to address the needs of summer visitors. That year, Fr. Frank Meyer and the trustees of St. Stephen's built Mary Star of the Sea chapel on the corner of Ferry and Orchard Roads (above). The same year, Trinity Evangelical constructed their Emanuel Chapel nearby (right). Despite the decline in summer visitors after 1914, Mary Star of the Sea continued operating in the summers until 1948, when the building was sold to the Grand Island American Legion.

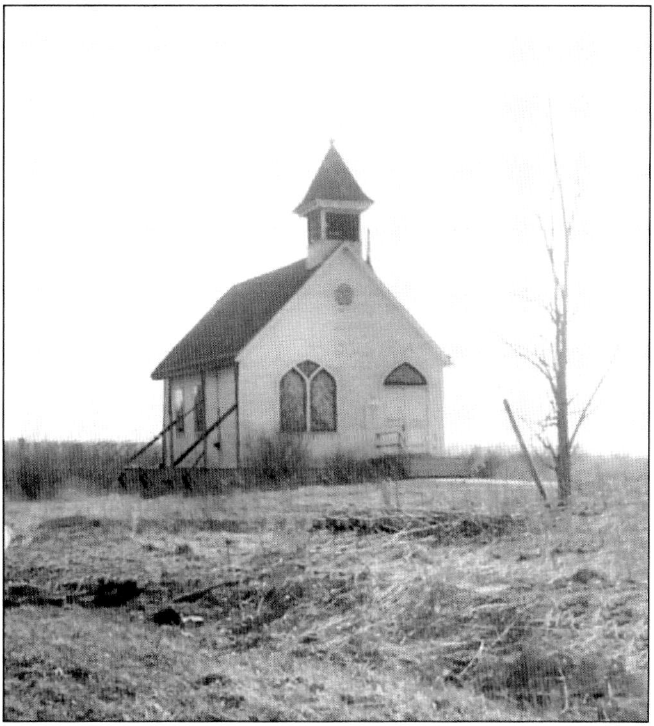

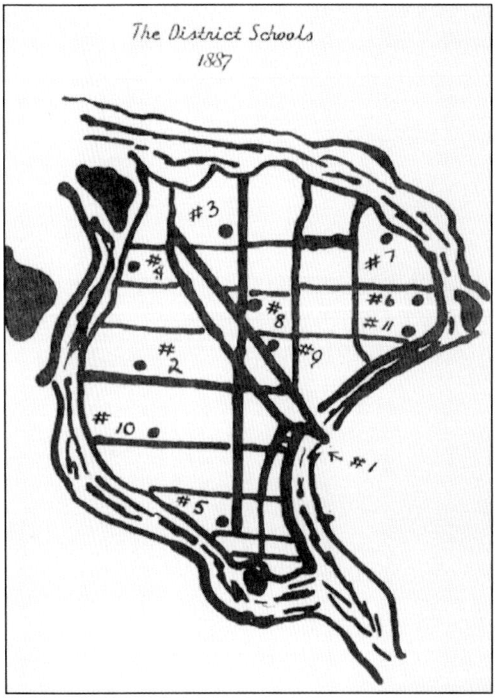

Until 1937, the island used a system of one-room and later some two-room schoolhouses to serve younger children. Ferries carried older students to mainland high schools, primarily Tonawanda and Riverside. In winter, that could be problematic. This map shows the location of the one-room schools in 1887, when the island's population was already starting to decline.

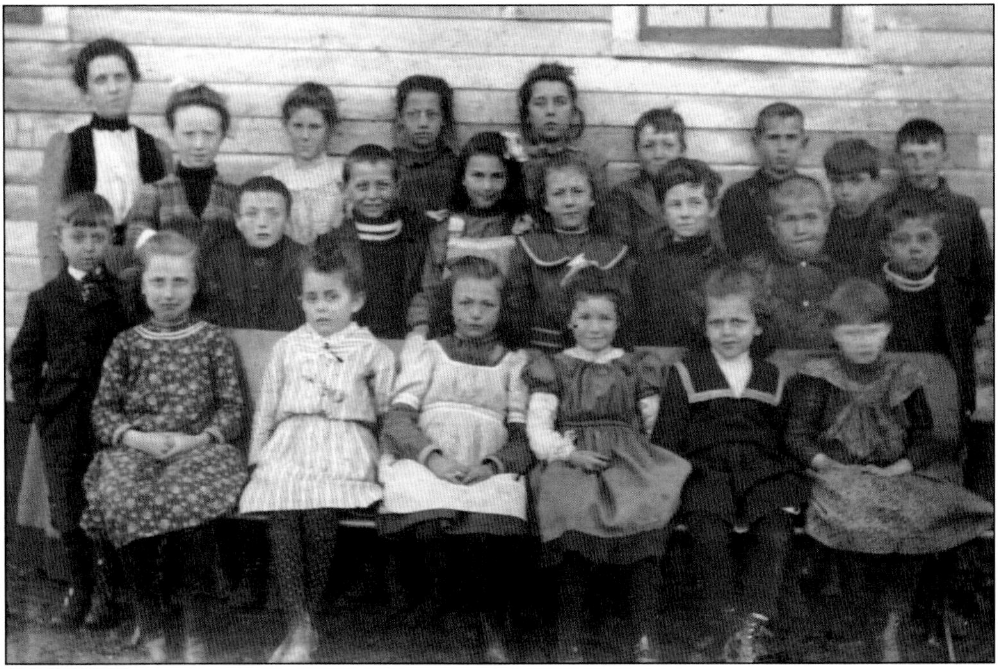

A typical school was one story, one room, one teacher, and a small class of students in first through eighth grades. One particularly cold winter, School No. 3 served only two students for a while because ice blocked students who lived on Buckhorn Island from attending. Until 1879, each of the 10 schools on the island was its own separate school district. In that year, the legislature passed a law creating a single Grand Island school district, and islanders elected the first school board: John Nice, John Staley, Lewis Long, Robert Gilbert, and Levant Ransom.

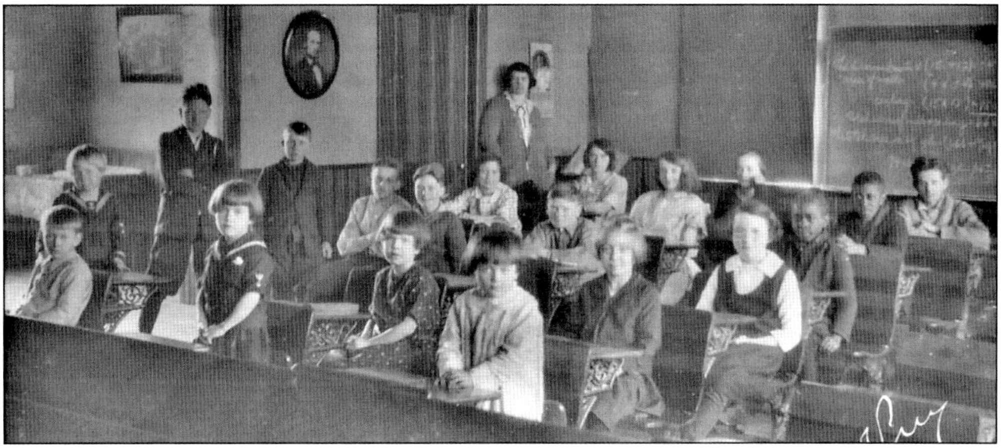

The pupils of School No. 5 on Bush and Baseline Roads are pictured here with their teacher, a Miss Lloyd, in 1923. They are (first row of desks on right, from front to back) Irene Santo, Mabel Webb, Bernice DeGlopper, Paul and George Williams, and Ralph Fitzpatrick; (second row) Arlene Yensan, Dennis Fitzpatrick, Lillis DeGlopper, and Sylvia Christman; (third row) Doris Yensan, Rodger Rawley, and Mildred Lang; (fourth row) Steve Santo, George Fitzpatrick, and Anna Webb; (standing) Mary and Fred Rawley, Walter DeGlopper, and Miss Lloyd.

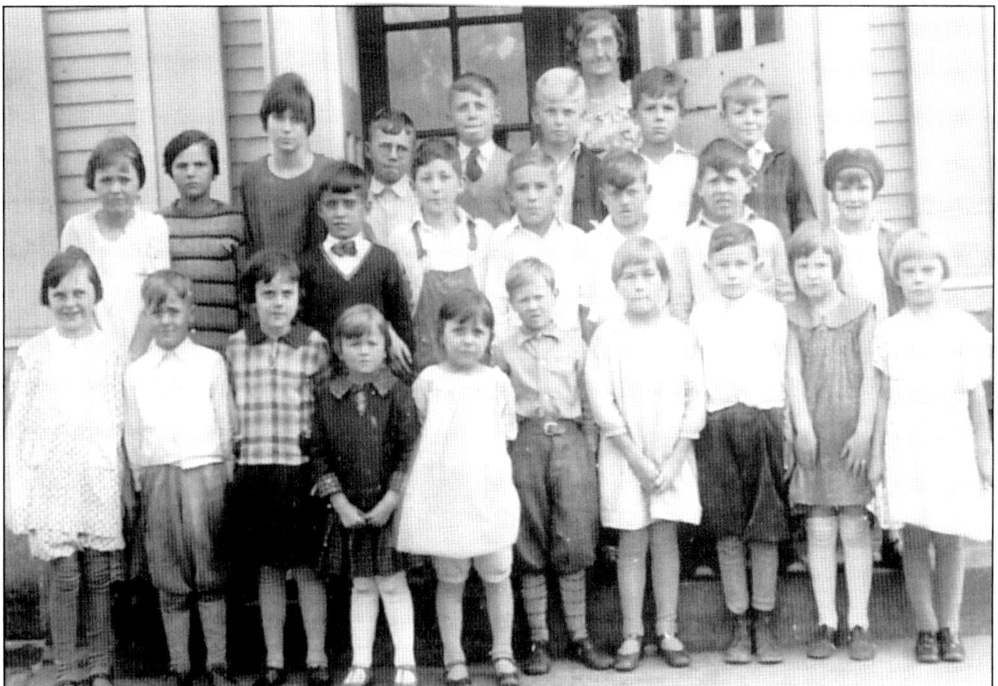

In 1929, teacher Margaret DeGlopper (back right) stands on the front steps of School No. 9 with her students. From left to right are (first row) Carola Long Freer, Clarence Schutt Jr., Betty Ziehm Yensan, Mesmer "Tootie" Maurer, Shirley Kreger Luther, Franklin Mesmer, June Christman Renwick, Harold Kaiser, Catherine Killian Long, and May Webb Eastman; (second row) Carlton "Joe" Killian, Harry Kaiser, James Stack, John Ralph Mesmer, Ralph Kreger, and Irene "Honey" Kaiser Daigler; (third row) Edna Schutt, Geraldine Schutt, Violet Schutt, Harold "Bud" Long, Ed Killian, Allan Kaiser, Billy Kaegebein, and Wally Killian.

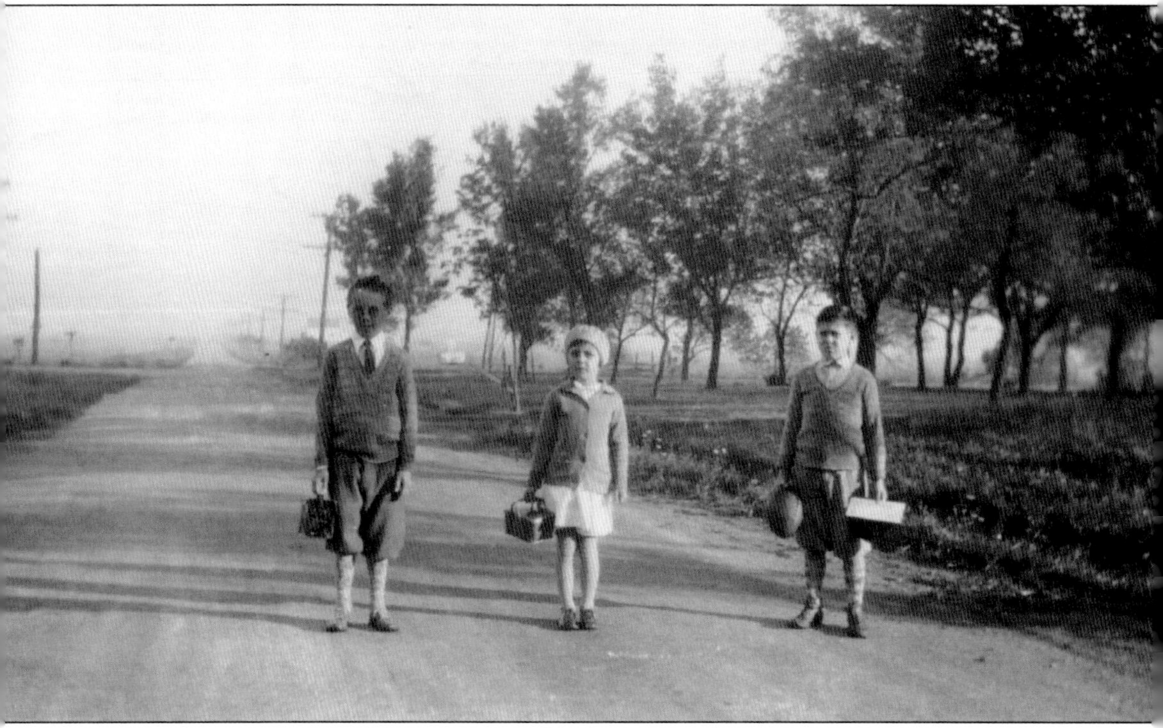

Until the construction of the first consolidated school in the mid-1930s, it was only natural that every student walked to school. In this early 1930s image, from left to right, Bud Long, Shirley Kreger (Luther), and Ralph Kreger are on their way to School No. 9, located at Baseline and Whitehaven Roads.

Five

A Watering Place for Buffalo

In the last half of the 19th century, Grand Island became the favored location for summer estates and private clubs dedicated to the relaxation and enjoyment of the wealthy from the mainland cities along the Niagara River. The island hosted a variety of hotels, resorts, and amusement parks enjoyed by the general population of the surrounding area.

The leading figure in turning Grand Island into a haven for the well-to-do was Lewis F. Allen, who arrived in Buffalo in 1827 to serve as secretary and financial manager for the Western Esurance Company. The young businessman soon began to purchase and lease significant tracts of land in the rapidly developing city. Allen's faith in the future of Buffalo as a major urban center inspired his many civic activities. He had an interest in agricultural experimentation, especially the breeding of shorthorn cattle. He first established his herd on his Buffalo land, but when he helped the East Boston Timber Company acquire its 16,000 acres of white oak forest on Grand Island, he also purchased 600 acres that became Allenton Farm, a new location for his cattle breeding and fruit cultivation. In 1858, he opened the Falconwood Club to Buffalo's elite. In 1863, Allen publicized his effort to give wealthy citizens what they deserved, publishing *Does Buffalo Need a Watering Place?*, along with his strong affirmative answer. Successful Buffalonians could move their families to the healthful and relaxing retreat for the summer and still conveniently commute to the city. And Allen was ready to contribute by making available for sale a portion of his own holdings, which included 10,000 feet of shoreline. Soon, mansions and private clubs began to spread along the island's shores. Riverlawn, the summer estate of Hon. Elbridge G. Spaulding, a prominent lawyer, banker, and politician, stood adjacent to the Allen's Falconwood property by 1870.

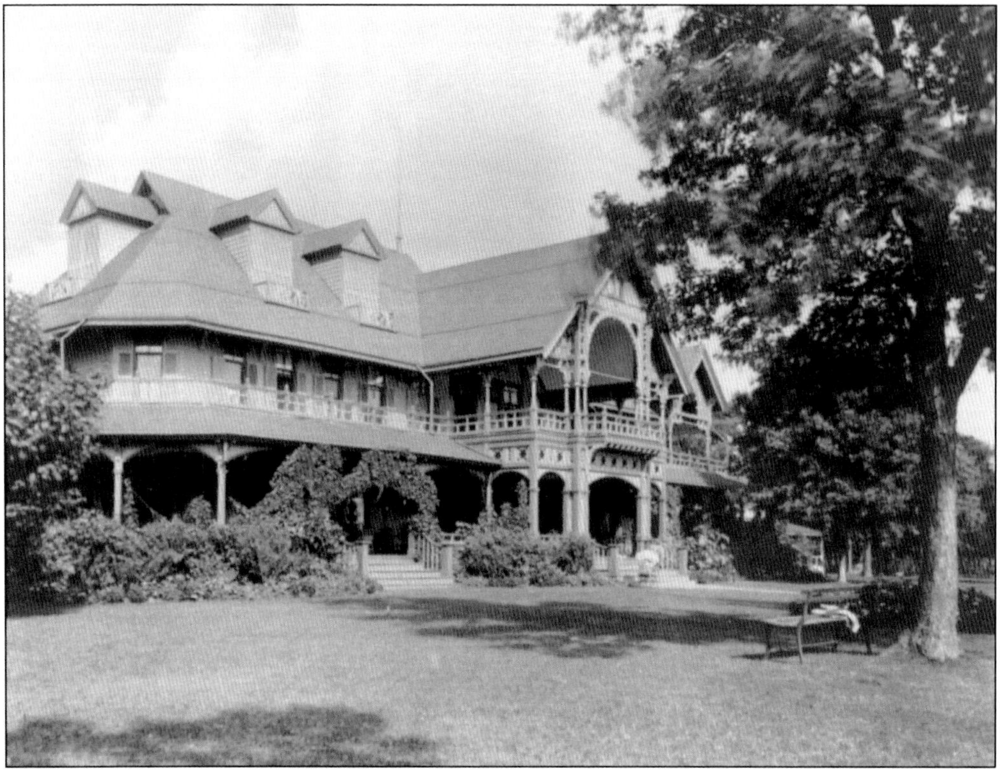

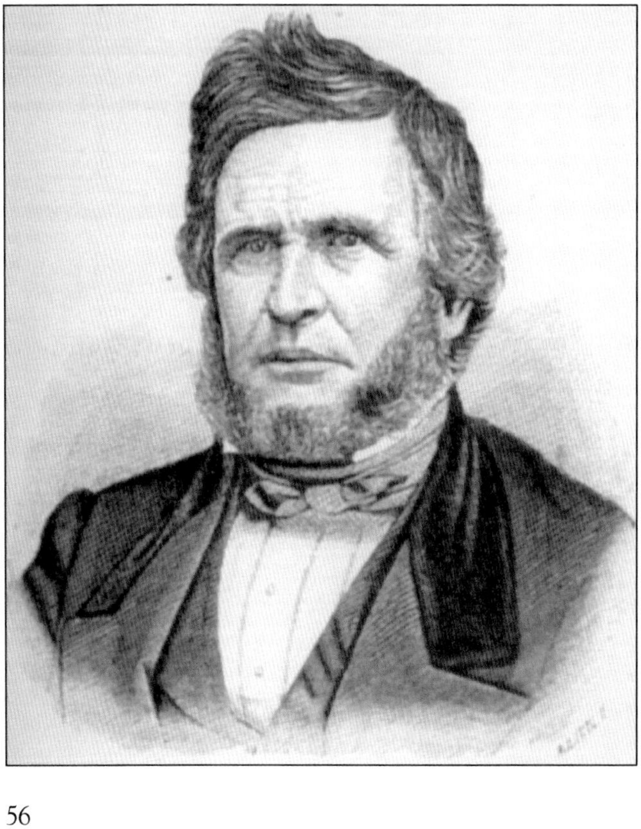

Pioneering Grand Island real estate developer Lewis Allen set aside a portion of his Allenton Farm and built what was thought to be a new Allen mansion, but instead it opened its doors in 1859 as the ornate centerpiece of a resort known as the Falconwood Club, named for the hawks and eagles that nested in the tall trees that covered much of the property. It was to be the first of many resorts and clubs that appeared on the island. Only 70 members could stay in the main building, but some had separate cottages. All could enjoy a breathtaking view of the West River and the Buffalo skyline. The property was destroyed by fire in the 1920s.

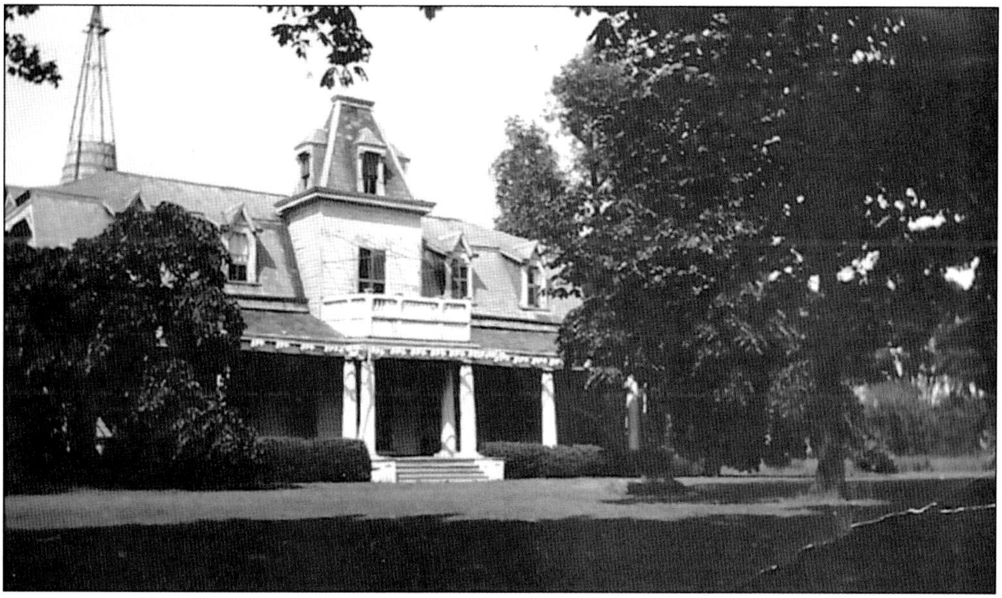

The Beaver Island clubhouse was built by a group of Buffalo sportsmen first known as the Jolly Reefers. In 1852, they incorporated as the Beaver Island Club and built their new clubhouse. Lewis F. Allen was one of the founding members and brought in his nephew Grover Cleveland (right), who continued to enjoy fishing and hunting on Grand Island even as his political career took him far from Buffalo. Later, the clubhouse became the home of Charles D. Marshall and was known as Marshall Mansion. The property was sold to the state as part of the Beaver Island State Park in 1935, and it was destroyed in 1941.

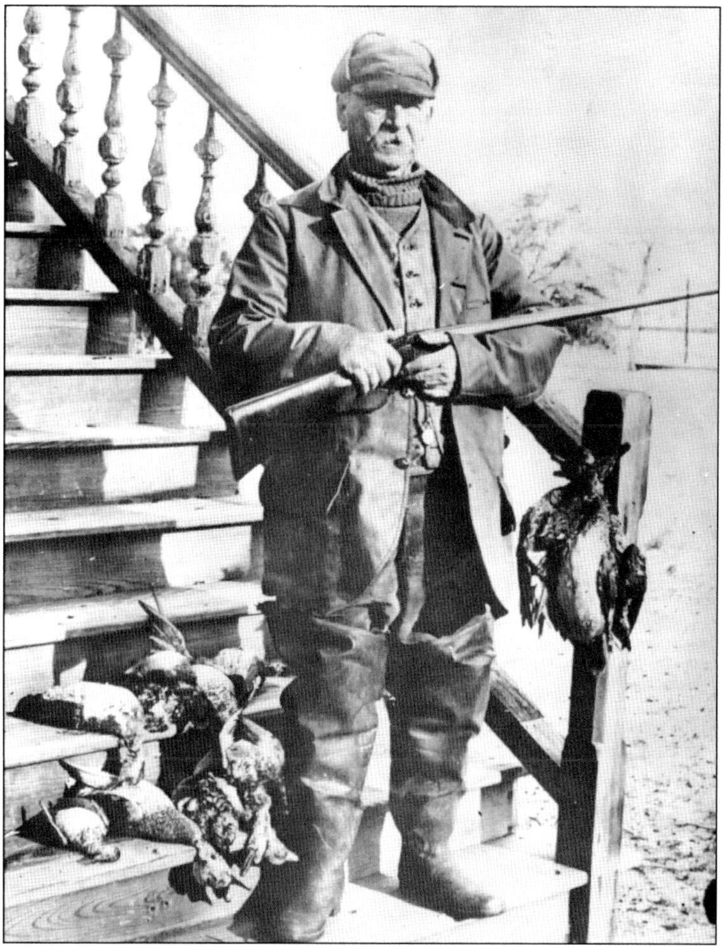

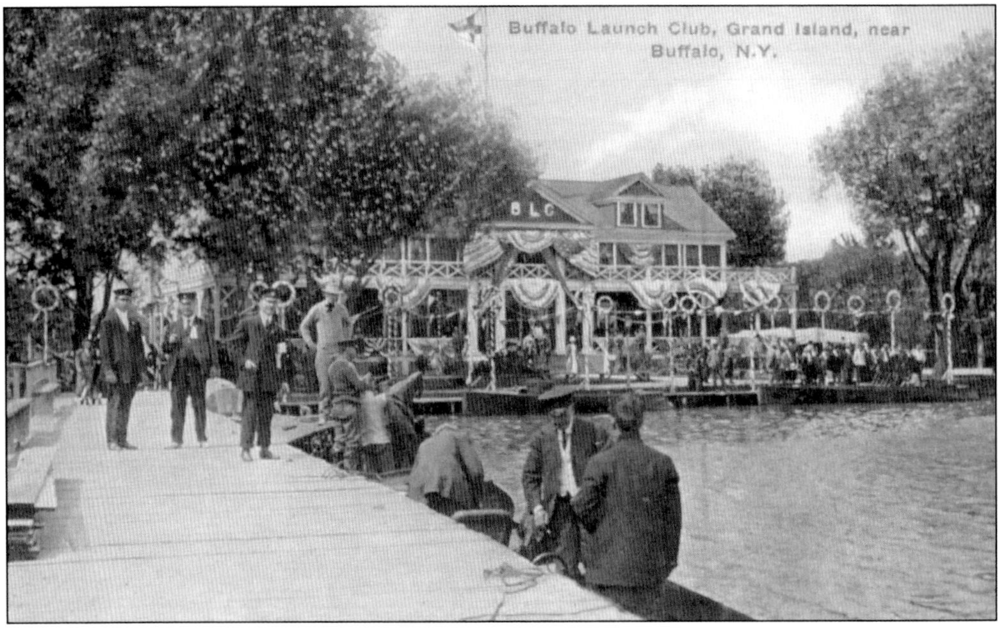

The last arrival among the private clubs of Grand Island was the Buffalo Launch Club, the first powerboat club in North America. Incorporated in 1904 at the instigation of Dr. Albert Hubbard, the group was not exclusive; they just wanted to share their passion for boat racing. Even before completing their clubhouse on the eastern shore of the island in 1906, they held their first regatta. These became annual affairs that attracted competitors from across America and Canada. They are shown below gathering at the Bedell House dock. Racing on the Niagara has continued, and the club still operates to this day.

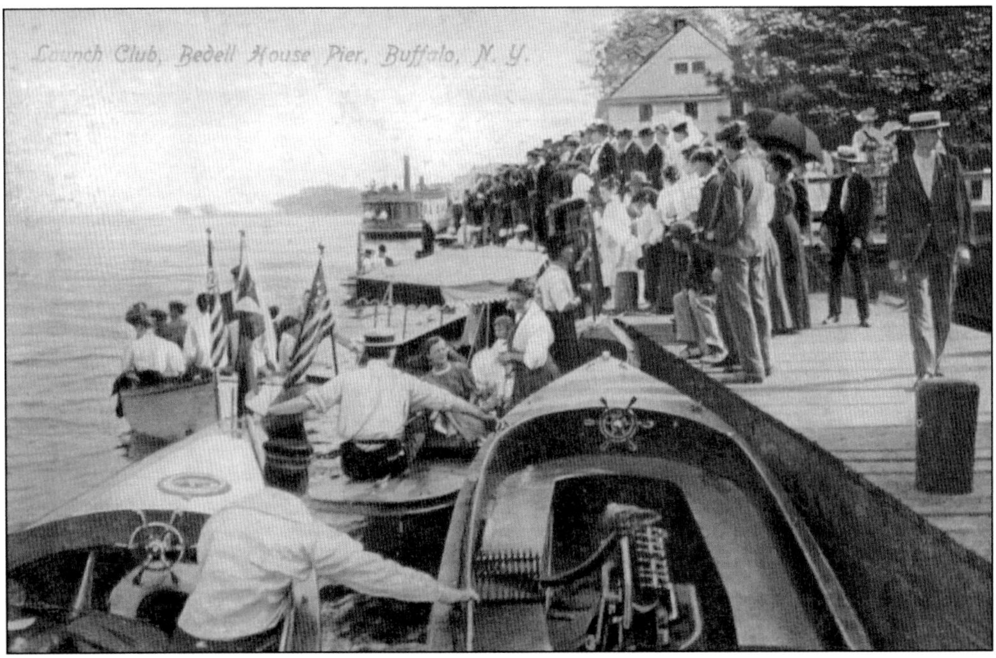

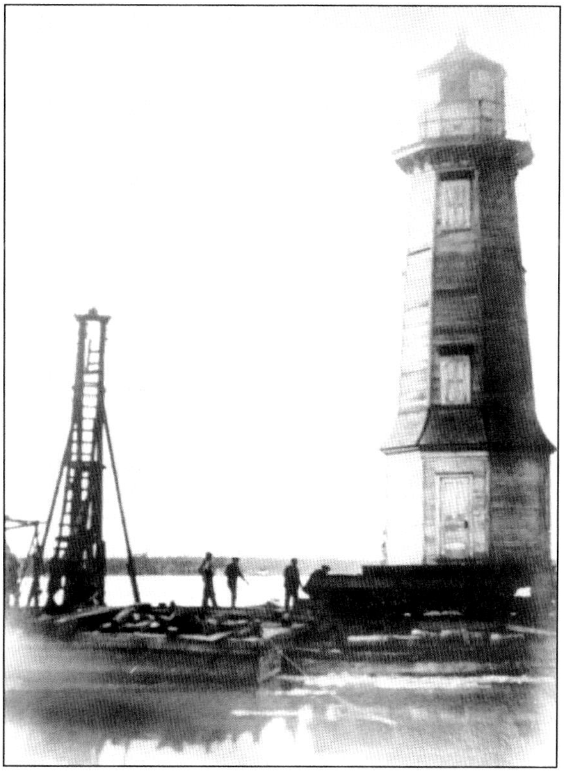

This 52-foot lighthouse was not always a feature of the Buffalo Launch Club. Older than the club itself, the lighthouse was built in 1885 and originally stood across the East River on Busti Street in Tonawanda. It was one of two lighthouses on the Niagara River that were to be dismantled in 1931. The club rescued the beacon and moved it across the river. It was not a long trip, but the move was not simple. The lighthouse is pictured here in transit to its new home. The original clubhouse burned the same year and was replaced with the current structure.

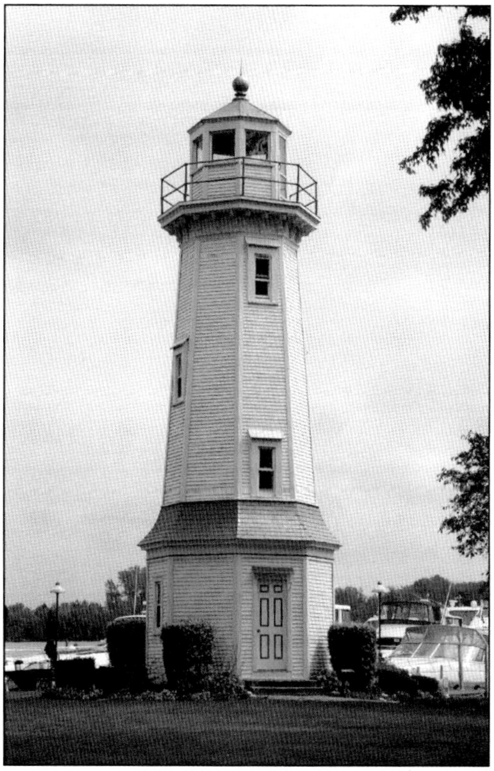

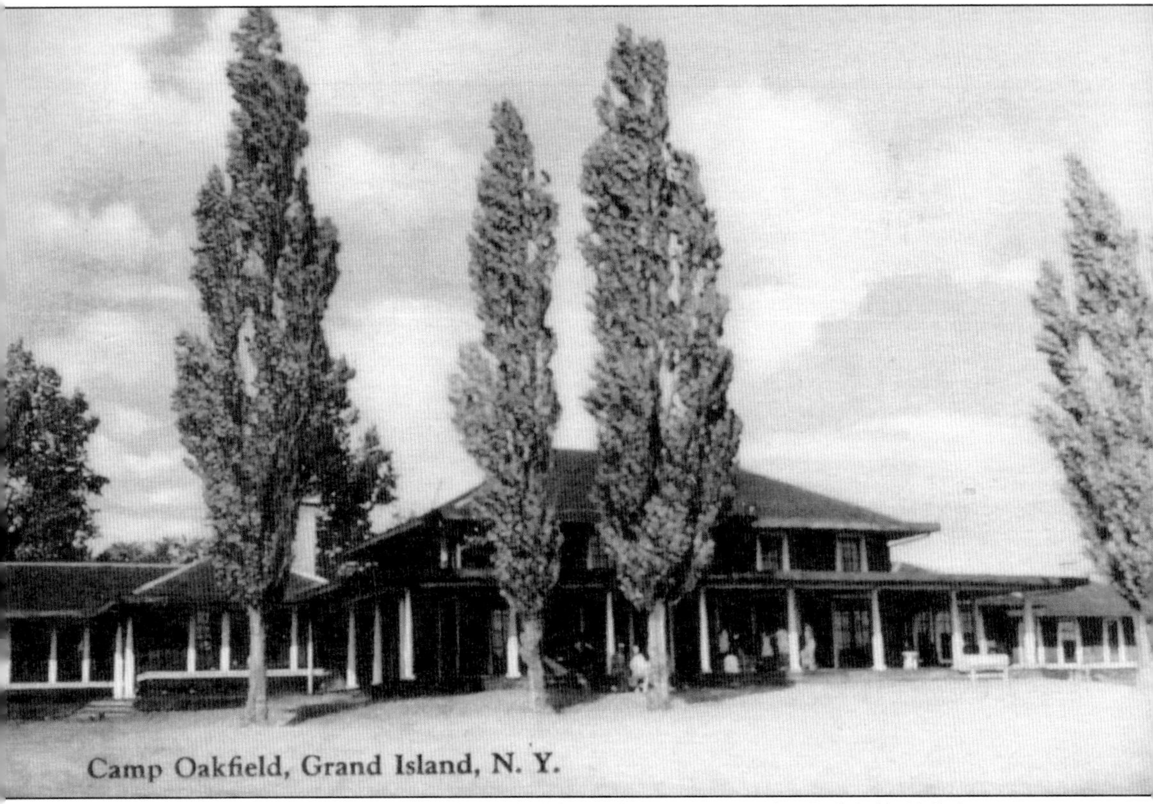

The largest of the private clubs at the end of the 19th century was the Oakfield Club, boasting more than 400 members. The four-story clubhouse opened in 1887 with 250-foot-long verandas on each floor. The lush interior provided large public spaces for the elite to gather and socialize. Individual rooms on the top three floors were finished in a manner suitable for the clientele. The extensive grounds included individual cottages built for some members, but there was still plenty of room for relaxation and outdoor activities with their families and friends. Members and guests arrived aboard the Oakfield Club's steamer, the *Lorelei.* In the early 20th century, the structure endured two fires. Membership dropped, and the property was sold to be replaced by the smaller, two-story Camp Oakfield, pictured here.

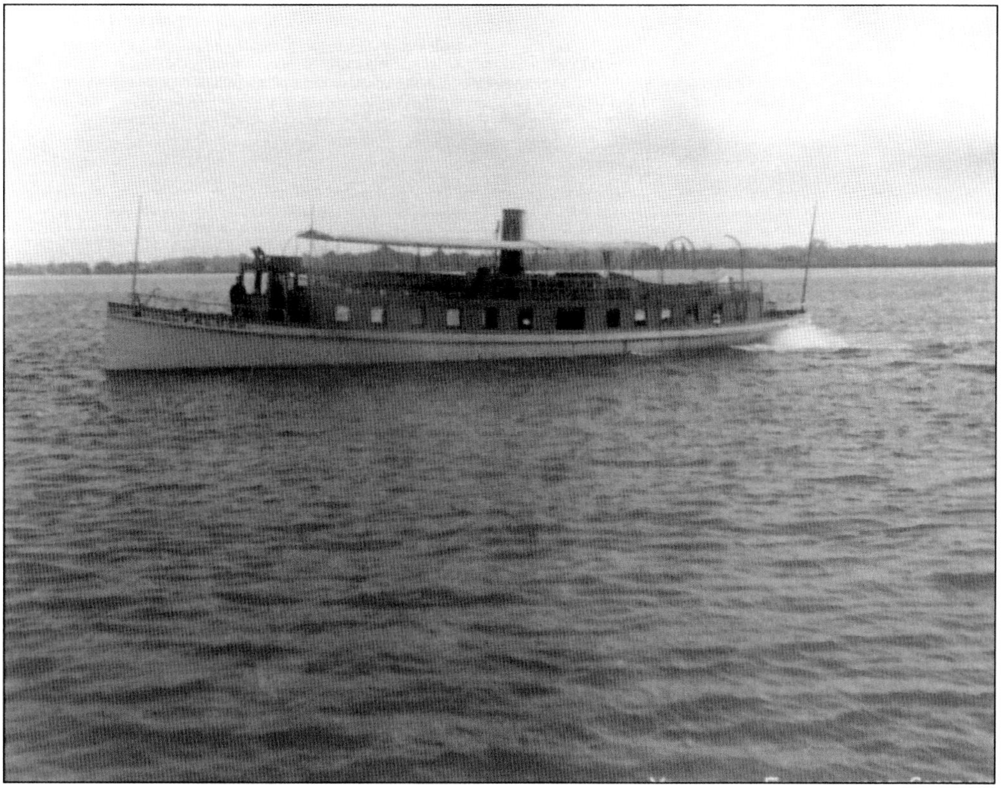

An important point in Lewis Allen's call for a watering place for Buffalo was the relatively easy connection between downtown Buffalo and the Grand Island retreat. Businessmen could move their families to the island for the summer and then commute to join them. A few members of the elite relied on their own yachts, but the Falconwood Club had its *Falcon* steamer to facilitate travel. Other private clubs followed suit. There were usually two decks: the lower enclosed and the upper with a soft top since most trips were made in warm weather. On both decks of the *Kittie Ditzel* it is possible to see the well-dressed passengers on their way to or from Grand Island.

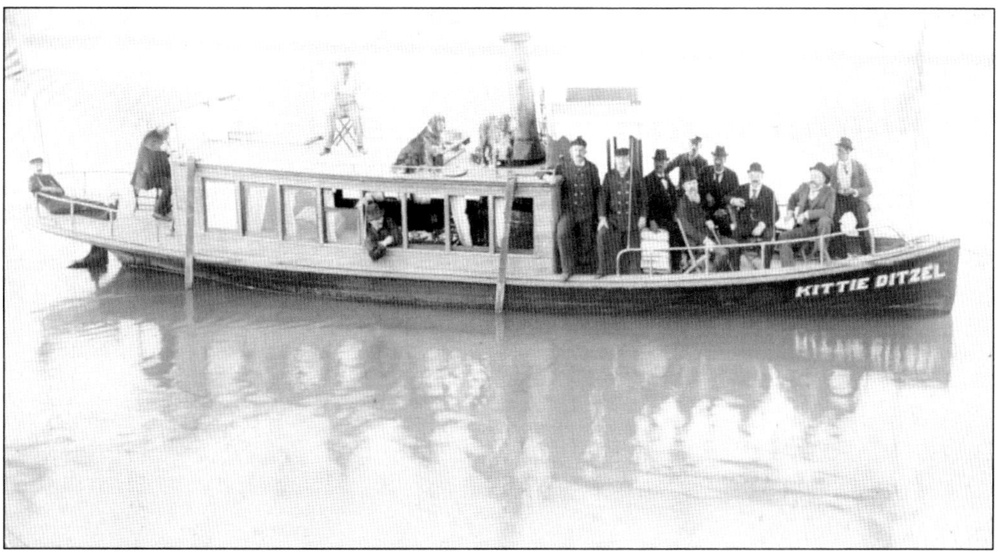

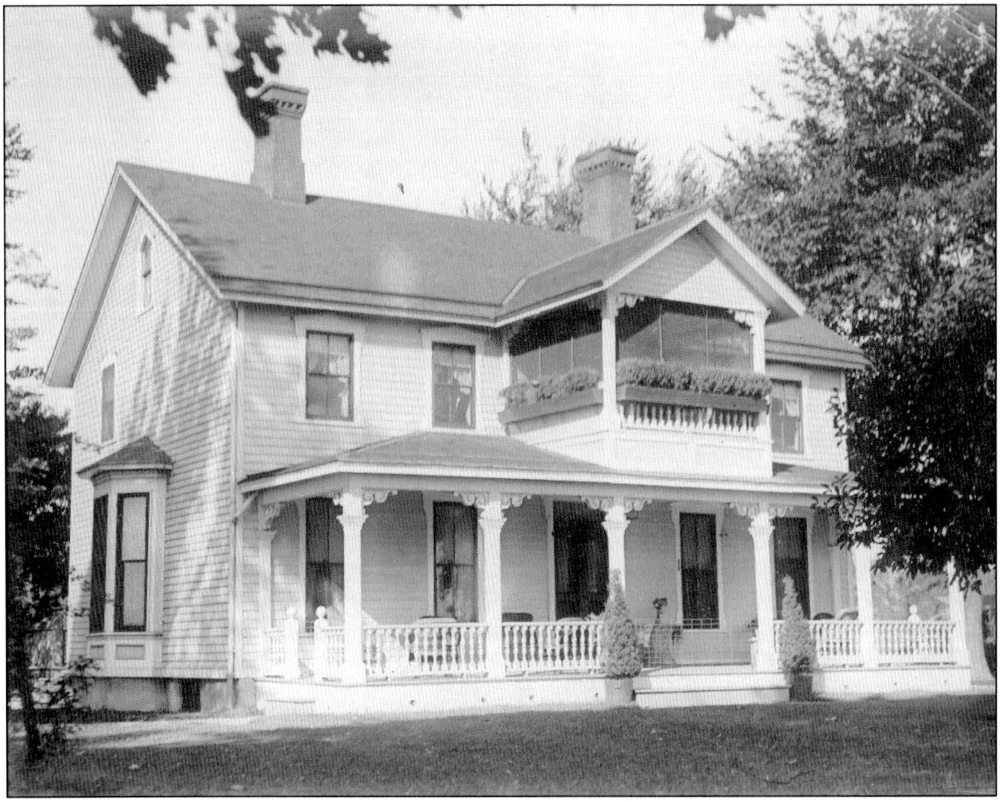

River Lea was built by Lewis F. Allen for his son William and his bride. It was one of just two houses that were spared when Beaver Island State Park was built on what had been Allenton Farm and the Falconwood property, including the Spaulding-Sidway estate. Today, it houses the Grand Island Historical Society. Above is the house before a fire in 1934, and below the formidable gates are pictured.

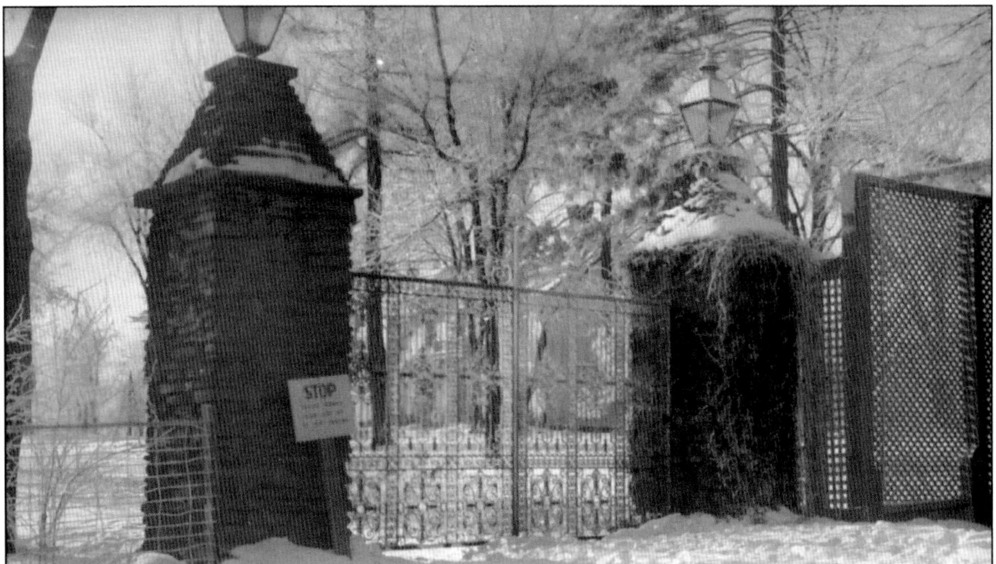

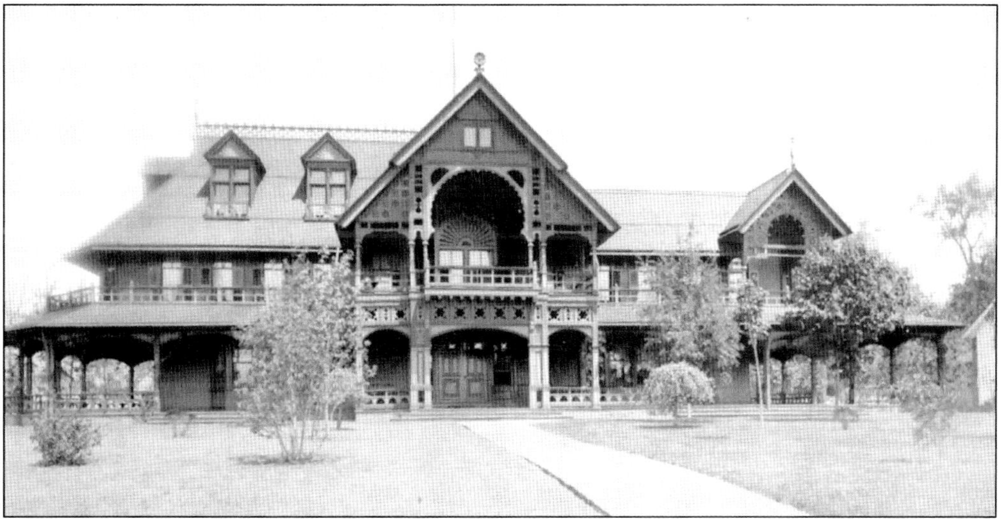

Elbridge G. Spaulding was first a very successful banker, mayor, and three-term member of Congress. He was instrumental in creating some of Buffalo's most important public institutions. By 1863, he was most famous as "the father of the greenback," the paper currency that allowed the Union to finance its side of the Civil War. Upon returning to Buffalo, he purchased a portion of Allenton Farm and began building his new house in an architectural style known as Victorian Stick. Spaulding maintained this magnificent property, including its outbuildings, for the rest of his life.

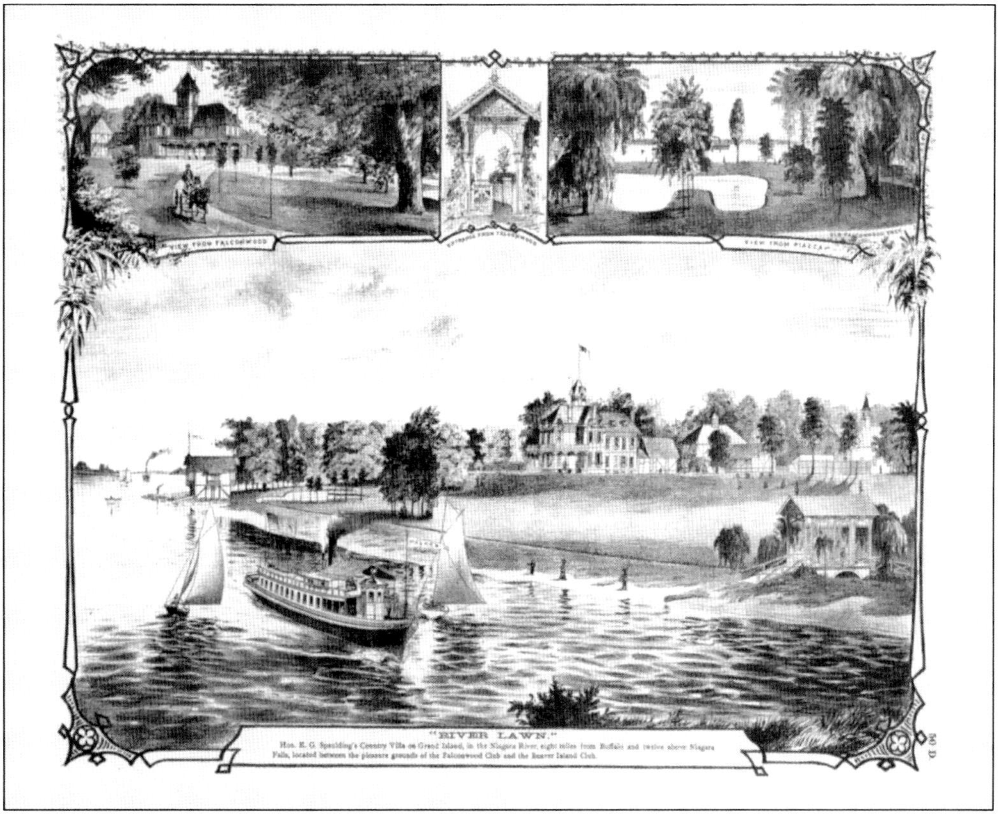

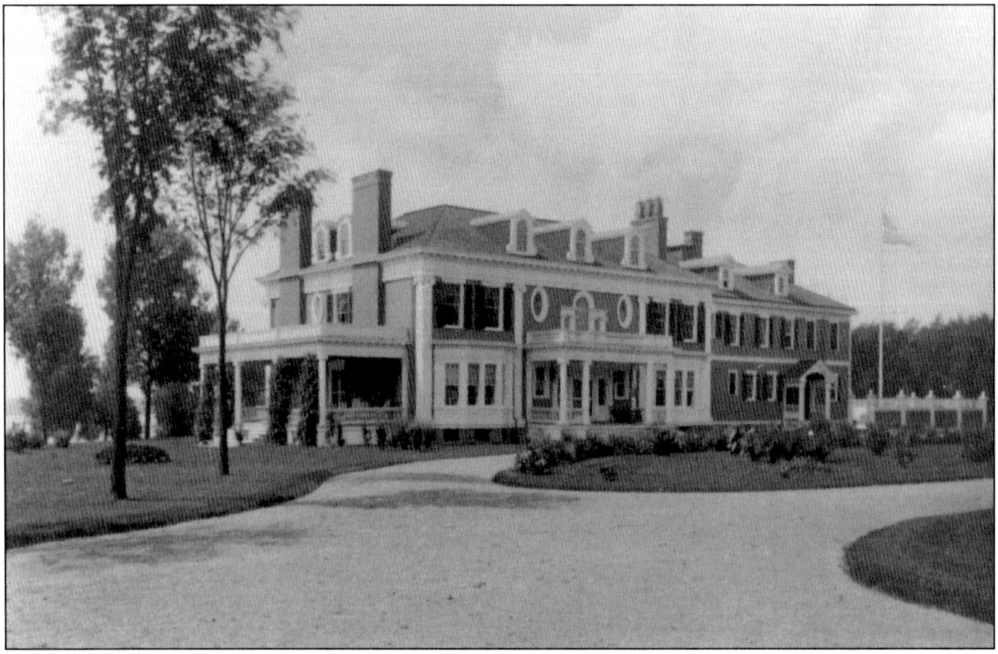

Spaulding's daughter married Franklin St. John Sidway, a prominent businessman and banker. Spaulding presented the Sidways with the opportunity to build their own house on a portion of his River Lawn estate in sight of his own house. During the 1880s, they took full advantage of that opportunity, constructing what many consider the grandest of the mansions built by Buffalo's elite. On the inland side, arriving guests would roll up their curved driveway to enter their impressive house. The Georgian-style Sidway home looked out over a spacious lawn that sloped gradually down to the river.

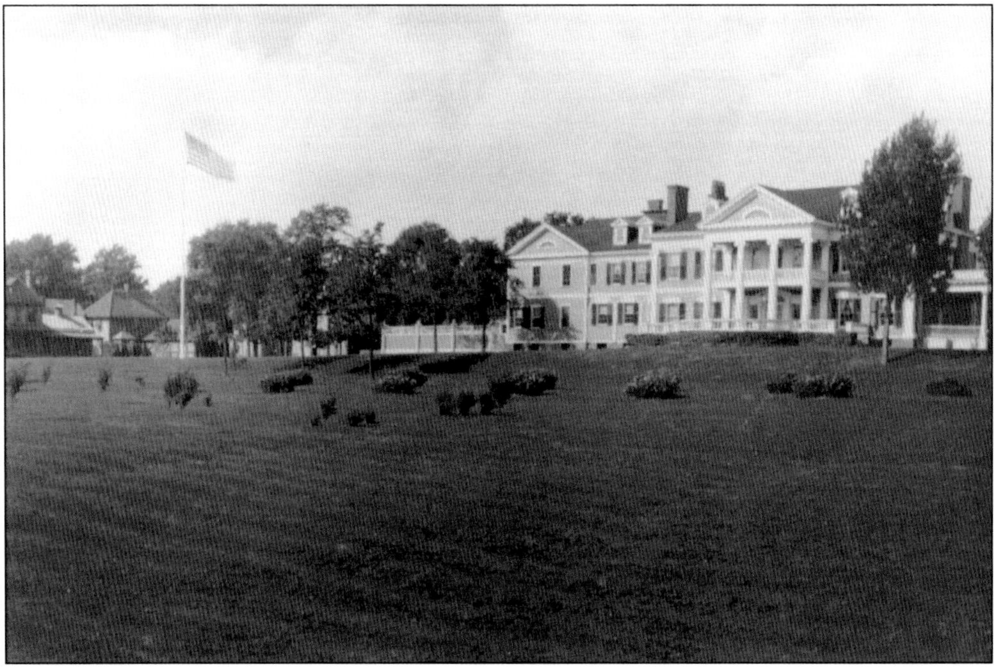

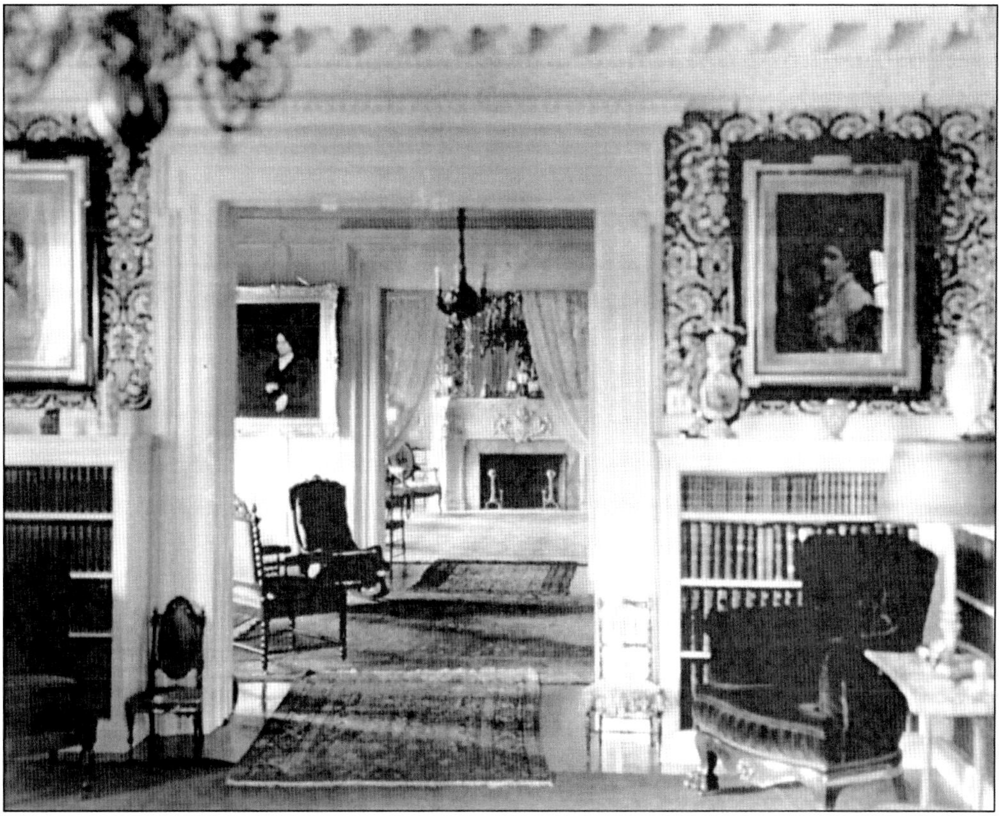

The exterior grandeur and beauty of the Franklin St. John Sidway house was matched by its interior. The rooms were filled with the exquisite Victorian and Edwardian furniture of the time. The dining room was trimmed with gold leaf as were the mirrors and doorways. The family maintained close ties to Grand Island and supported its continued development. Charlotte Spaulding Sidway christened a large ferry bearing her name, and her children's financial support for the first consolidated school on the island led to its being called the Charlotte Sidway School.

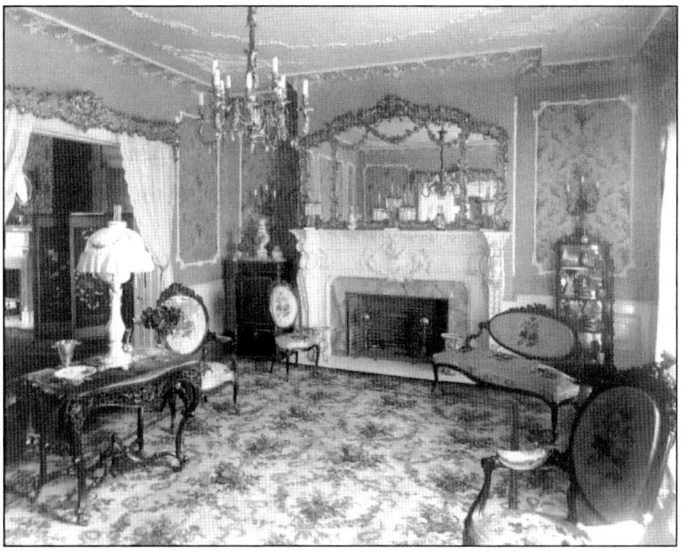

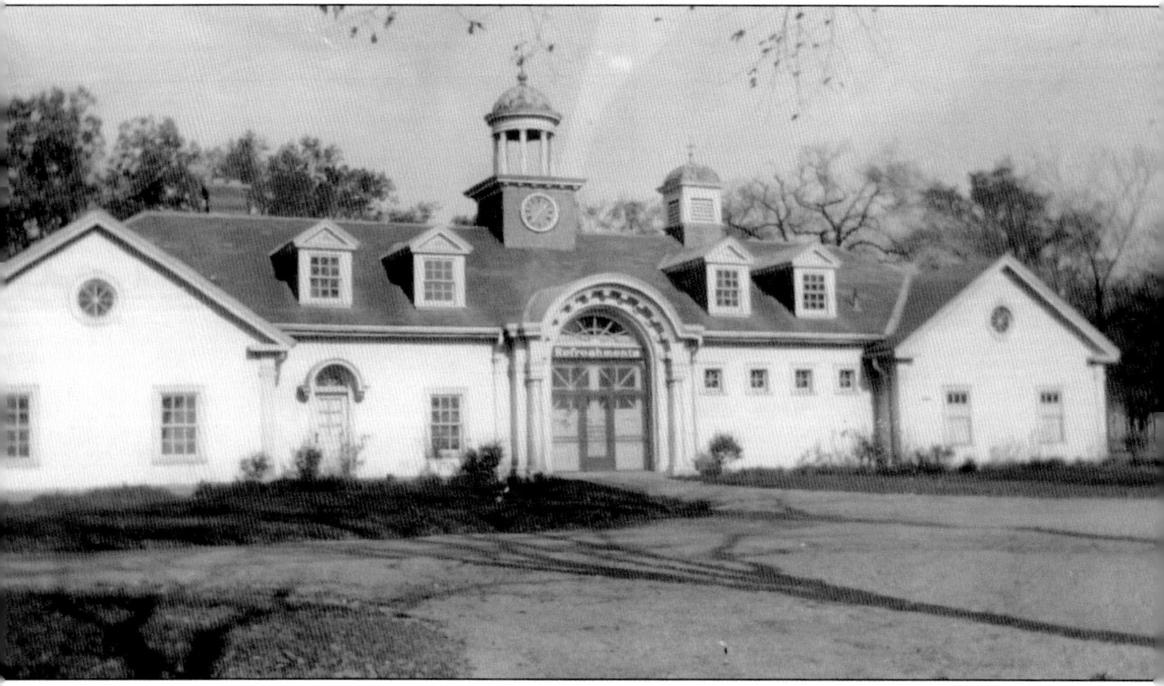

A house as grand as the Sidways' on Spaulding's River Lawn estate required equally elaborate outbuildings like this coach house. In the days before automobiles, families like the Sidways had to house and care for their teams of horses as well as the vehicles they needed to get around the island. No expense was spared in providing for those animals. The coach house was just another sign of the commitment of the Spaulding and Sidway families to the island they made their summer home. When New York State Parks Department took over the private property at that end of the island, the Sidway home was demolished, but the coach house was spared temporarily, becoming a restaurant at the new park until the casino opened in 1939.

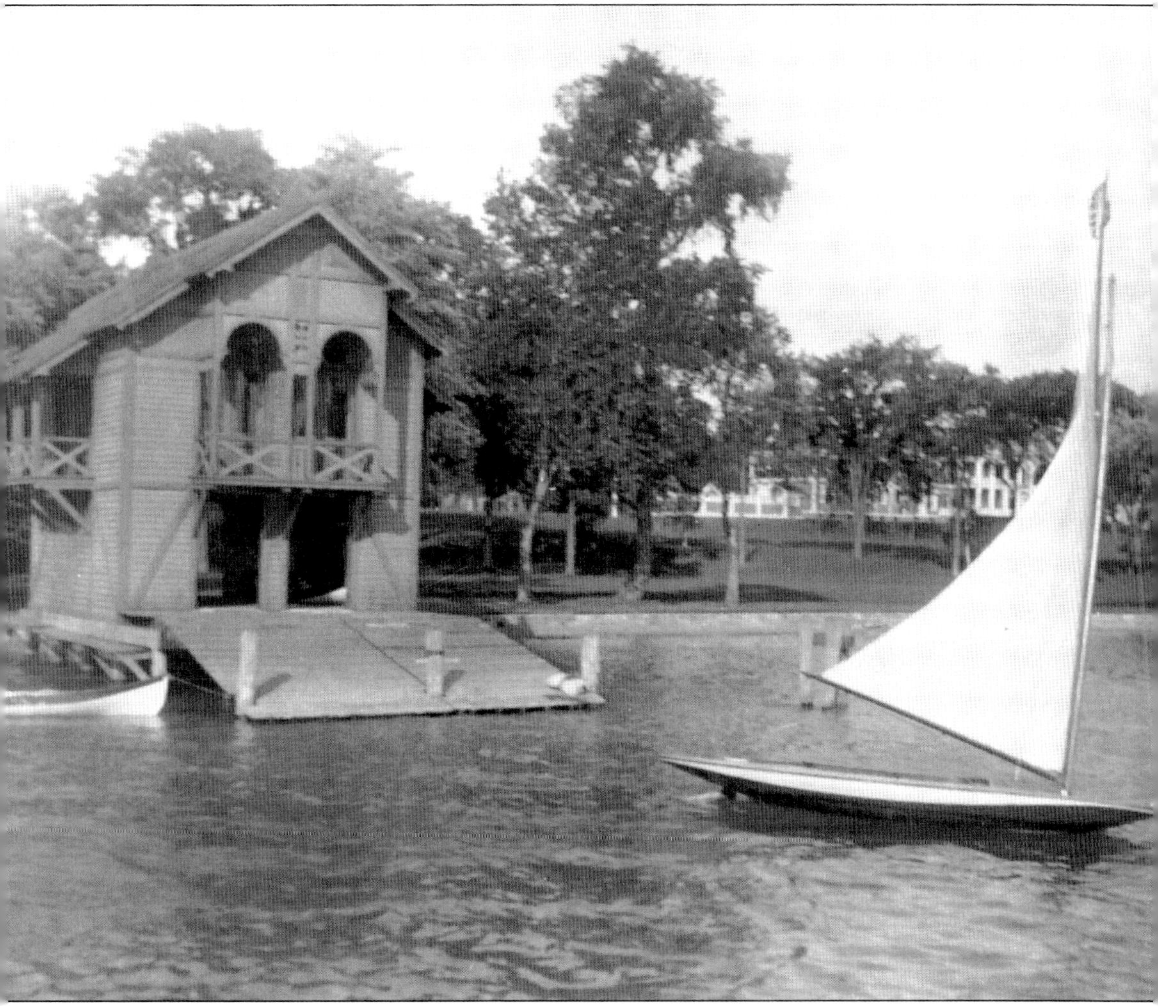

When Spaulding built the house on his River Lawn estate around 1870, he also constructed a boathouse similar in style. Today, it is one of the last remaining structures from the original River Lawn compound, thanks to one of his descendants. In 1935, when Beaver Island State Park was being planned for the site, the boathouse was floated downriver to be relocated at the property of Spaulding's grandson Franklin St. John Sidway, where it sits today. In July 1998, local preservationists and members of the family celebrated the addition of the Spaulding-Sidway boathouse to the National Register of Historic Places.

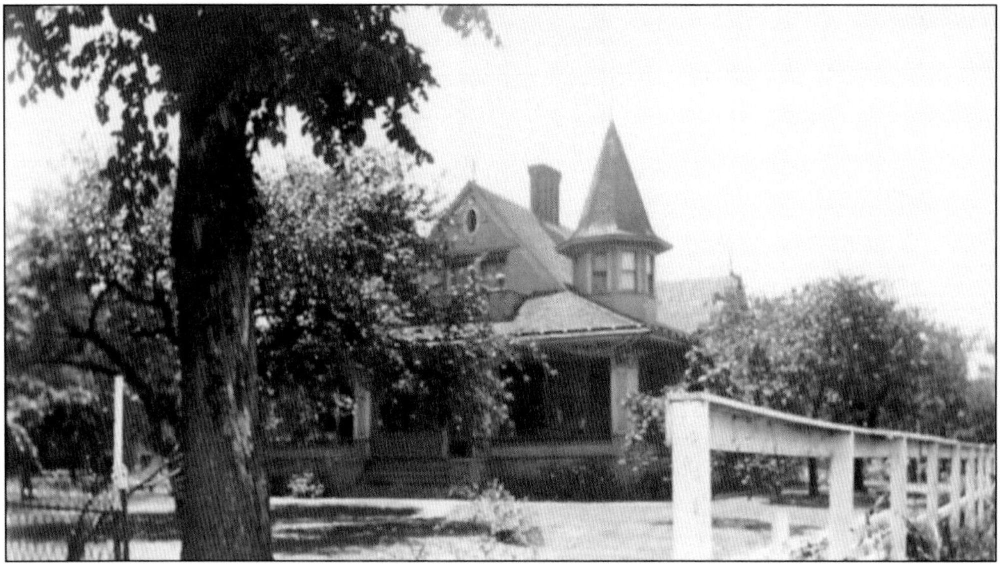

Not all of the old houses were torn down in the name of progress. In 1890, Fred Fenster built Queensdale Cottage on East River Road in Ferry Village, and Clem Scheuerman purchased it soon after. It became known as the Davern House as Davern's Tavern was across the road.

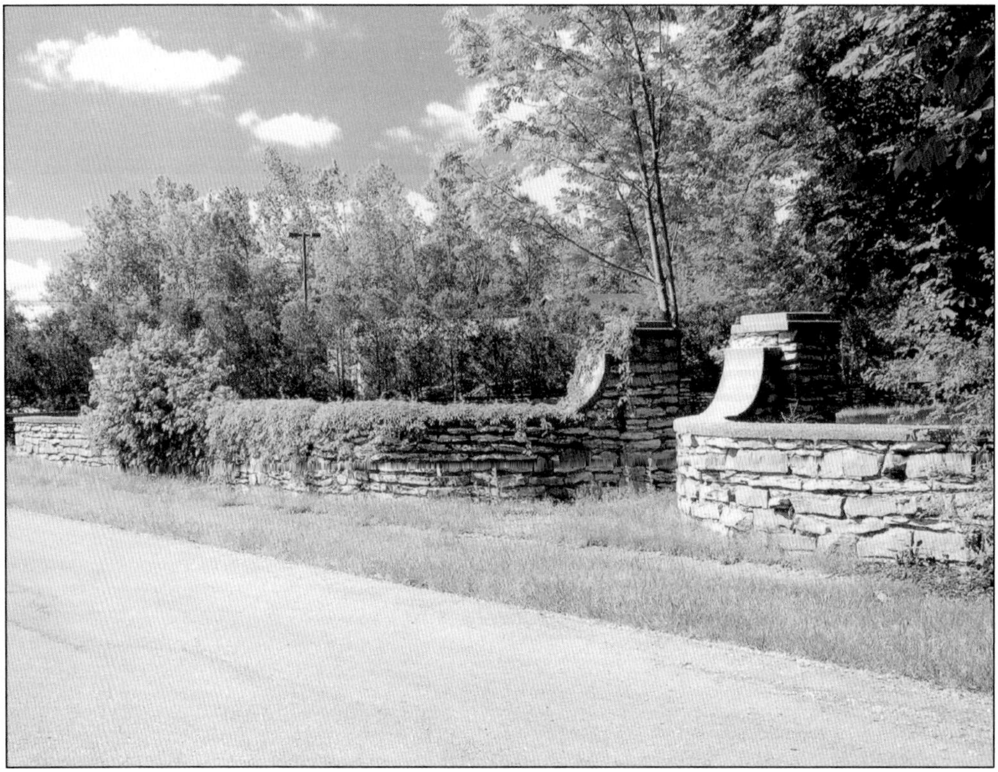

These gates are what remain of the Grand Island estate of Frank J. Offerman, a prominent Buffalo sports and business leader during the 1920s and 1930s. He owned the Buffalo baseball club as well as other businesses. Visitors to his island house included national baseball figures and governors Al Smith, Franklin Roosevelt, and Herbert Lehman.

Six

Golden Era

Grand Island's appeal as a beautiful place for urban residents to get away was not limited to the elite. What is sometimes called the "golden era" began in the late 1800s and lasted into the 20th century. It seemed to begin in 1877, when Ossian Bedell opened one of the first of the hotels that came to dot the island. There were already smaller summer boardinghouses, and hotels like the Sheenwater and Edgewater appeared over the next decades.

Summer breezes and the natural environment were the main attractions, but man-made entertainment soon began to appear in the form of picnic grounds and amusement parks. The first was attached to John Graf's Niagara View Hotel on the East River. Edgewater Park, Electric Beach, Elmwood Beach, Sheenwater, and Eagle Park soon joined it in providing a recreation spot for fraternal, religious, and social groups who could reach it by means of the boats owned by the resorts, hotels, and parks. Cruise ships carried visitors around the island to view the sights.

Golden eras do not last forever. The success of the popular attractions seems to have contributed to the departure of the owners of the large summer homes who relocated to the shore of Lake Erie. By the early 20th century, the amusement park fad was also beginning to fade. An incident in 1912 put a dark cloud over what remained. Overloaded with one of the many celebrating groups, the dock at Eagle Park collapsed as the last ferry approached. Of the more than 100 people who fell into the West River, 37 died.

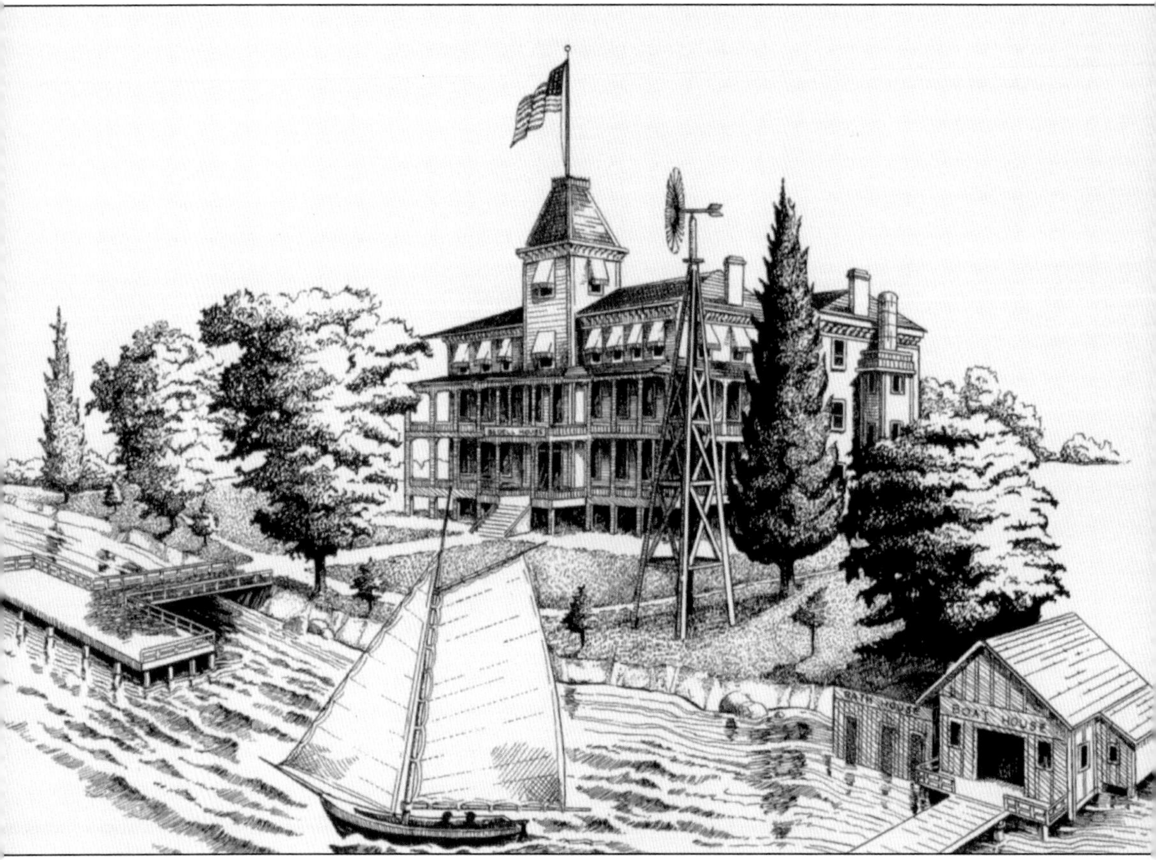

Ossian Bedell aspired to make a Grand Island retreat available to a larger portion of the population. The original Bedell House, shown here, opened in 1877. Its overwhelming popularity required additional construction within two years. A fire destroyed much of that building in 1886, but a larger Bedell House opened the following year. The 240-acre property provided the hotel with fresh produce and dairy products as well as room for guests' relaxation and outdoor activities. Some arrived in their horse-drawn carriages by ferry and rode along tree-lined roadways to the hotel entrance. The essential water connections—the docks and ferries—are evident. The rebuilt Bedell House lasted until 1935, when another fire destroyed the main hotel.

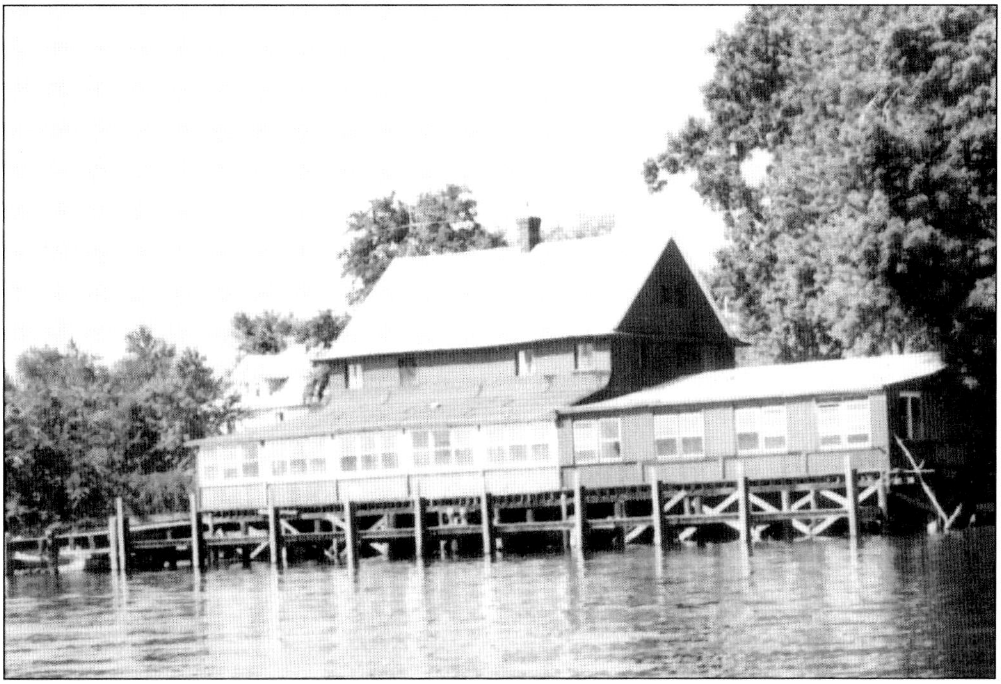

The Bedell House Annex was one of the first additions to the hotel property, and it escaped the fire that destroyed the hotel in 1886. Since its dock was the main point of arrival for visitors to the island, unsurprisingly its large bar remained busy. A 1935 fire finally destroyed the hotel building, but the annex bar continued to operate. The opening of the bridges that same year, which ended the ferry business and greatly reduced foot traffic near the bar, did not kill it. Clarence "Paddy" Fix owned the property, but it had a variety of operators over the years. Lou Mayer took over in 1952. The bar closed when the annex finally burned in 1988, but the notice in the sesquicentennial book indicates how much it is still missed.

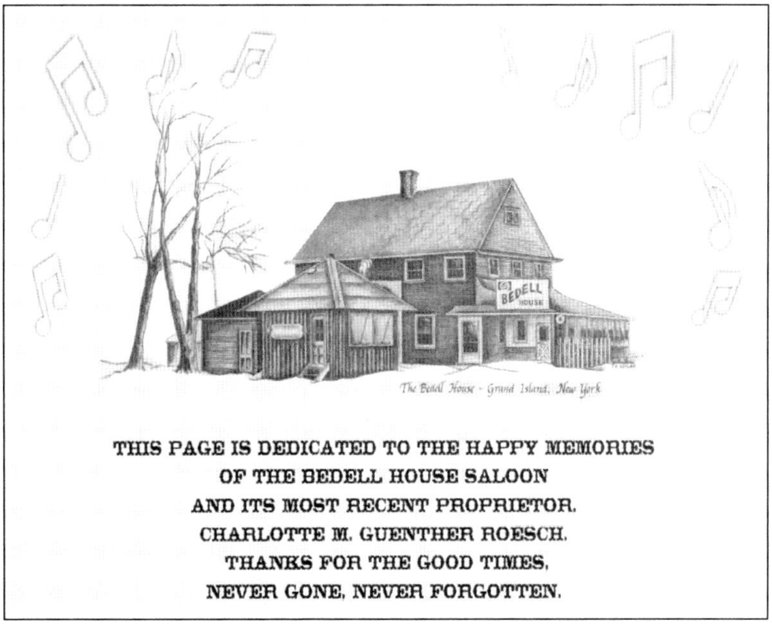

THIS PAGE IS DEDICATED TO THE HAPPY MEMORIES
OF THE BEDELL HOUSE SALOON
AND ITS MOST RECENT PROPRIETOR.
CHARLOTTE M. GUENTHER ROESCH.
THANKS FOR THE GOOD TIMES,
NEVER GONE, NEVER FORGOTTEN.

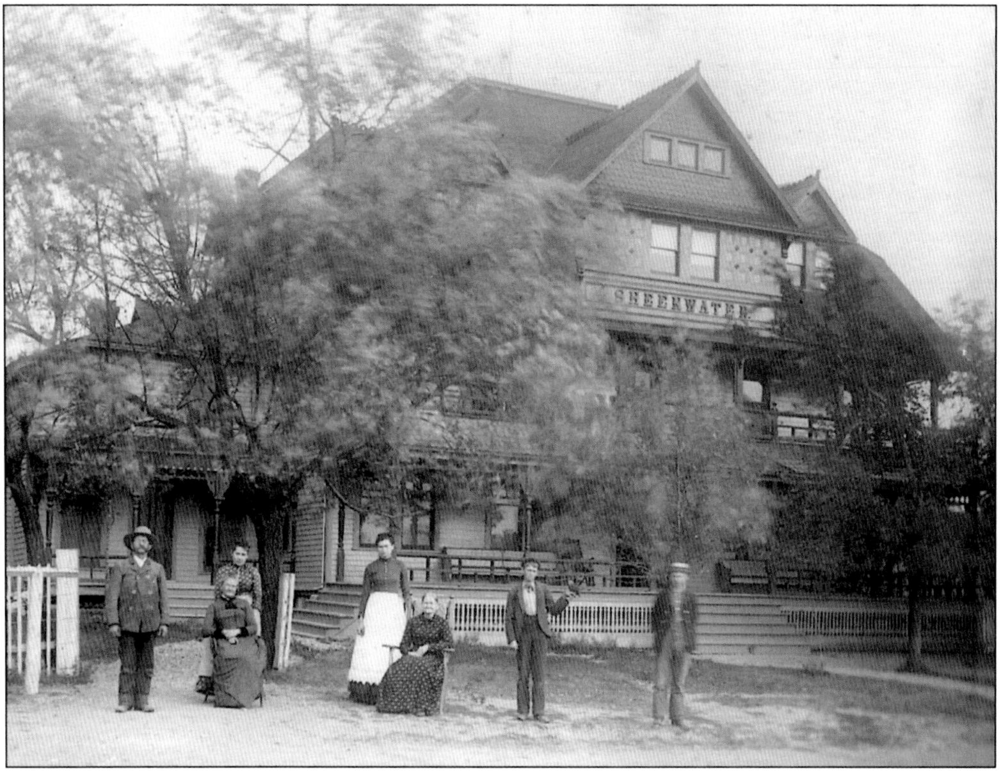

The operation of the clubs, hotels, and amusement parks took a lot of work. The Howard family and others are pictured standing in front of their hotel, the Sheenwater. Oliver Cromwell Howard is shown above with, from left to right, Anna Blackmore Howard, Elizabeth Johnson Howard, Annie Albert, unidentified, Charles Bartlett Howard, and unidentified. The photograph below, taken in back of the building, features, from left to right, Annie Albert, Anna Blackmore Howard, Charles B. Howard, Clarence (infant), and unidentified.

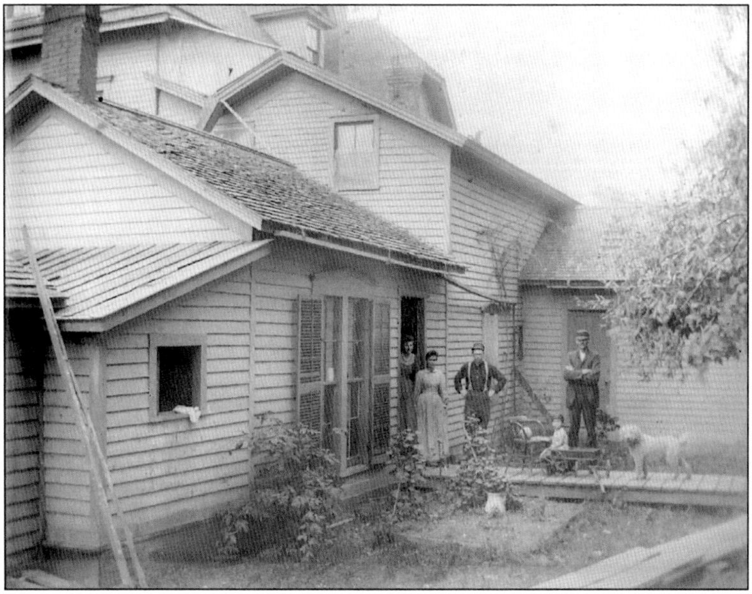

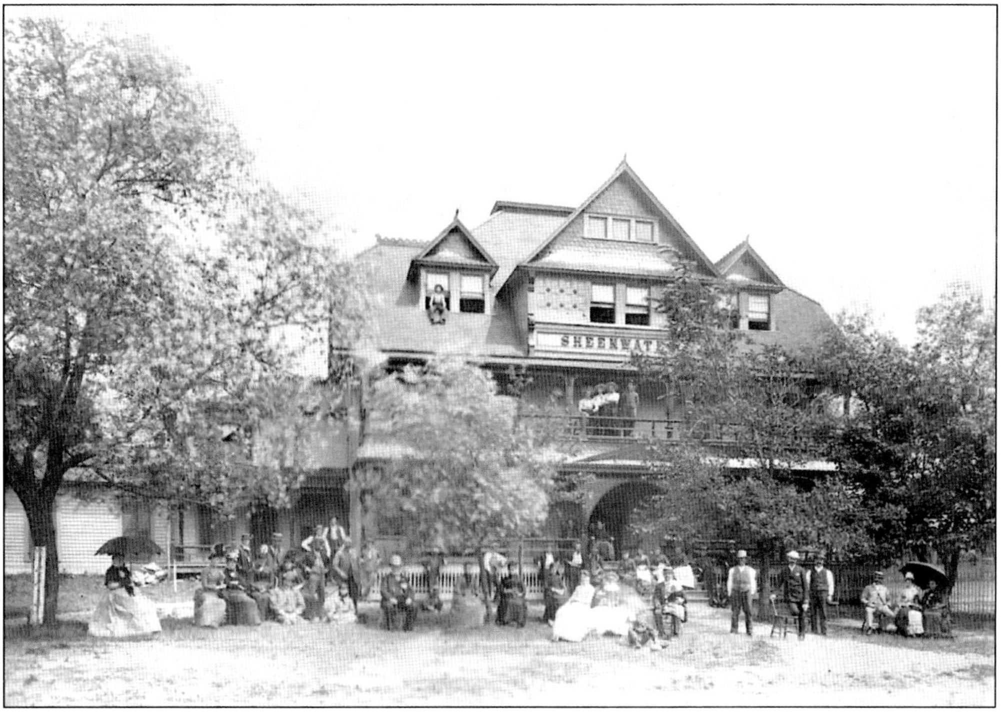

Pictured here during 1880, the Sheenwater on West River at Love Road featured the first electrically lighted amusement park in America and included a wooded area for quiet relaxation. Guests had an easy stroll from the dock to the hotel where they could enjoy the view of the West River and the spectacular sunsets from the upper floor windows and veranda. Hard times and declining business during the 1930s Depression caused the Howards to sell the Sheenwater, and most of the family moved to Canada.

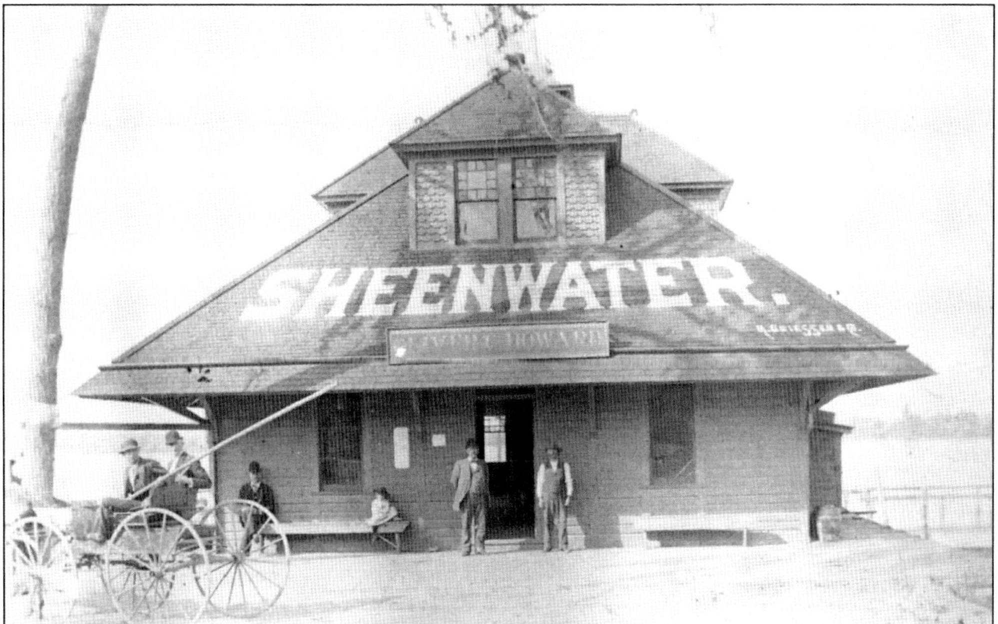

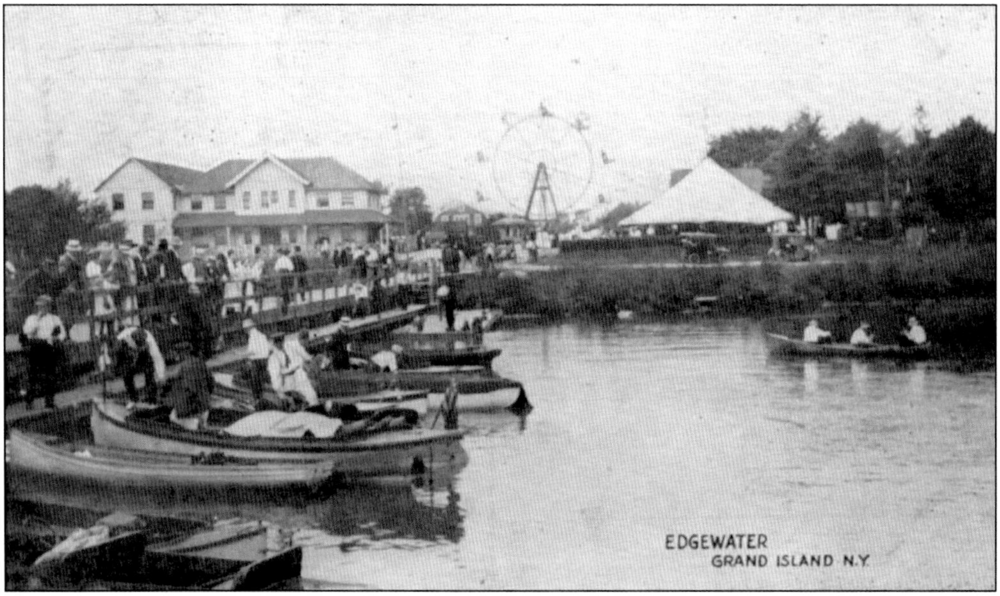

The Edgewater Hotel, located on East River Road, enjoyed decades of success under the management of its builder, William E. Voetsch, who bought the land in 1886 and developed a hotel and amusement park. A Ferris wheel can be seen behind the hotel. In 1892, the original three-story building, like many of the structures of the period, fell to a fire. It was replaced by a two-story building that lasted until 1974. A Buffalo native, Voetsch tried other real estate ventures on Grand Island, notably Electric Beach, a project he abandoned when it failed to enjoy the success of Edgewater.

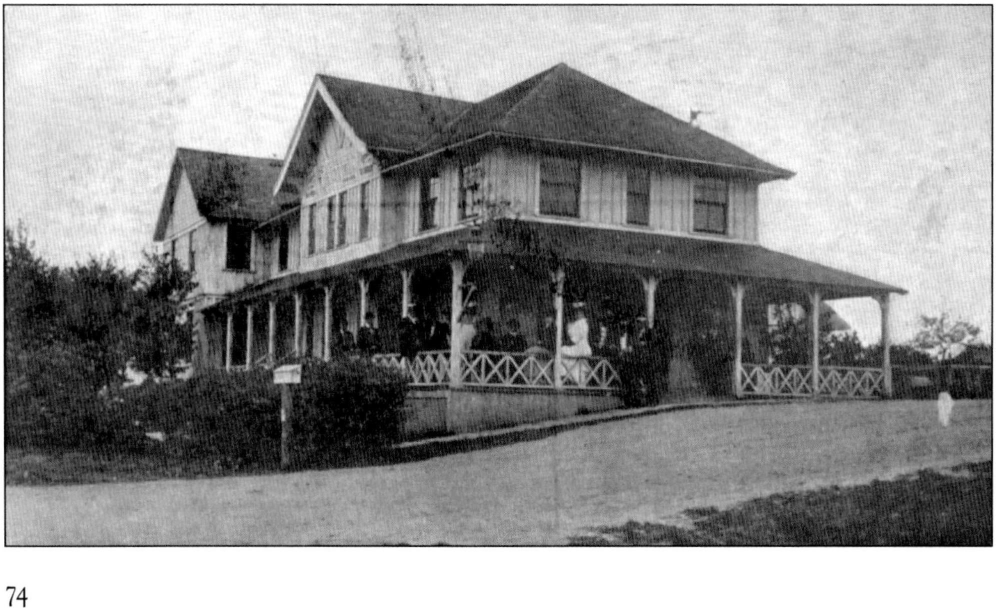

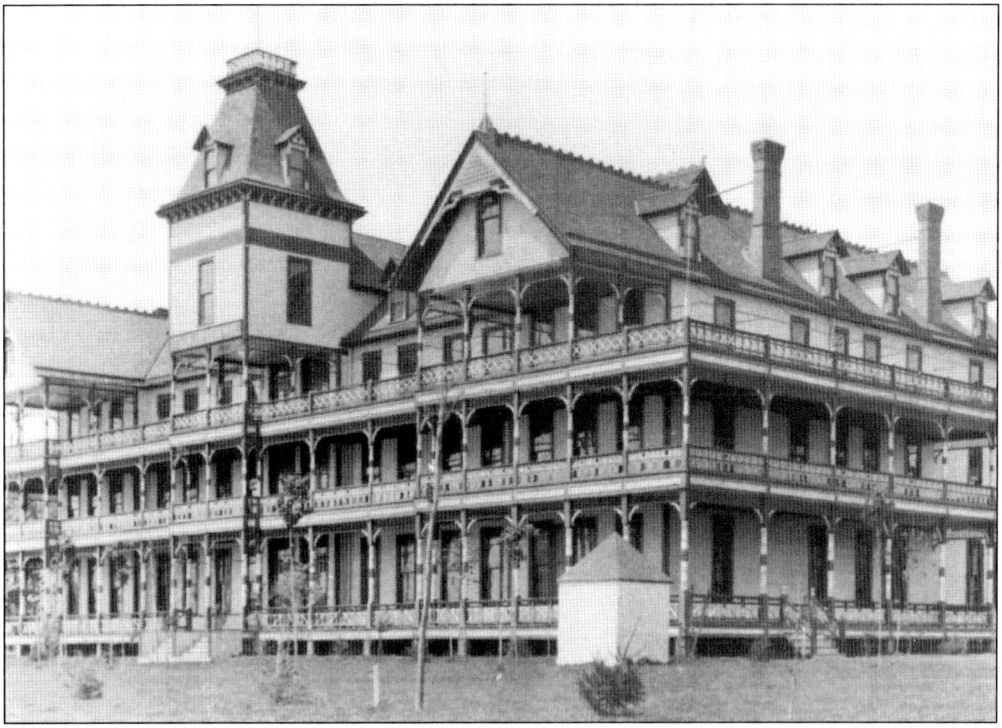

The McComb House, later the Island Club, was another well-known inn on the West River. Built in 1887, it sat on a 90-acre tract that included a farm to supply fresh produce and wooded parklands leading down to the river. Guests came from Buffalo aboard the *Huntress*. Well endowed with gingerbread wooden trim, the hotel featured broad verandas for viewing the river and surrounding landscapes. On summer weekends, crowds packed its dock on their way to fill the four-story inn to capacity.

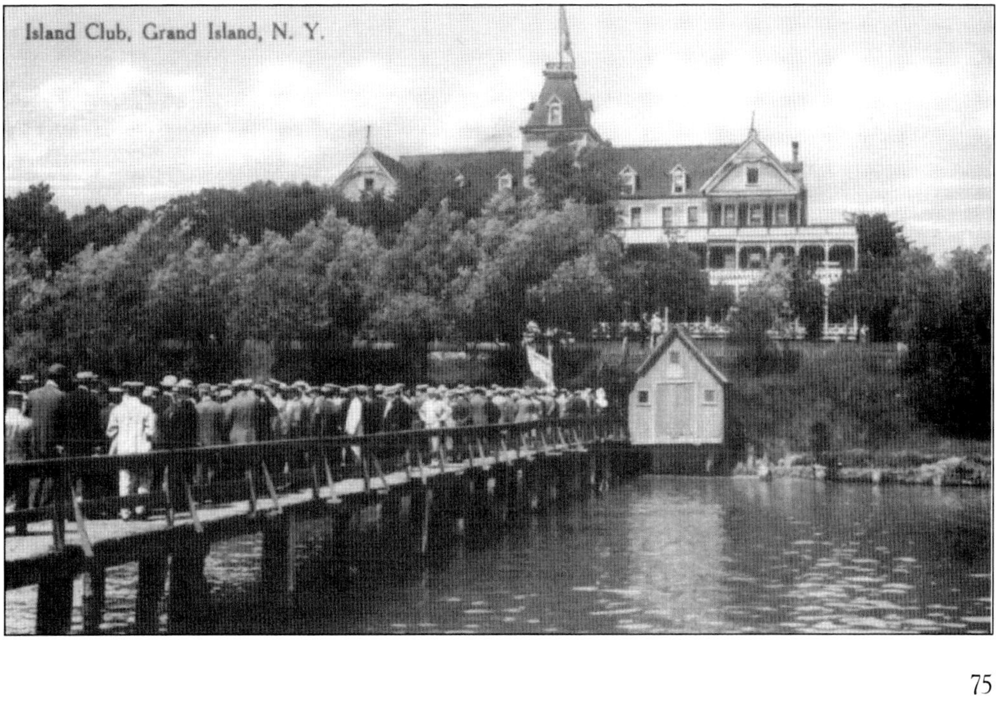

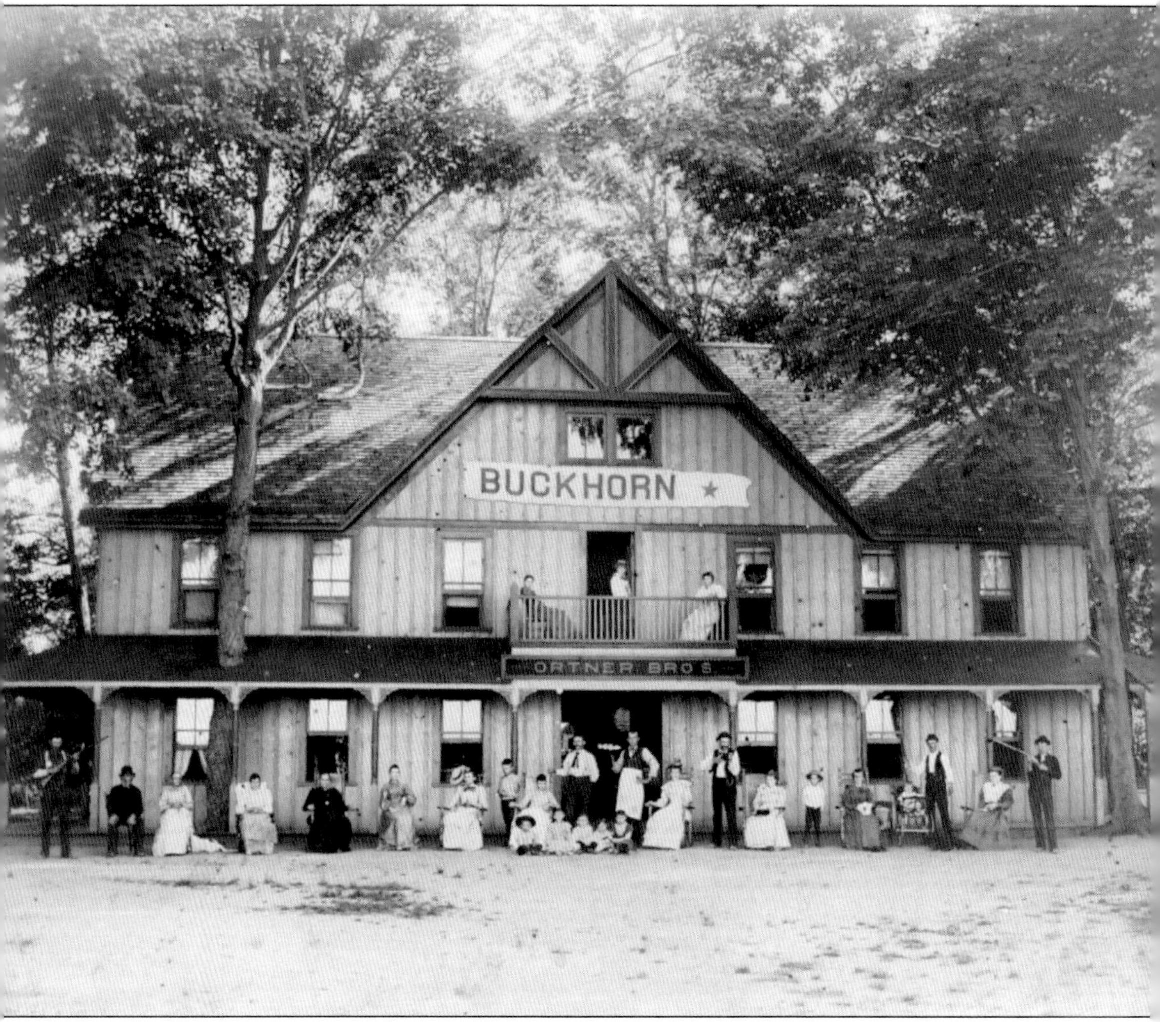

One of Grand Island's hotels set itself apart—literally. The Ortner brothers' Buckhorn Hotel sat on a separate island, Buckhorn Island, at the north end of the main island across the narrow Burnt Ship Creek. Guests and staff pose in front of the building, which was smaller and more rustic than most of the hotels located on the east and west shores. Buckhorn Island remained a place primarily used for hunting and fishing. The guns of the men at either end of the group on the ground level are clearly visible. In the 1930s, the Civilian Conservation Corps was put to work clearing the marshes around Burnt Ship Creek. Later, New York added the island itself to make Buckhorn Island State Park, a great nature preserve.

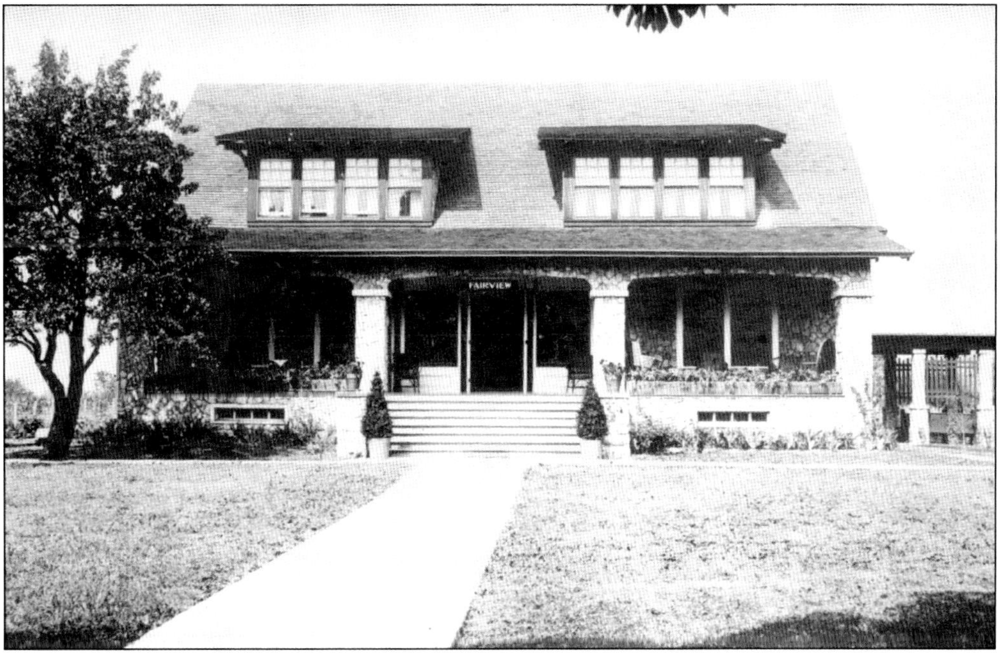

Visitors came to Grand Island for many different experiences. Some wanted a quieter time in places like the Fairview, pictured above in 1914. Others came to frequent the numerous bars and taverns that dotted the shores. These places did well even in the off season, and the locals had their favorites. At his boathouse and restaurant, John Volz offered boats for rent as well as the opportunity to enjoy a fish fry.

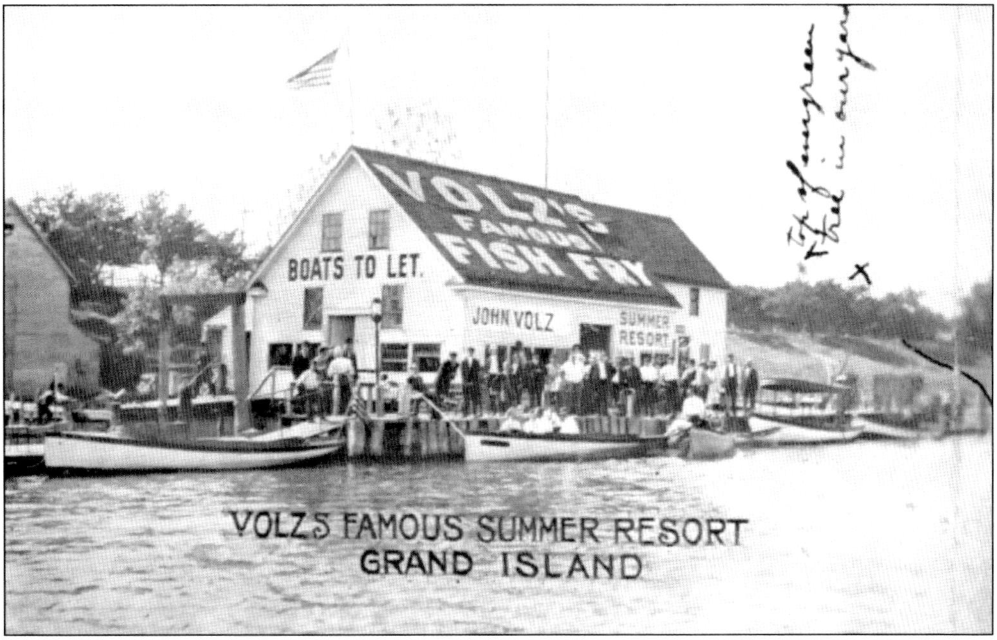

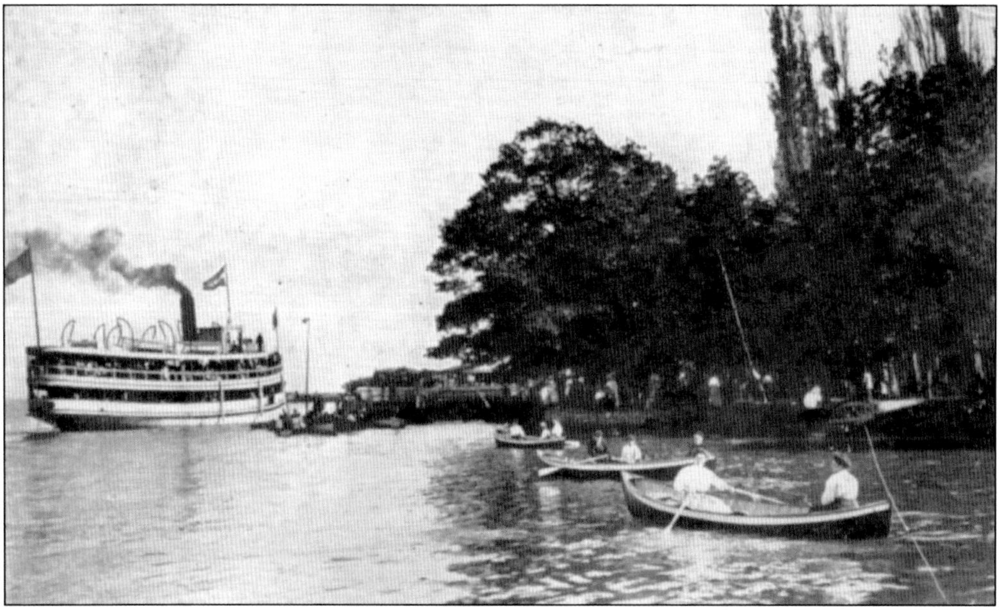

It was not just ferries and yachts that kept the docks of Grand Island crowded during the summer months. All manner of boats moved visitors from the mainland to the many attractions on the island. No doubt many came to enjoy the water in an ideal setting like the one pictured below, but getting there sometimes required navigating not only the river currents, but also masses of their fellow travelers. For the first century after American settlement on the island, it was always about the boats.

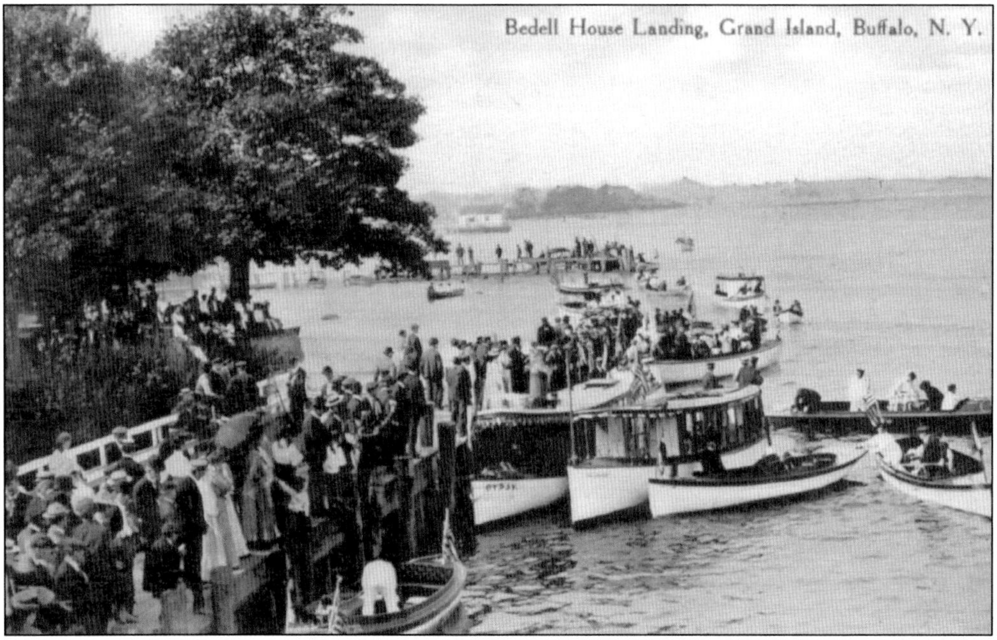

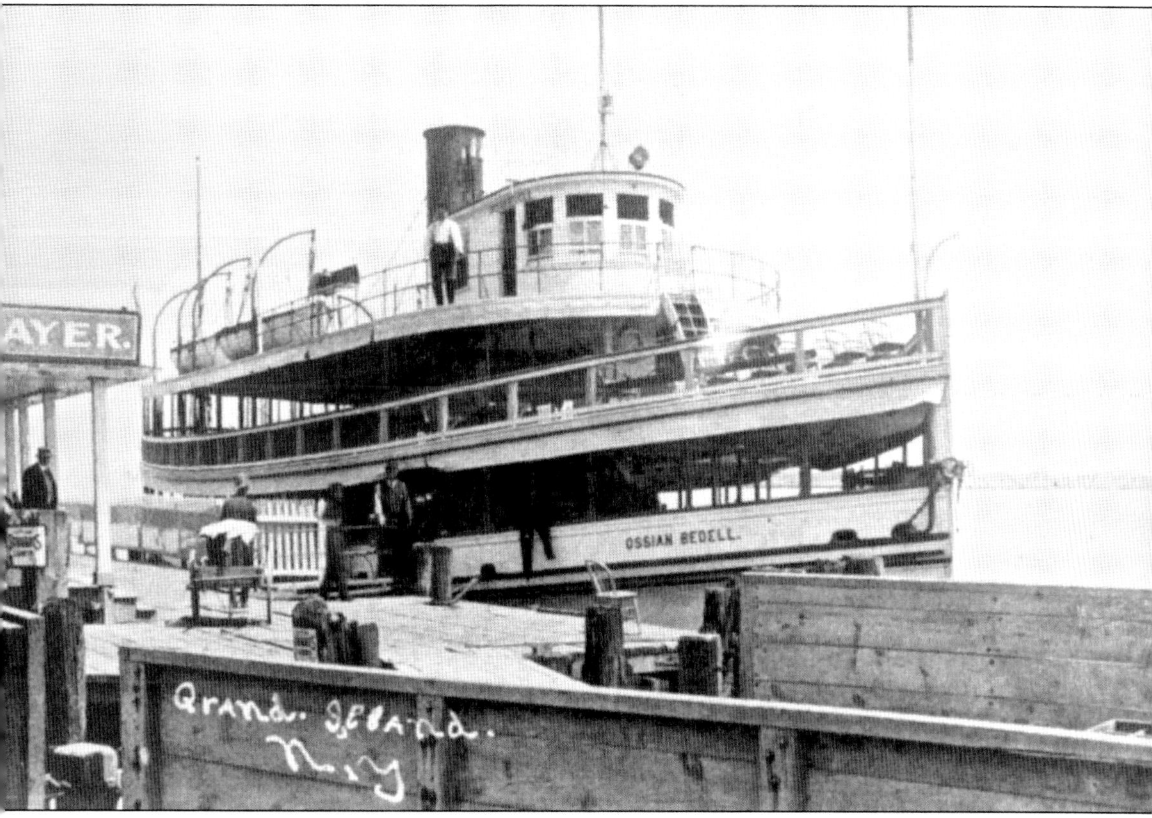

To accommodate their clientele, hotels relied on ferries, many owned by the hostelries and clubs to serve their guests exclusively. The Falconwood Club had the *Falcon*; the Edgewater Hotel, its *Edgewater* ferry; McComb House, the *Huntress*; and the Oakfield Club had the *Lorelei*. Bedell House dock, the main point of arrival and departure, was served by the *Allenton*, the *Silver Spray*, the *Canadian*, the *Americana*, and others. The *Ossian Bedell*, shown at the dock of the Bedell House Annex, was named for the owner of the hotel. This 296-ton boat was built in 1901 at the Buffalo Dry Dock.

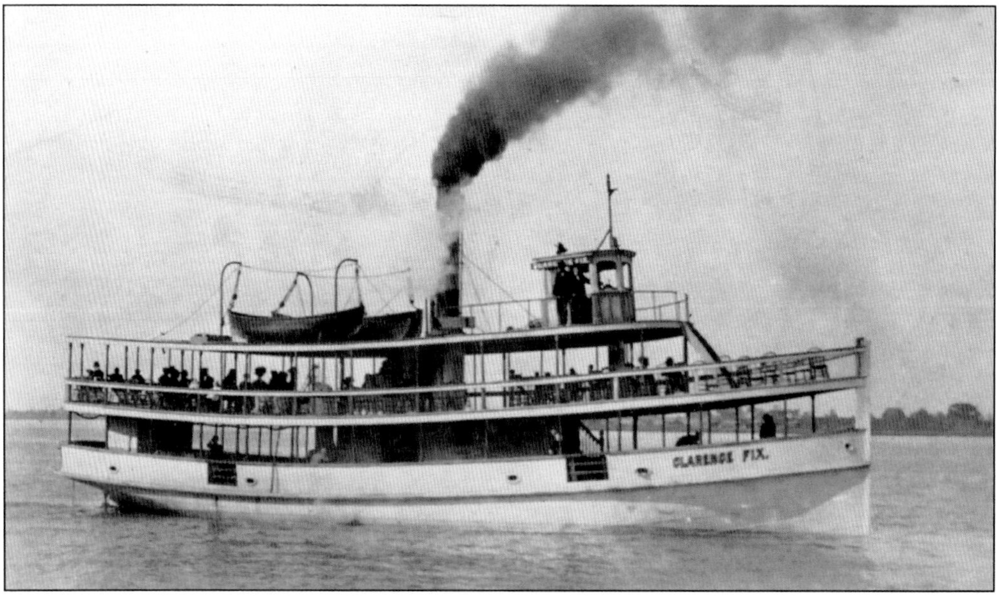

The ferry *Clarence Fix* was named for Clarence "Paddy" Fix, at one time owner of the Bedell House and the large Fix Bros. Towing Company fleet. For decades, the Fix clan dominated Grand Island's key connection to the rest of the world. The *Seabreeze* stayed busy as part of the Fix Bros. fleet of passenger ferries serving Grand Island and other destinations on the Niagara River and Lake Erie. Even after the bridges made ferries unnecessary, Fix took visitors on cruises along the island's shore. He died at the helm on one of those trips in 1945.

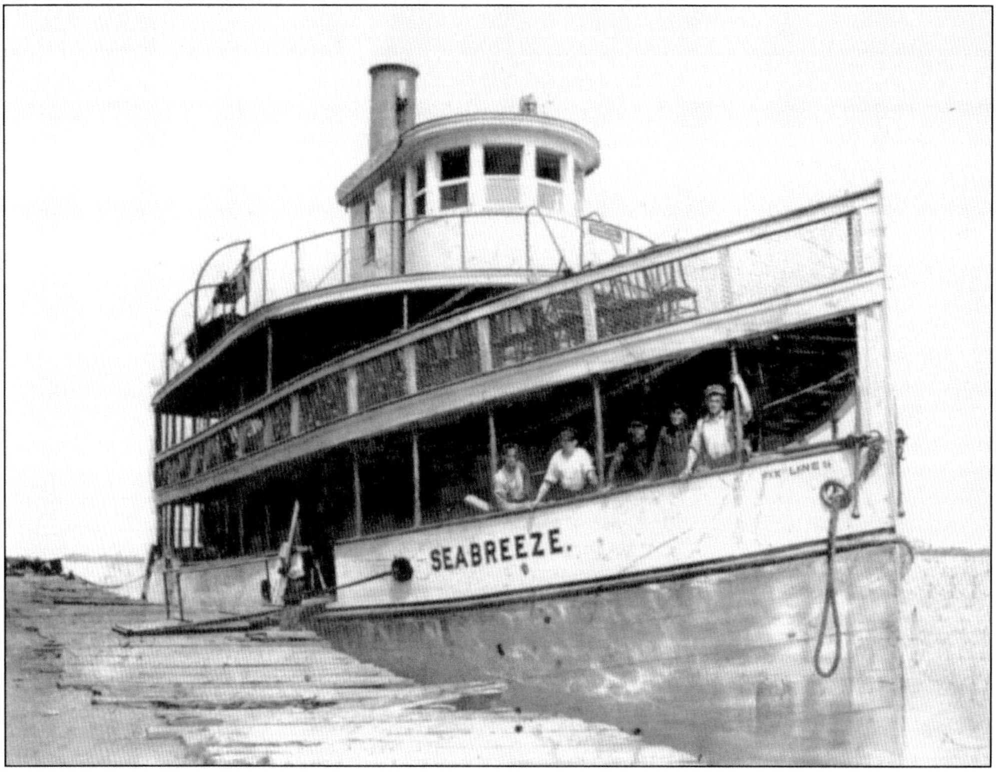

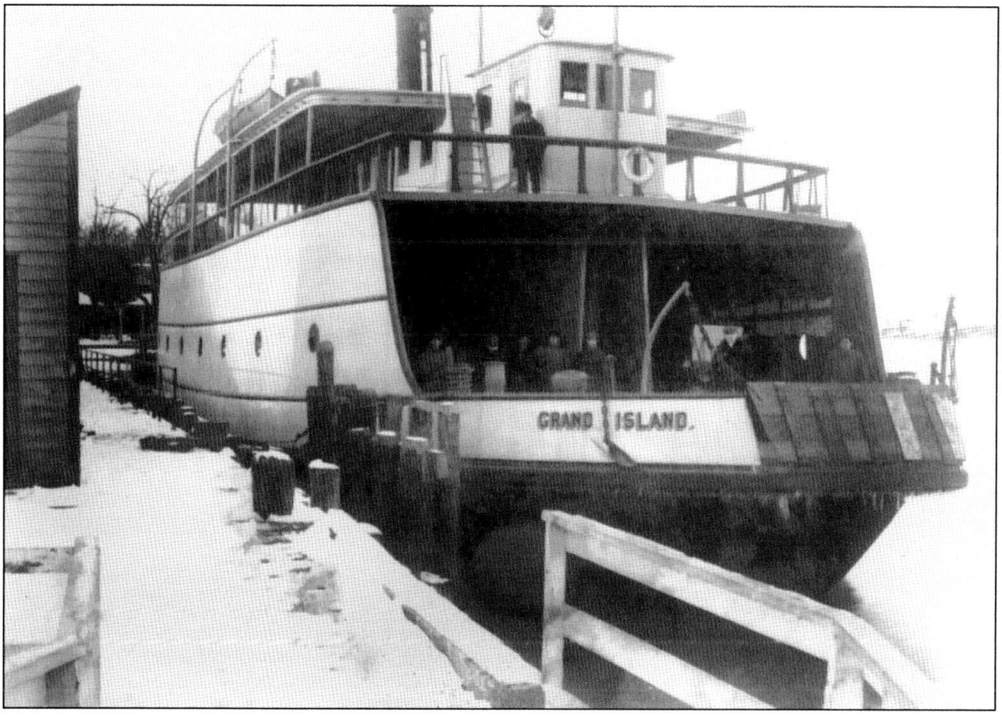

Until the completion of the first set of bridges in 1935, Grand Island was heavily dependent on a diverse fleet of ferries and other boats. Its first ferries were chartered in 1825 and, along with a mixed fleet of other boats, remained the island's only connection to the mainland for some time. The *Grand Island* was one of the largest and latest. This car carrier serving Buffalo was built in 1901. After the bridges made the ferries unnecessary, the *Grand Island* was later used as a "sand sucker," or dredge. The *H.W. Long* was named for Grand Island supervisor Henry W. Long in 1918. It carried passengers to and from the Tonawanda shore.

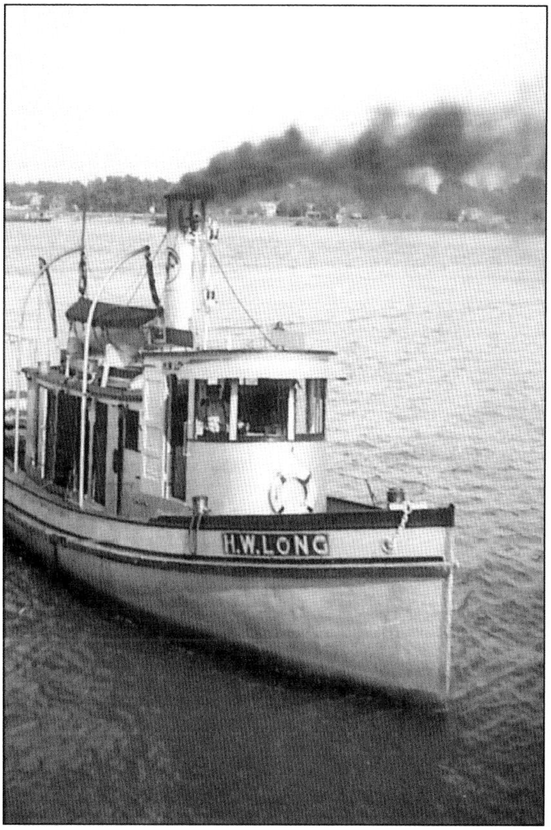

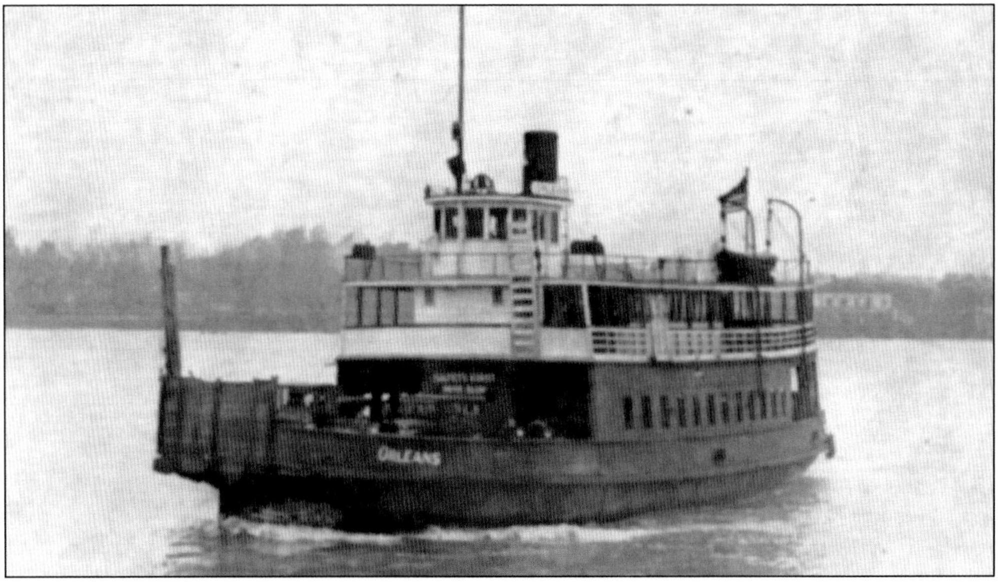

The *Orleans* was built in Quebec, Canada, in 1898. From 1916 until 1931, several different companies used her to service routes between Buffalo and Fort Erie. In 1931, Charles Fix purchased the *Orleans* to serve Grand Island. She continued to serve in that capacity until 1955, when she was severely damaged while laid up at the Fix Dock on the island. Later that year, she was scrapped.

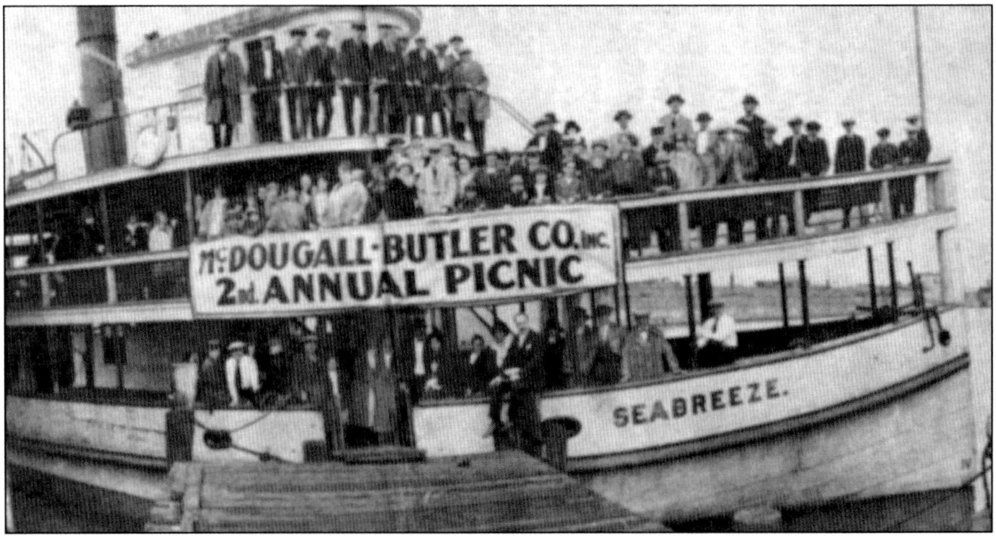

This crowd arriving at Grand Island on the *Seabreeze* is a perfect illustration of the fact that the island's boats had multiple purposes. They were often chartered for daylong events like this company outing. During the summer months, these kinds of outings were common and an important part of the golden era.

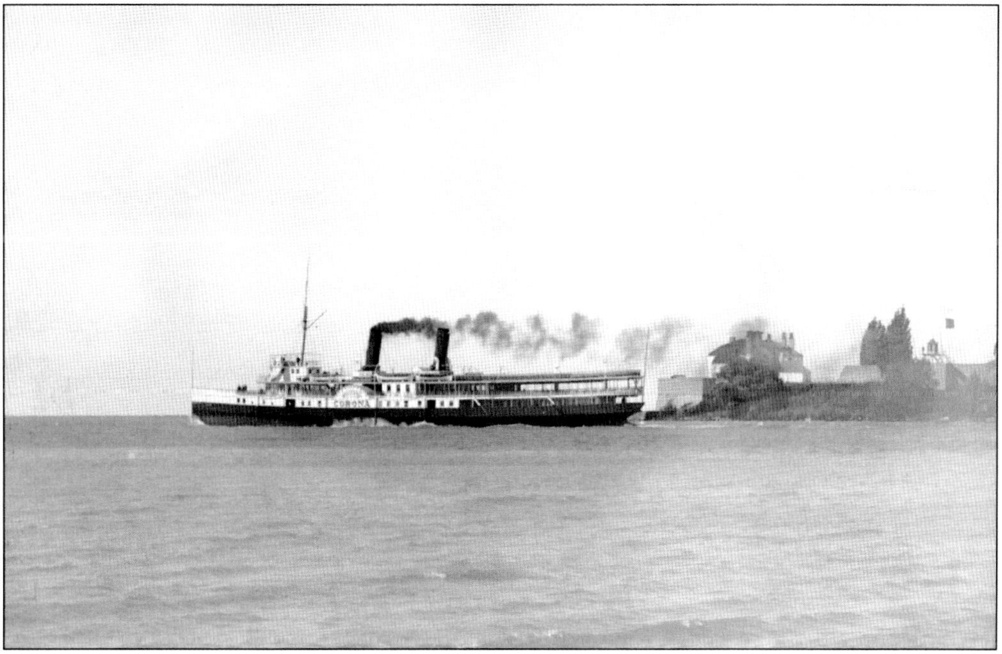

Edgewater Park had its own steamer, the *Edgewater.* In addition, visitors to the park arrived on the *Corona*, the *Silver Spray*, the *Clarence Fix*, the *Lottie Koerber*, the *Seabreeze*, or the *Dorothy*. In 1898, the *Corona* burned and sank by the park's pier; its smokestacks in the East River are the only visible remains.

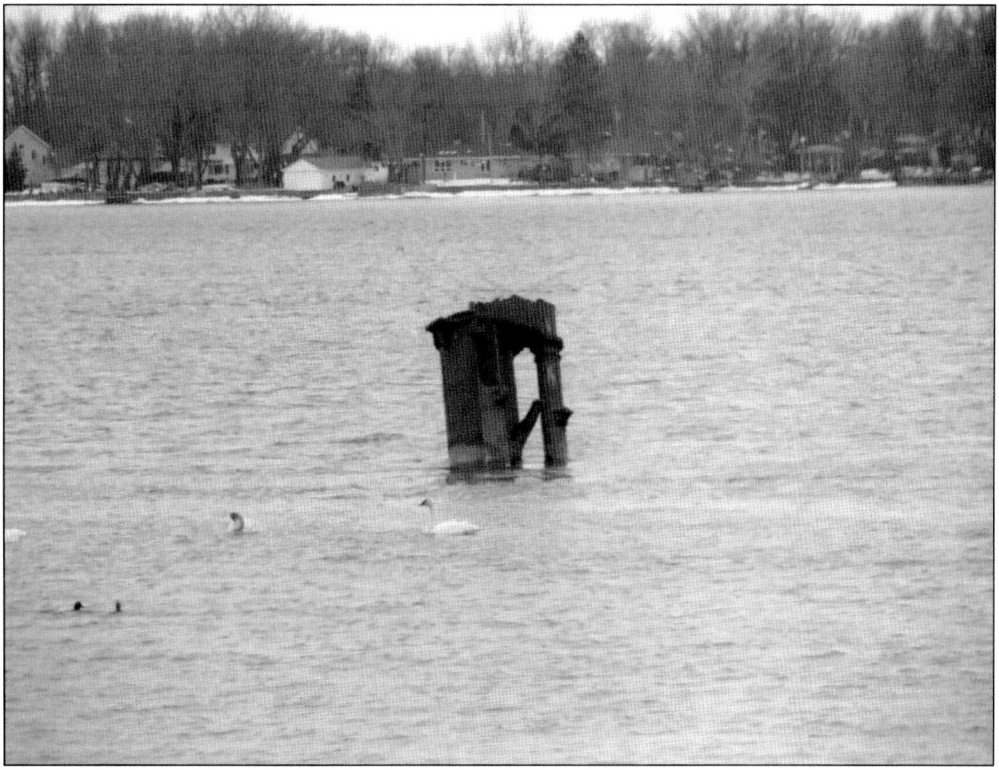

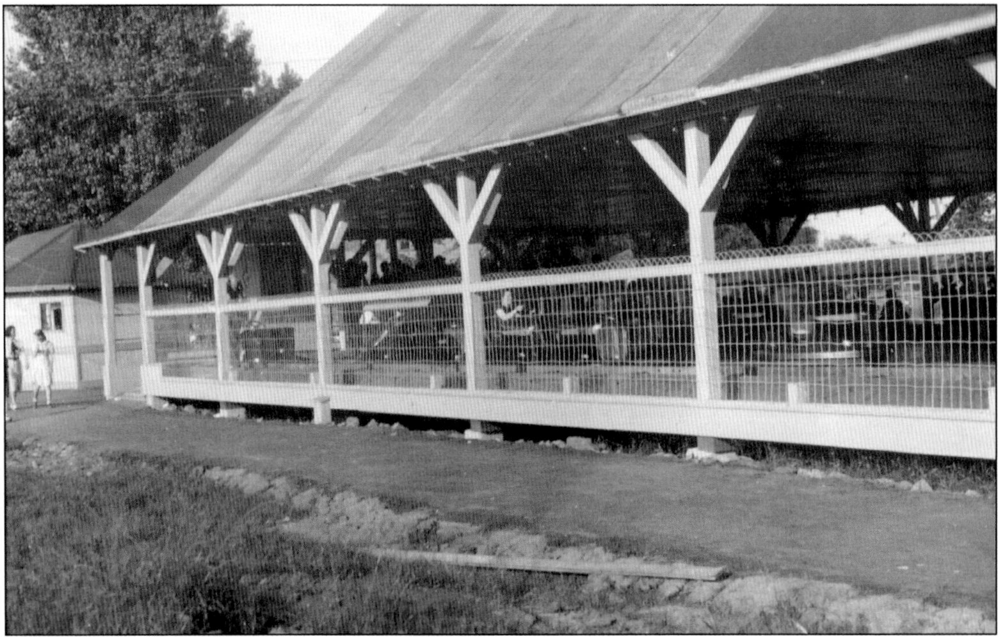

During Grand Island's golden era, individuals and groups of all sizes made their way to the island to enjoy the great variety of activities available. Many different family, social, religious, and business groups made a day on the island an annual affair, crowding the ferries and docks on summer weekends. Rides like the bumper cars and the merry-go-round at Edgewater Park were among the options for those picnicking on the grounds.

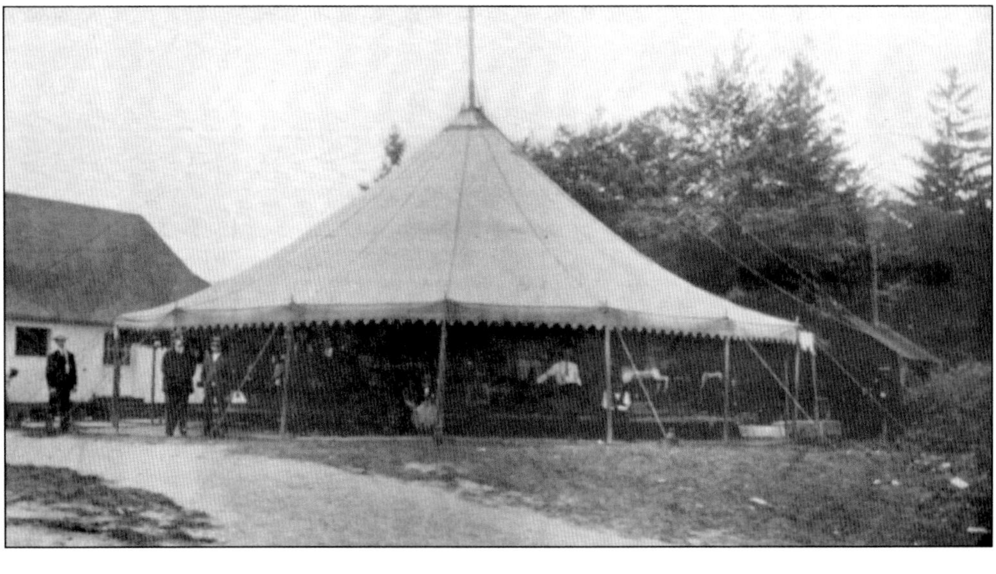

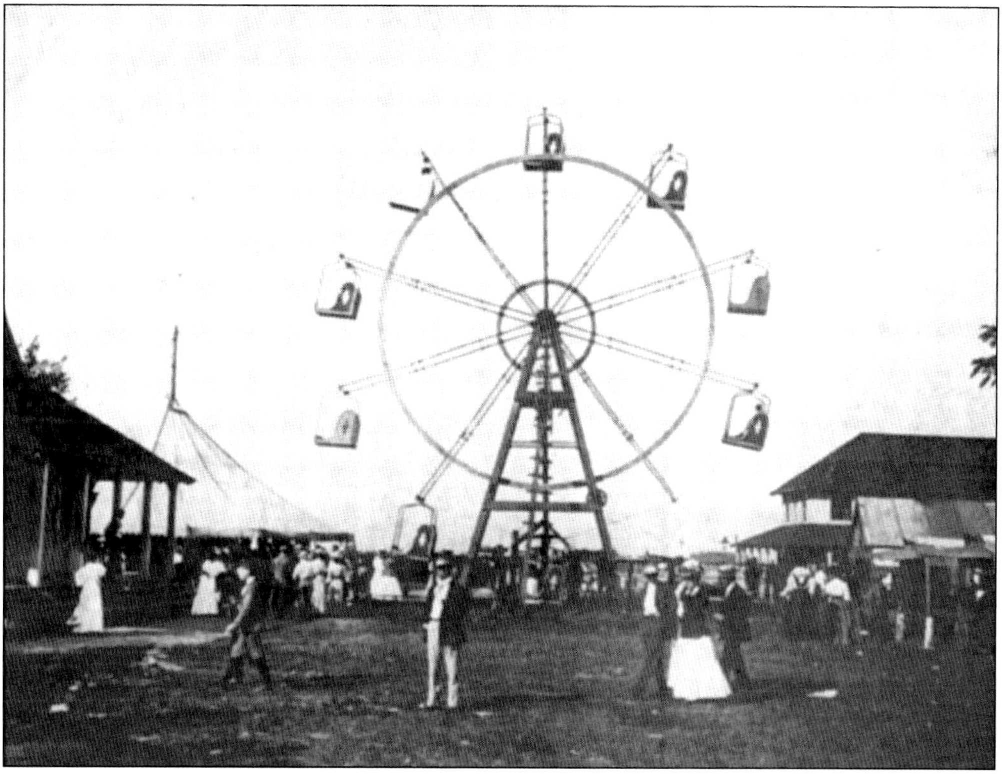

Edgewater Park featured a wide variety of attractions, including rides like the Razzle Dazzle, a Ferris wheel. A new building was constructed after an 1892 fire, and six bowling alleys were added. Other rides joined these in the late 1930s, after the family sold the property to a New York City company. Island residents were welcomed to the chamber of commerce's annual Harvest Festival, which was often held at Edgewater Park.

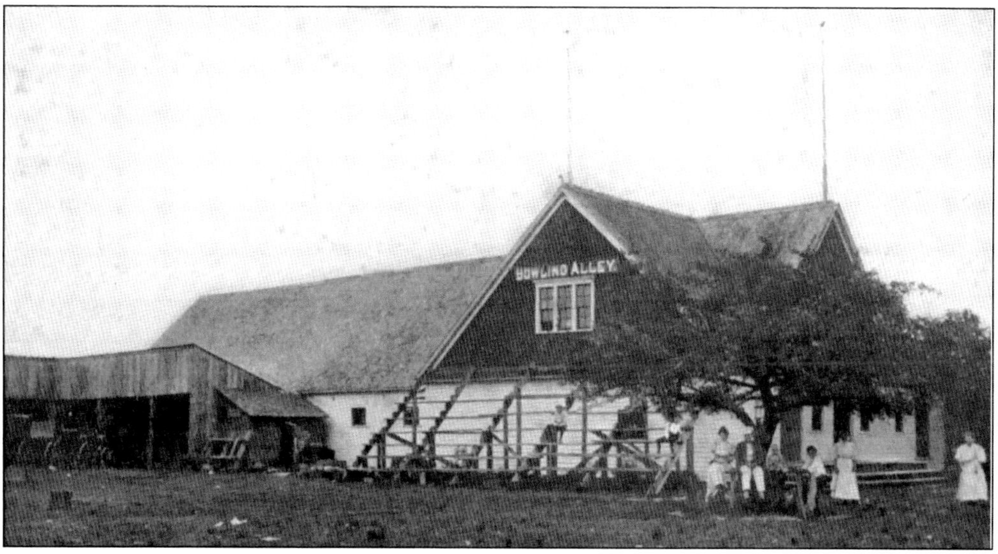

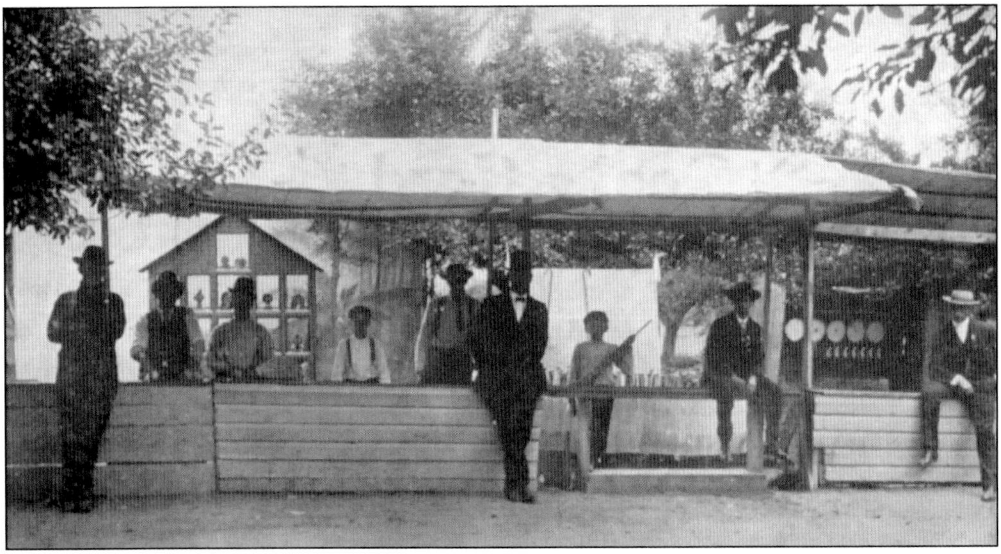

Along with the popular carousel and the Bump-de-Bump, an indoor undulating slide, Edgewater Park had a shooting gallery, dance hall, food stands, a popular bar, and boating, fishing, bathing, and baseball. Carnival-like games were available on the grounds as well. There was always something new to try. When a New York City company took over the property in 1937, it added a miniature train.

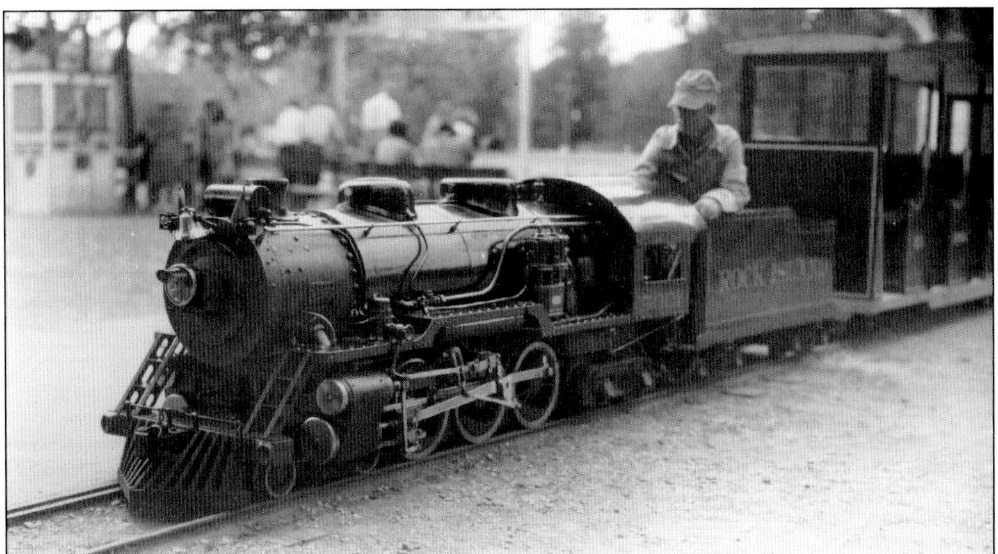

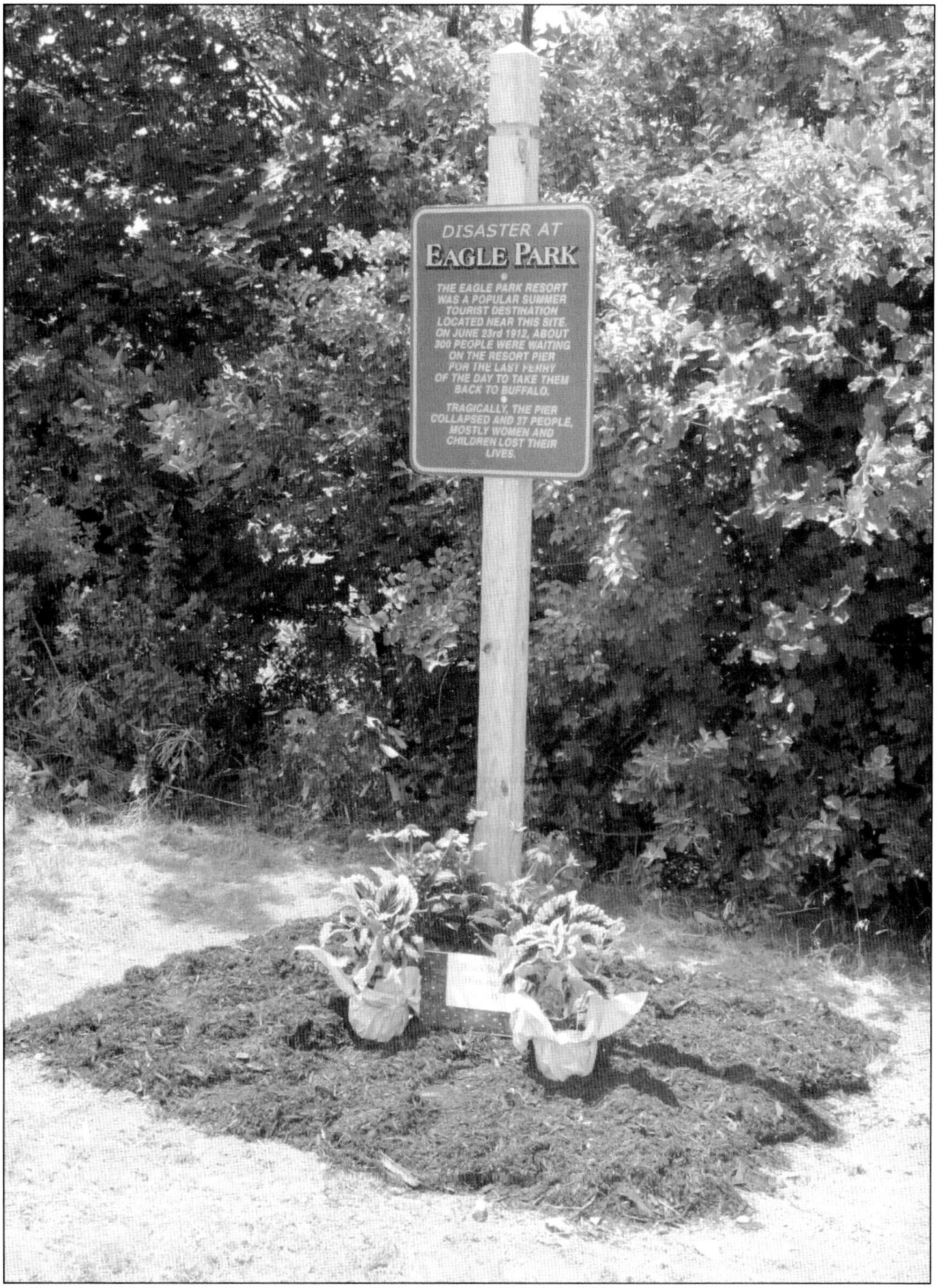

Some resorts, like the Edgewater and Sheenwater, were associated with hotels that began to open in late 1870s; their guests stayed for days. Others like Eagle Park, opened in 1889 by Henry Cook, were freestanding and primarily served day-trippers who came to the island on the various ferries. Many belonged to social or civic groups that made a tradition of annual trips to celebrate the summer. Along the west branch of the Niagara River, Grand Island and New York recognize and remember the worst tragedy in island history.

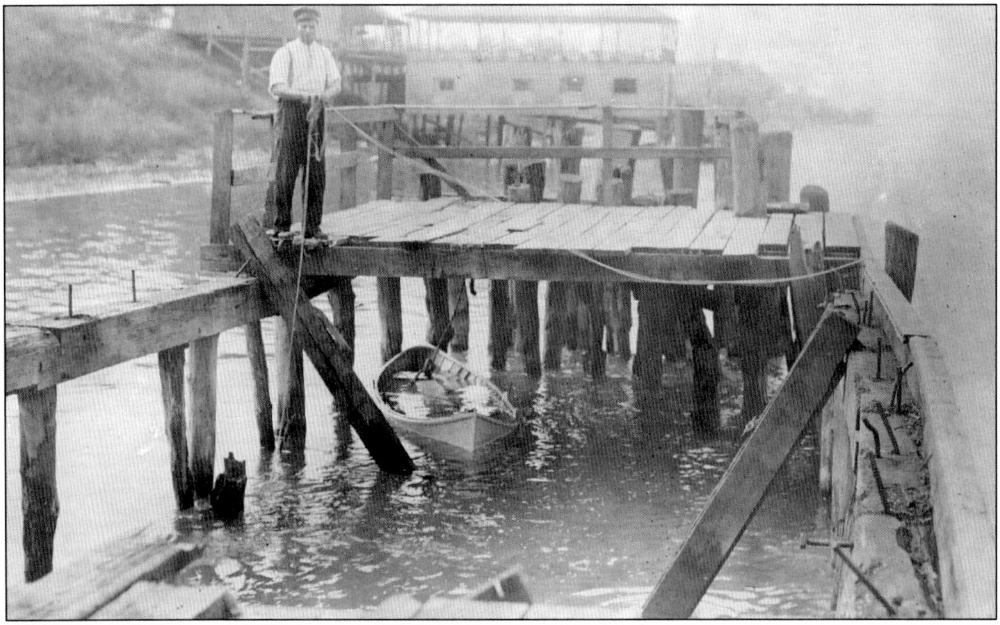

On June 23, 1912, the Foresters' Lodge from Black Rock made its annual day trip to Eagle Park. Some members left in the afternoon, but many stayed to catch the last ferry just at dusk. As the tug *Henry Koerber* and its barge approached with Capt. Frank Fix at the helm, some 250 revelers crowded the dock, singing and swaying. Workers tried to get them back, but it was too late. Before the barge touched it, 50 feet of the dock collapsed, hurling more than 100 people into the river. When the search for bodies ended and the inquest was held, the death toll was set at 37. The golden era was already ebbing, but the bad publicity from the Eagle Park disaster seemed to seal its fate.

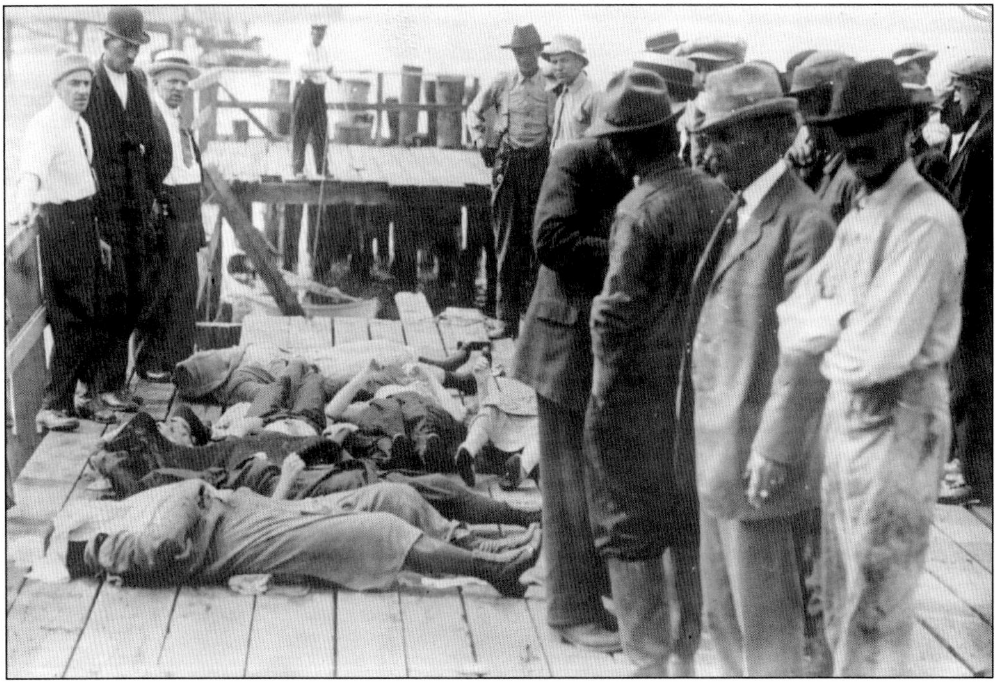

Seven

From War to War

The end of the golden era coincided with the coming of World War I. Grand Island's year-round population had been shrinking since 1880, a decline that accelerated after 1900. As the automobile became a principal means of transportation, life sped up in the United States, but without cheap and easy access to the mainland, the limitations of the island became increasingly evident. Everything cost more in terms of time or money or both. Young people wanted more opportunities than the island could offer. More than ever, the island was a farm community, and the 1920s was not a great time for farmers anywhere.

The onset of the Great Depression was a disaster for most Americans, but at the same time, it triggered the end of Grand Island's population decline and marked the beginning of its transformation. In response to the economic crisis, both state and federal governments began trying to create jobs through increased spending on public works, particularly infrastructure. The Civilian Conservation Corps (CCC) had a camp on the island, and the Works Progress Administration (WPA) was also present. The state built Beaver Island State Park on the former Spaulding-Sidway estates, and West River Parkway was built to bring back the island's traditional appeal as a resort area. Most importantly, the response to the crisis finally opened the door to something local leaders had been unsuccessfully seeking for decades: bridges to the mainland.

The long-awaited transformation began immediately after the completion of the first bridges, but it slowed down substantially with the United States' entry into World War II. In that emergency, everything focused on winning the war, and like other communities, Grand Island made its contribution and paid a high price. But at the end of the war, islanders could celebrate not only victory, but also the prospect of renewed and sustained development as the postwar population and the resulting opportunities soared.

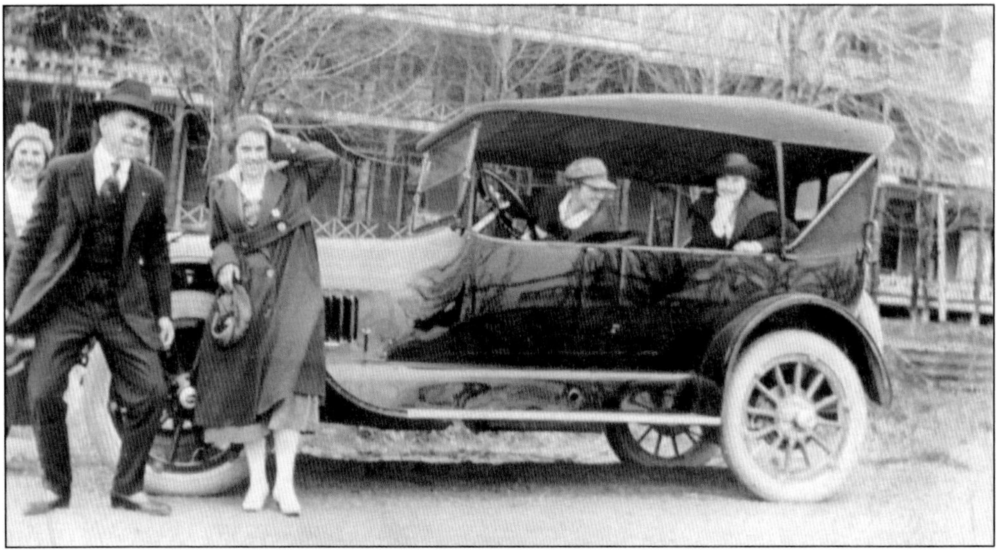

In the 1920s, the Automobile Age began in earnest for Americans. Grand Island residents still relied on ferries to connect with the mainland, but more and more cars began to come to the island to stay. The Roaring 20s are remembered as a time for fun, and the photograph above of the Long family reflects the spirit of greater freedom evoked by the car. From left to right are unidentified, Alvin Long, Ethel Long Ricketts, Mabel Long Kreger (behind the wheel), and Julia Braunschweig Long. In the image below, the woman is driving, and she and her male passenger have traded hats to make the point even clearer. They seem to be making a joke, but women did get the vote that decade.

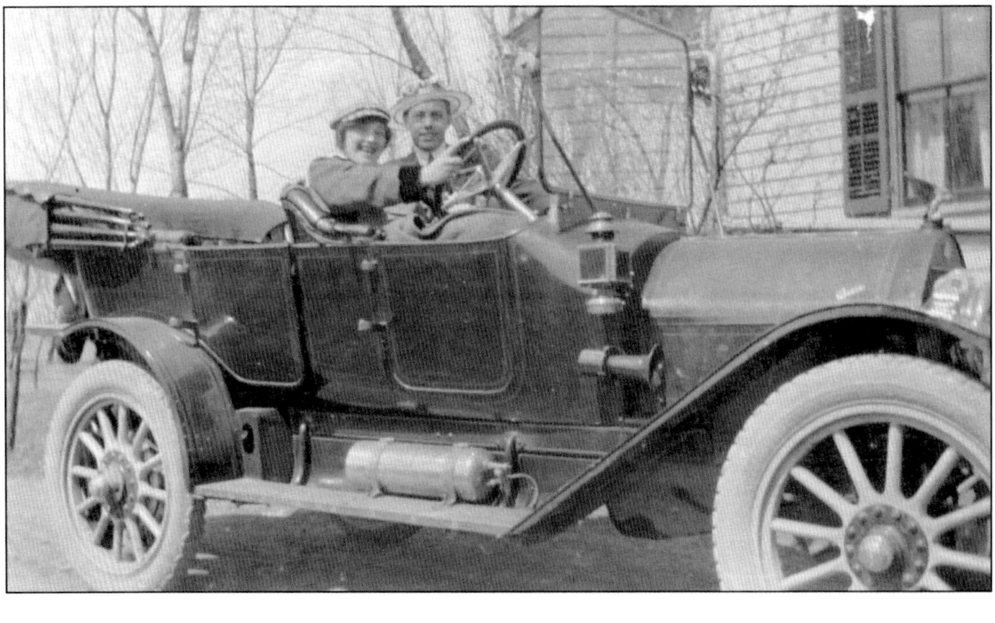

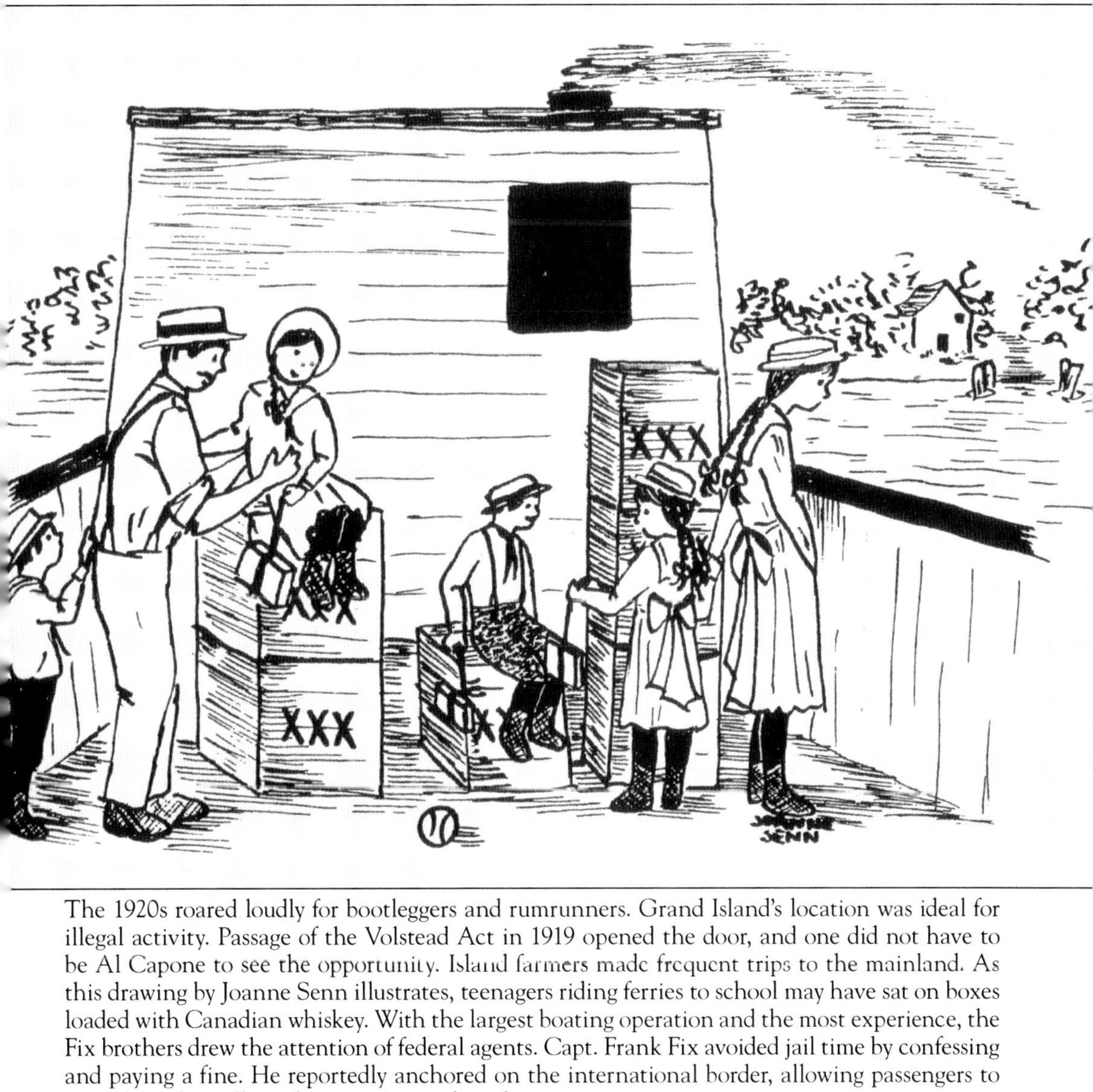

The 1920s roared loudly for bootleggers and rumrunners. Grand Island's location was ideal for illegal activity. Passage of the Volstead Act in 1919 opened the door, and one did not have to be Al Capone to see the opportunity. Island farmers made frequent trips to the mainland. As this drawing by Joanne Senn illustrates, teenagers riding ferries to school may have sat on boxes loaded with Canadian whiskey. With the largest boating operation and the most experience, the Fix brothers drew the attention of federal agents. Capt. Frank Fix avoided jail time by confessing and paying a fine. He reportedly anchored on the international border, allowing passengers to get a drink by walking from port to starboard.

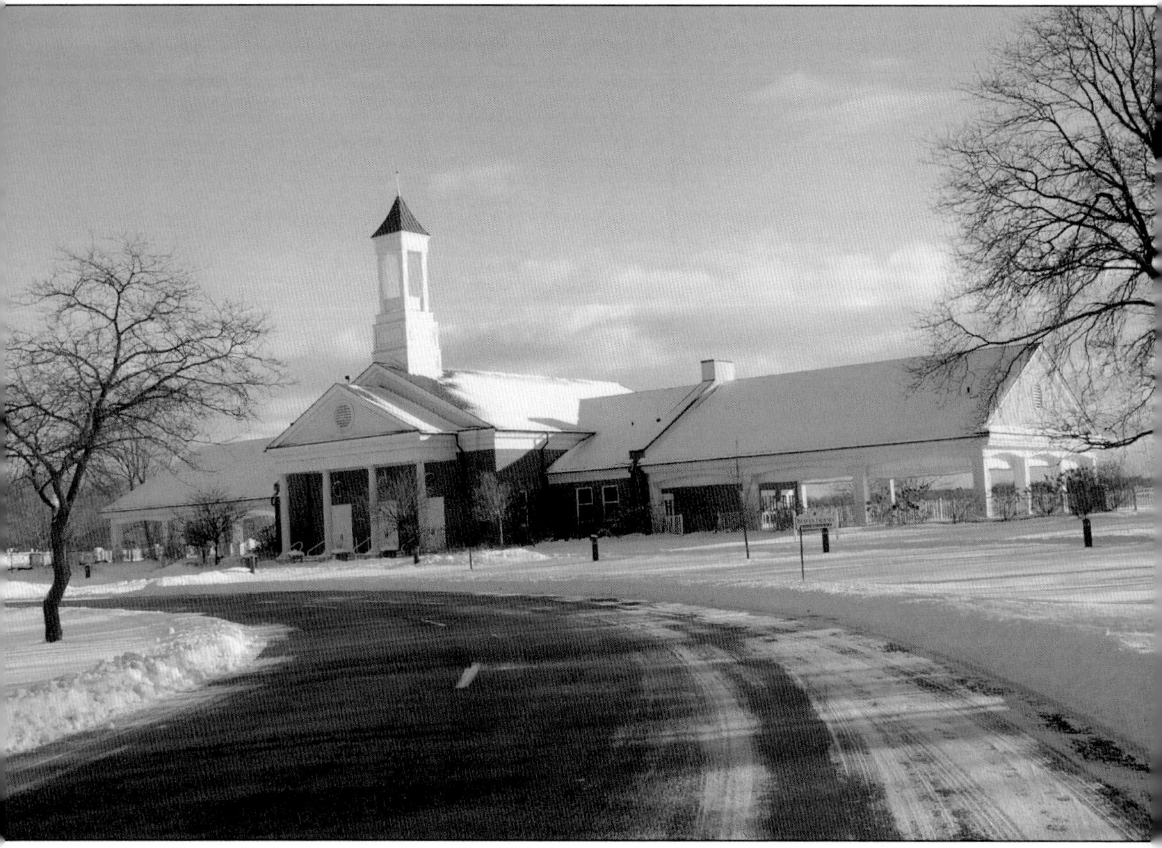

Even before the Great Depression started, New York began efforts to restore Grand Island to its role as western New York's summer playground. It acquired land at both the north and south ends of the island. Buckhorn State Park would be on the north. Beaver Island State Park at the south end includes the smaller Beaver Island. Attractions were limited when the park first opened in 1935, but with the completion of the bridges, a new casino building and beach changed that dramatically. Opening for the Independence Day weekend in 1939, the park served over 5,000 bathers. Enhanced by the addition of 10,000 tons of sand, the beach created a steady and gentle slope into the Niagara River. Cars packed the parking lot, and the snack bar in the new casino building was overwhelmed. The original building was lost to fire in 1992, but the current Beaver Island Club soon replaced it.

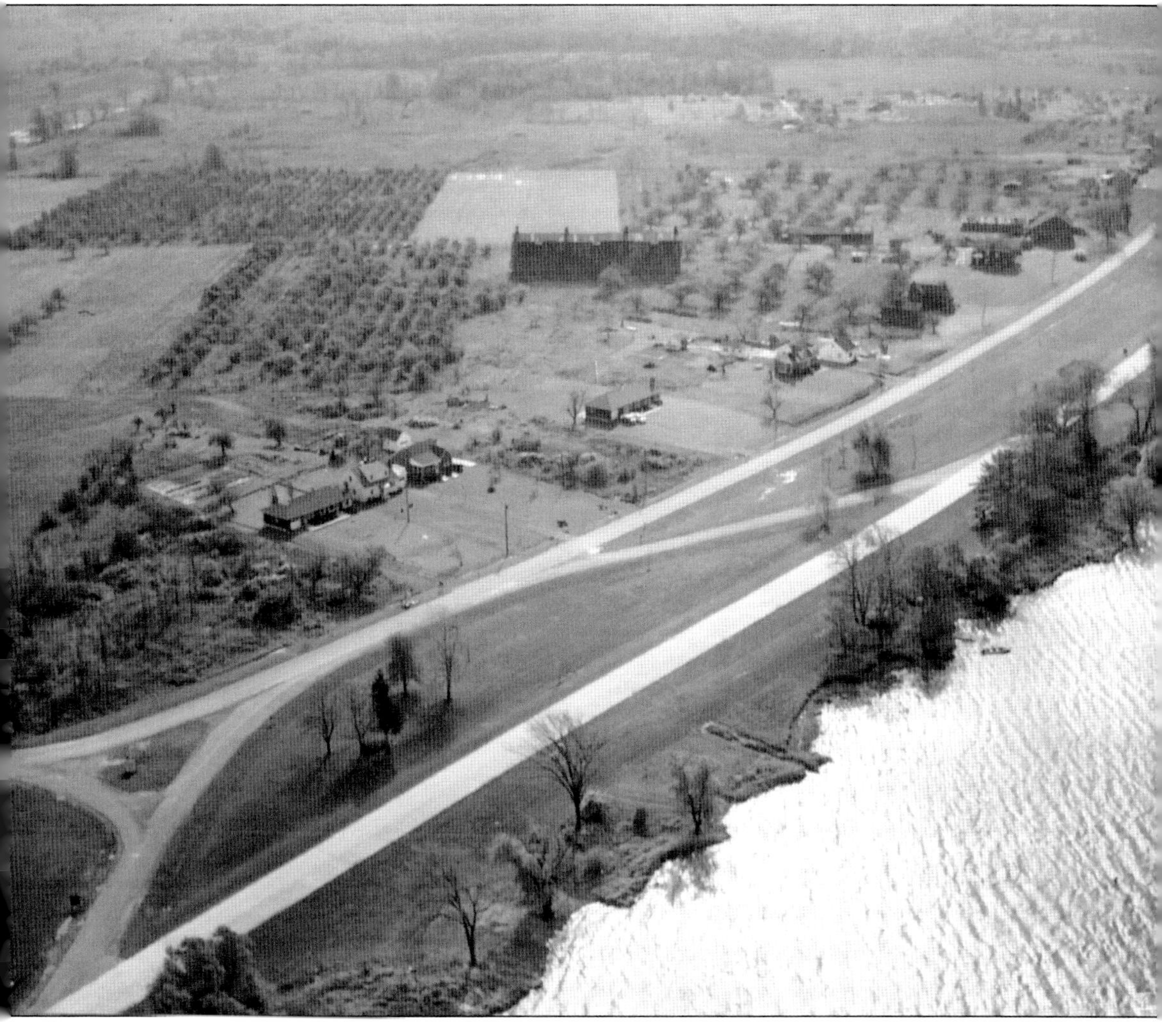

While building facilities at Beaver Island Park, the state began development of Buckhorn State Park on Burnt Ship Creek at the north end of the island. Much of the work was done by the CCC, a federal program designed to employ and educate young men while helping to support their families. They lived in barracks erected near Buckhorn Island. To connect the two new parks, work on the West River Parkway began. The parkway was part of the deal for the bridges, but it was not welcomed by everyone. In acquiring riparian rights to land along the planned route, New York forced homeowners to sell their waterfront property so their houses could be eliminated, leaving a trail of resentment among neighbors along the scenic roadway.

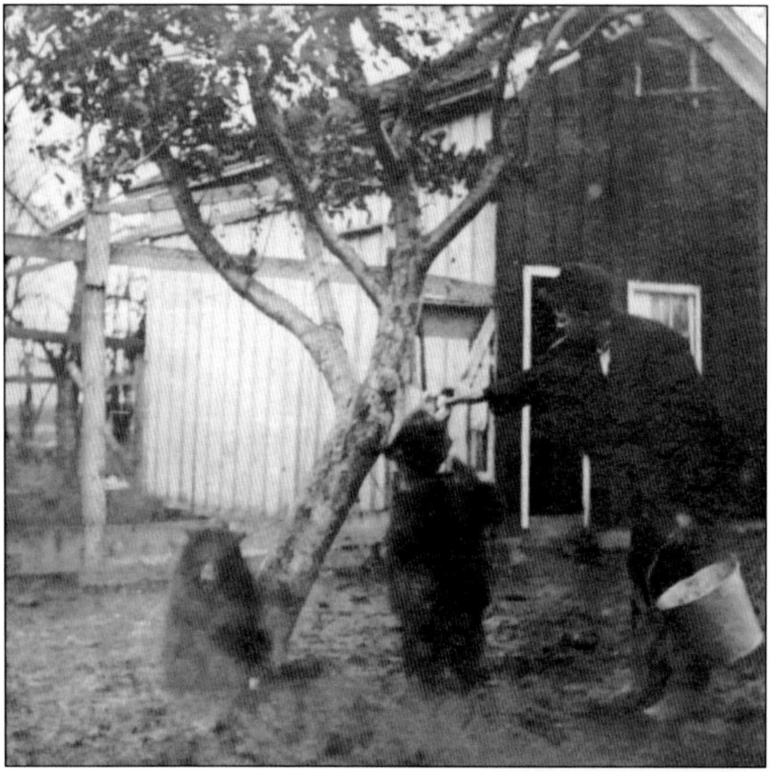

Several cinnamon bears at the new Beaver Island State Park was one of the more unusual attractions there. Ed Staley is shown here feeding them in their pen behind property that was previously the Harvey estate.

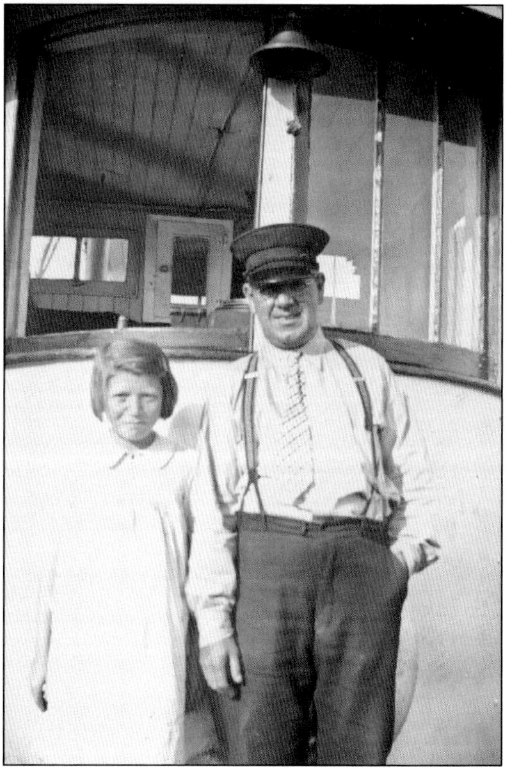

Art Welch worked as the engineer on a ferryboat captained by Capt. Frank L. Fitzsimmons. Here, Welch's daughter, young Shirley Welch, poses with the captain in front of the wheelhouse of the ferry. That must have been a very exciting day for her.

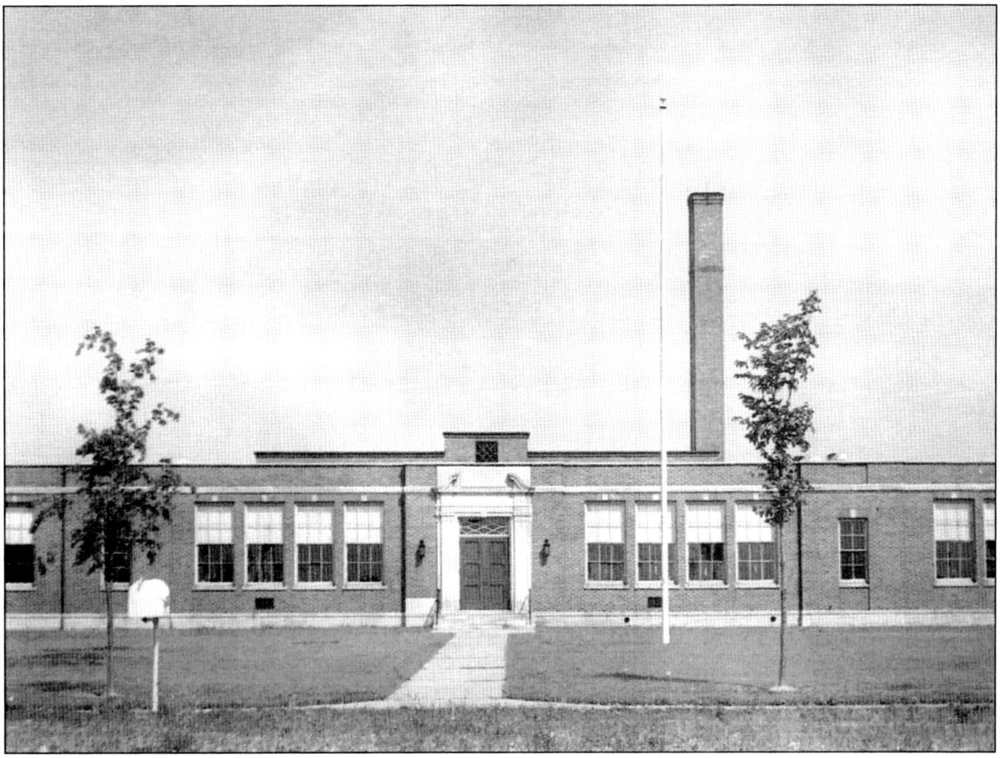

As the rest of America was stuck in the Great Depression, Grand Island was experiencing amazing changes. The completion of the first bridges to the mainland coincided with another major development, consolidation of the island's collection of one- and two-room schools into the Charlotte Sidway School, which opened in February 1936 and graduated its first class in 1937. All students in grades one through eight would now learn together. In the graduation portrait for the class of 1938, members of several well-known families appear.

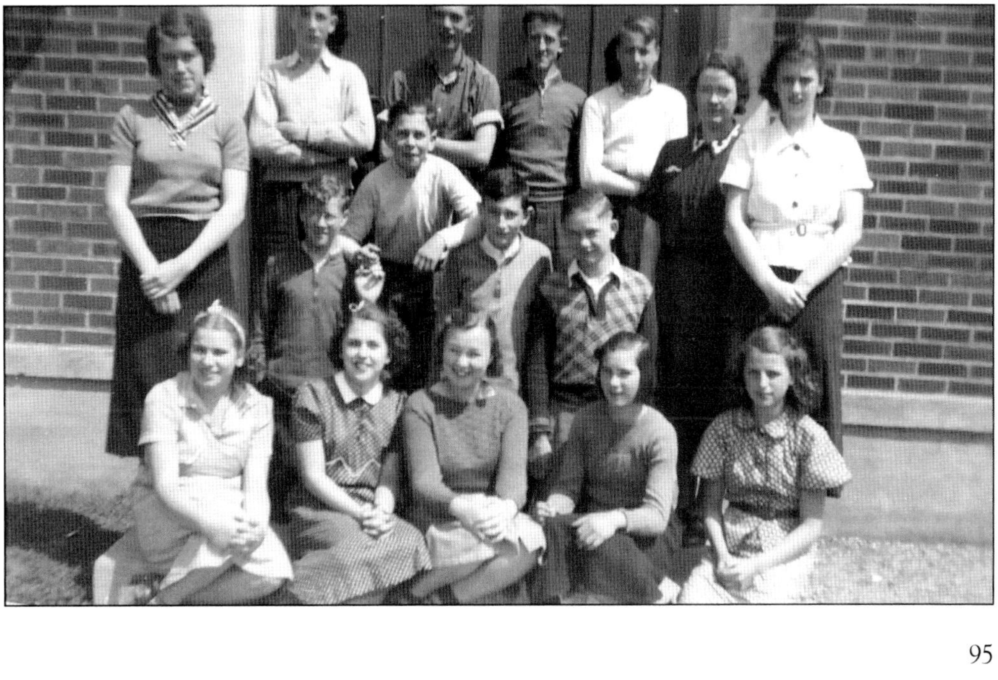

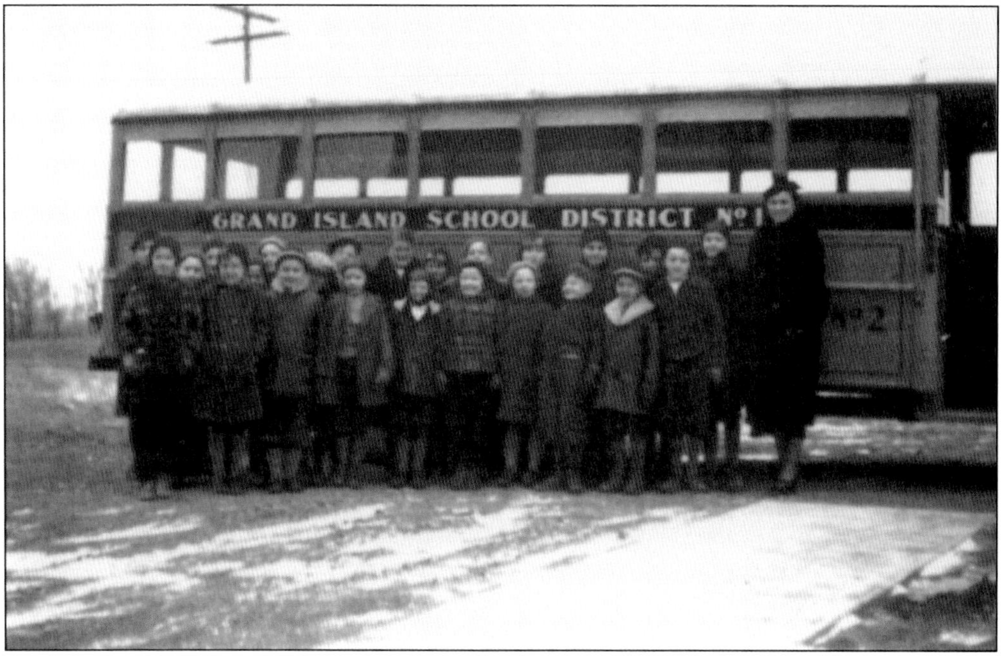

The completion of the first bridges, in 1935, ended Grand Island teenagers' dependence on unreliable ferries to get to mainland high schools. Older students would continue to attend mainland schools, but now they would travel by bus rather than ferry. The school district bought its first bus to facilitate their travel to and from school. It relieved them of the exposure to the elements as well as the uncertainty about river travel. As time passed and the population grew rapidly, a whole fleet soon became necessary.

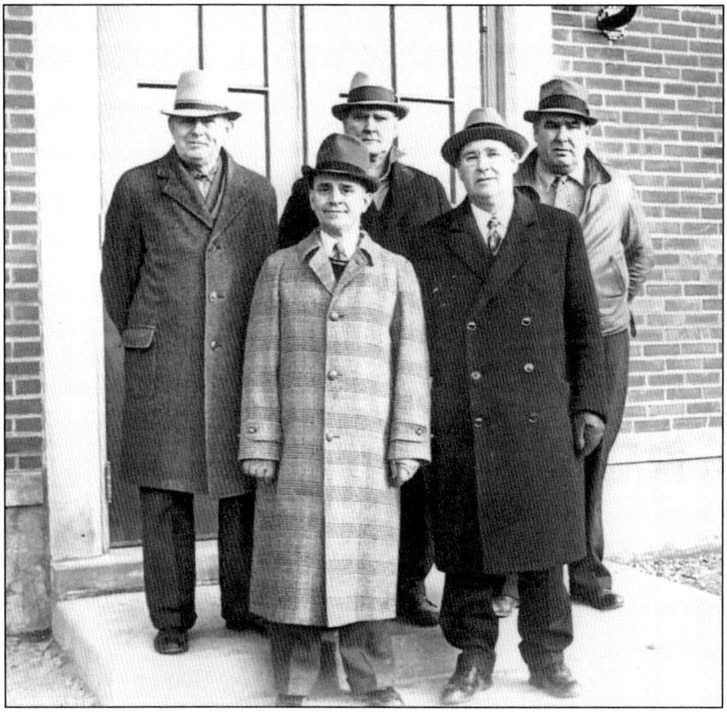

The year 1937 was a busy one for the Grand Island School Board. Like everyone else, they were adjusting to the new world opened up by the bridges. Additionally, they were in charge of completing major changes to the school system. Members are, from left to right (first row) Fred Grehlinger (president) and William Kaegebein (clerk); (second row) Hebert Ashley, Arthur Killian, and Henry Schutt.

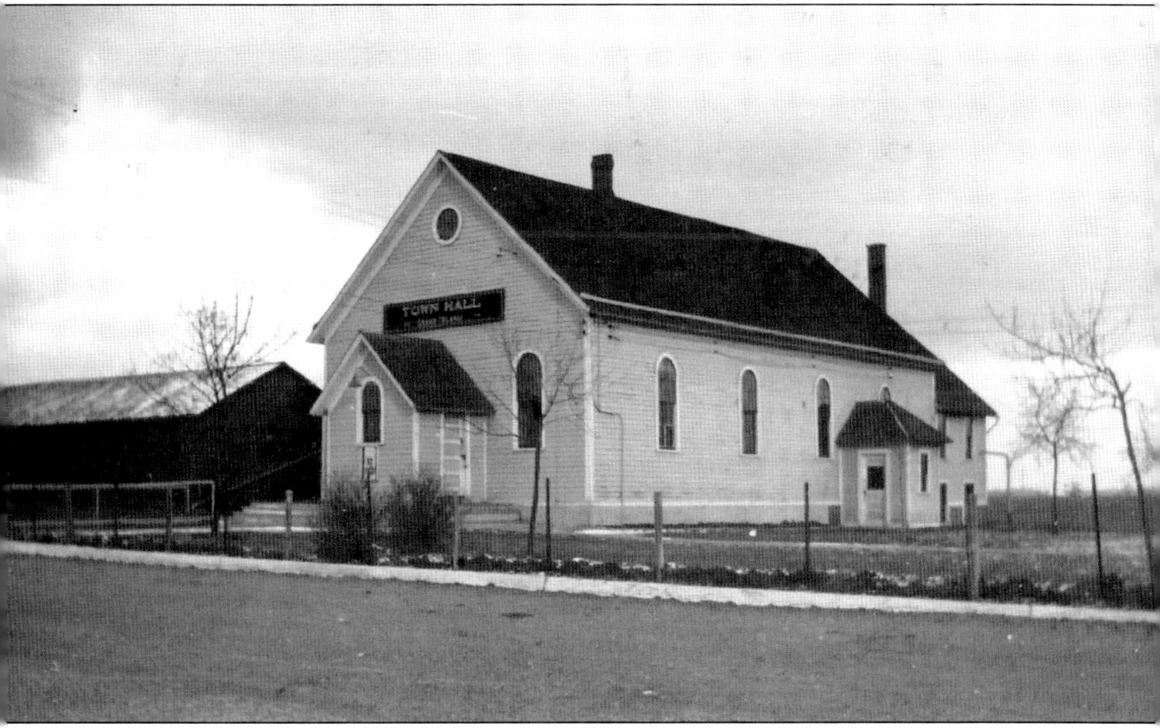

On a small island, fire is a great threat. Many of Grand Island's historical buildings are gone because of fires. Before the establishment of the island's fire company, bucket brigades drawing on farmers' wells were the usual means of fighting fires. If a fire required a larger response, off-island fire departments could be called in, but until there were bridges, they were usually too late. After the bridges were completed, population growth increased the need for a local fire department. After a meeting at the home of supervisor John Mesmer, the State of New York granted a certificate of incorporation for the Grand Island Fire Company in April 1938. When the town government moved into the former School No. 9 later that year, the fire company with its 53 volunteer members took over the original town hall. The town purchased the island's first fire truck soon after formation of the fire company.

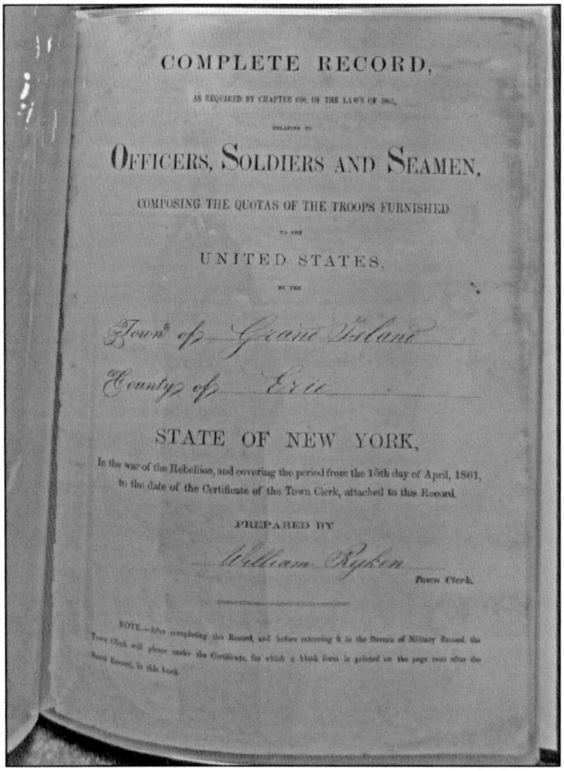
COMPLETE RECORD,

RELATING TO

OFFICERS, SOLDIERS AND SEAMEN,

COMPOSING THE QUOTAS OF THE TROOPS FURNISHED

TO THE

UNITED STATES,

BY THE

Town of Grand Island

County of Erie

STATE OF NEW YORK,

In the war of the Rebellion, and covering the period from the 15th day of April, 1861, to the date of the Certificate of the Town Clerk, attached to this Record.

PREPARED BY

William Ryken

Town Clerk.

Grand Island has sent its citizens to serve in all the nation's wars. The title page of a recording of all who served in the Civil War is shown. These men from Grand Island gave their lives during the war: John Bedell, Lucius Scott, Paul Seibert, George Bartrum, Duncan McInnes, Philip Duringer, Jacob Shoemaker, Clemence Neumyer, George Zeem, John Warren Kent, and Philip Diermeyer. The total population of the island in 1860 was 954.

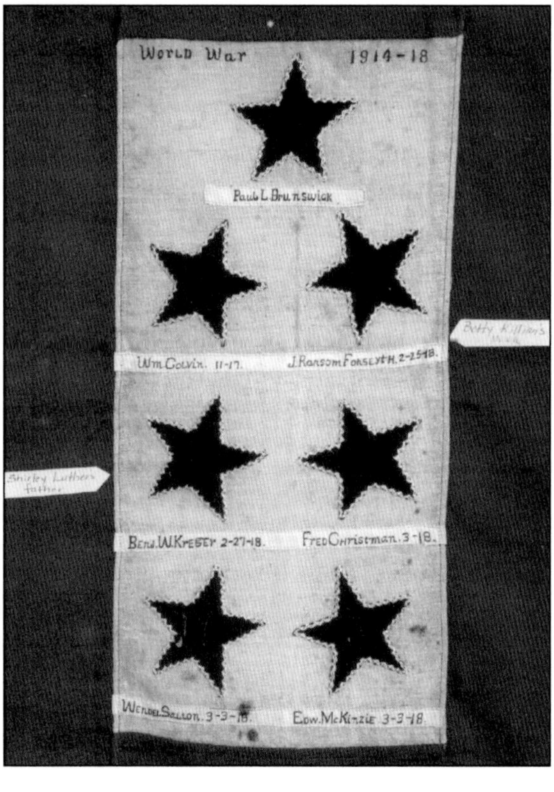

This wall hanging was made to honor members of Trinity EUB Church serving in World War I. The only islander killed in that conflict was Edward Pierce. The toll in World War II would be much higher: Charles DeGlopper, Eugene Dinsmore, William Gillen, Francis Goodchild, William Rhode, Howard Salton, Charles Smith, and George Smith. In World War II, service flags with blue and gold stars became too numerous.

Charles N. "Charlie" DeGlopper (left) went into military service when the United States entered World War II. A private in the 82nd Airborne Division, he fought in the North African and Italian campaigns before joining the Normandy invasion. As part of the 325th Glider Infantry Regiment, he flew in behind enemy lines. When his platoon was cut off from its company, DeGlopper volunteered to provide covering fire so the rest of the platoon could escape. Shooting his automatic weapon, he moved into the open to draw enemy fire. Badly wounded and bleeding, he continued to fire until his platoon was safe. He died there and in 1946 was posthumously awarded the Medal of Honor. Known as the "Gentle Giant" at home, he is shown with Sgt. Kirby McDonald. Below, DeGlopper's father attended the renaming of an army transport ship in his son's honor.

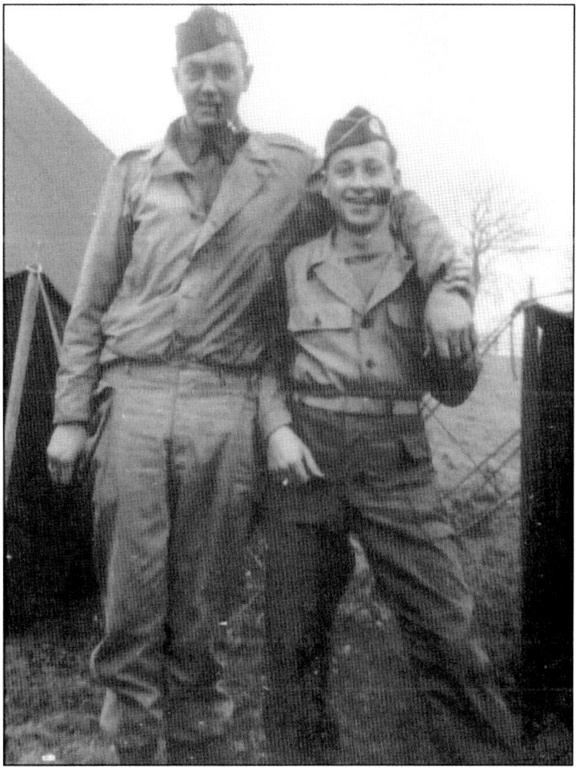

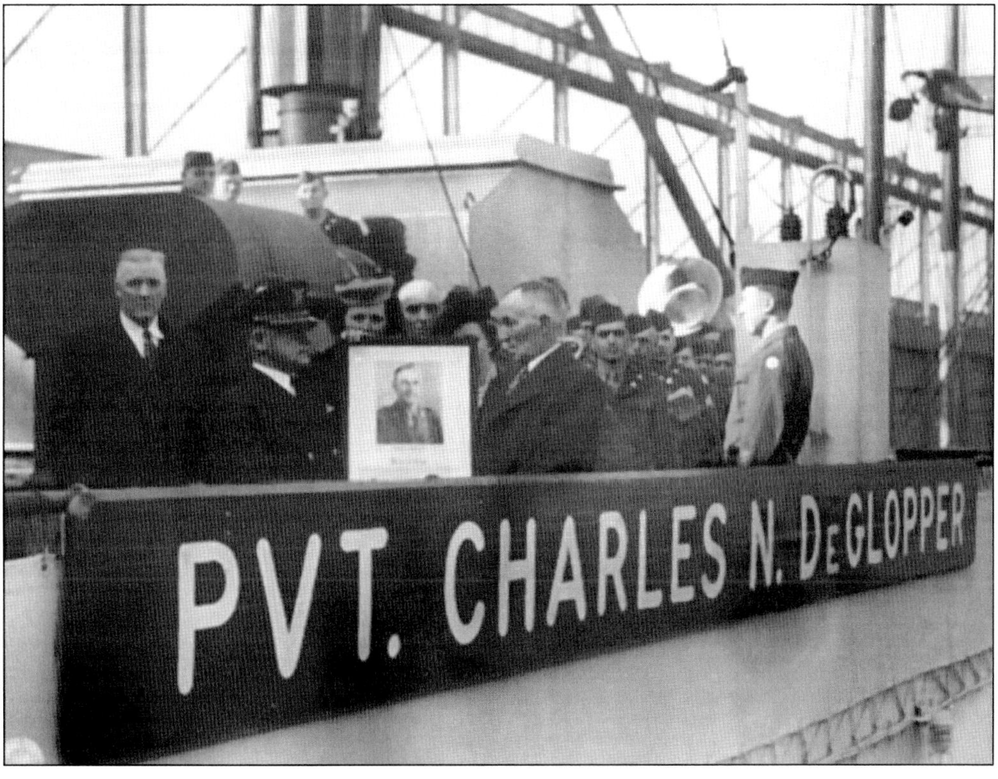

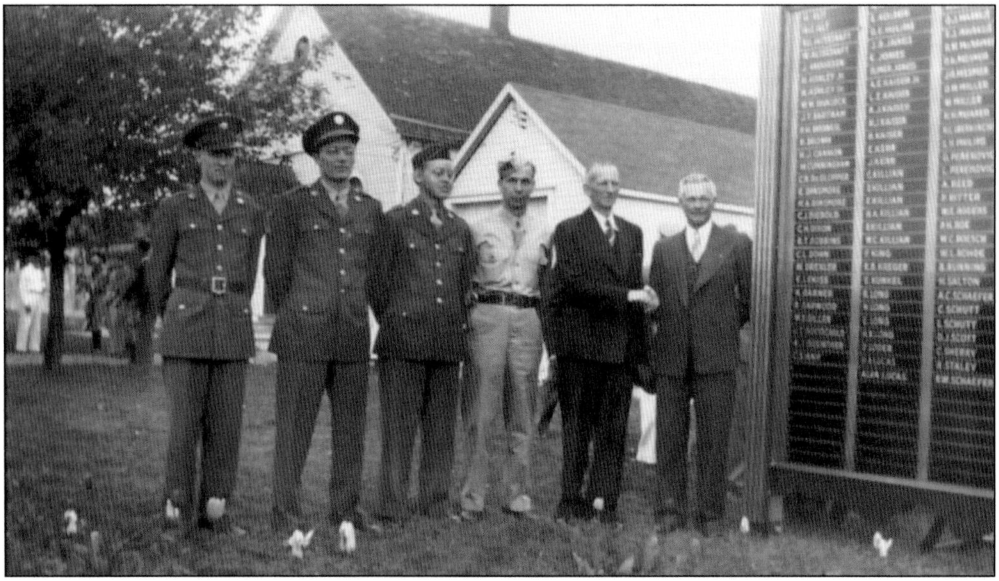

On June 1, 1943, a large plaque listing all of the Grand Island citizens serving in the armed forces in World War II was unveiled near the original town hall, at that time the fire hall. In the photograph, three of the men whose names are on that plaque are seen here. From left to right are Joe Anderson, Franklin Mesmer, and Donald Killian, whose names appeared on the list; Raymond R. Summers; town superintendent Reginald Long; and Horace French. One of the many ways Grand Island citizens joined with their fellow Americans to support the war effort was a scrap metal drive.

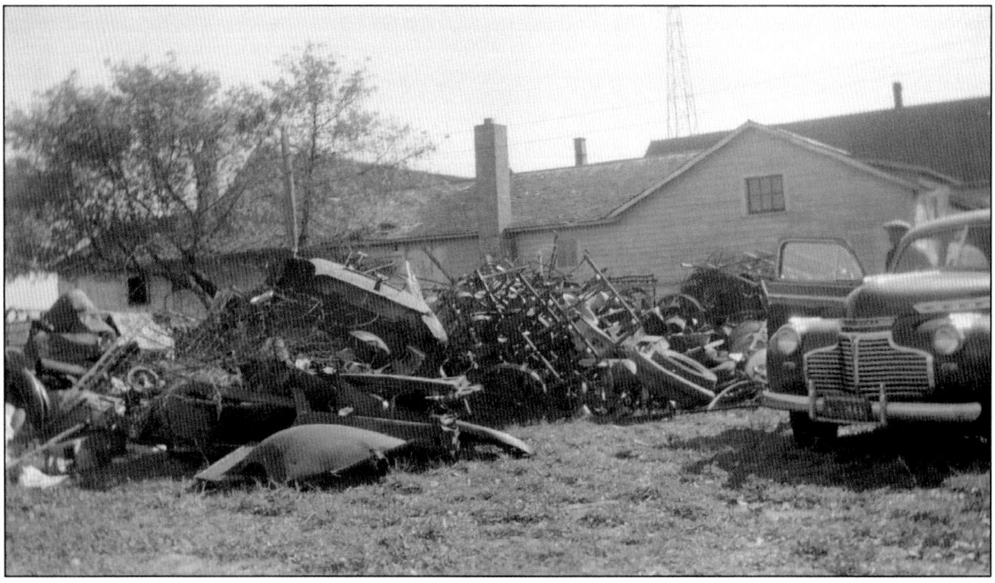

Eight

Why Is It So Hard to Build a Bridge Here?

Grand Island's most distinguishing characteristic has been its most obvious—it is an island. Until well into the 20th century, that meant a level of isolation that greatly affected when and how it developed. The difficulty in connecting to the mainland made it less attractive for many ordinary purposes. At the same time, the isolation helped make Grand Island unique, inspiring ideas that would not have been considered in more convenient locations.

During the 19th century, the Erie Canal and railroads tied the Niagara region ever more closely to the East Coast, but for Grand Island that connection continued to require an additional boat ride. Long after its mainland neighbors joined the seamless network of the national economy, Grand Island remained off the beaten path.

As time passed, the island's citizens naturally sought a more fixed and dependable connection to the mainland, particularly to the two cities above and below it on the Niagara River. The full development of the town required it. However, realizing that goal was no easy matter. Building a bridge of the required length is a giant undertaking, both economically and structurally challenging, but at least in the case of Grand Island, the politics were even more daunting. The New York State Assembly acted to license the first ferry service almost as soon as it opened the island for private ownership. Building a bridge took a century longer.

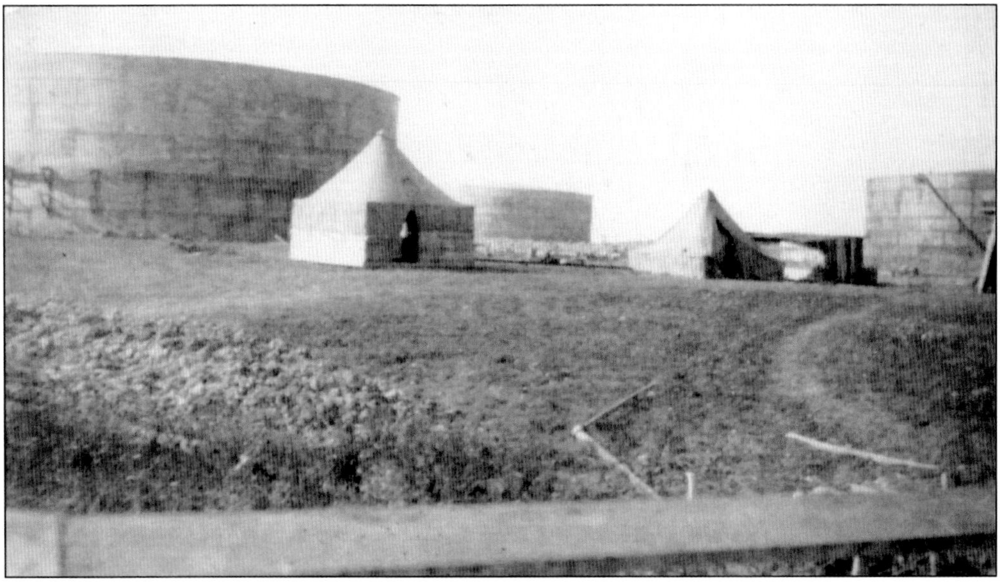

In 1923, the American Niagara Railroad Corporation obtained the right to build two bridges connecting New York to Ontario by way of Grand Island. Simultaneously, the New York Central Railroad planned to put its main Buffalo terminal on the island. Standard Oil Company erected storage tanks and a dock to accommodate tankers. The bridges were never built, and all projects withered away.

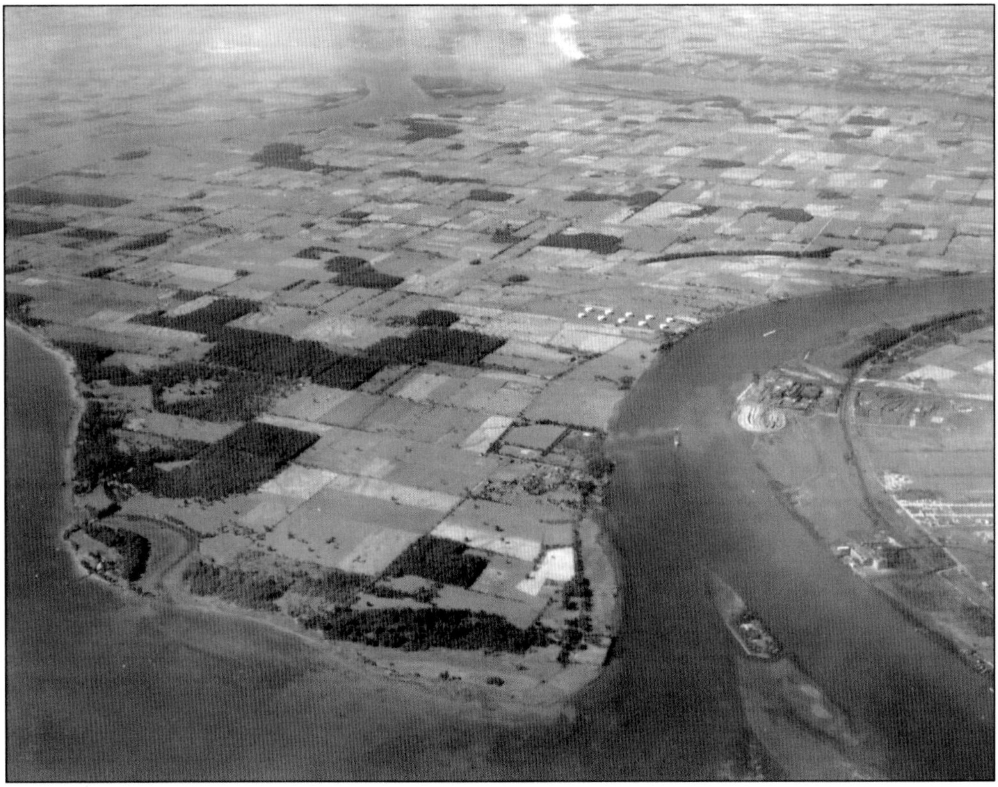

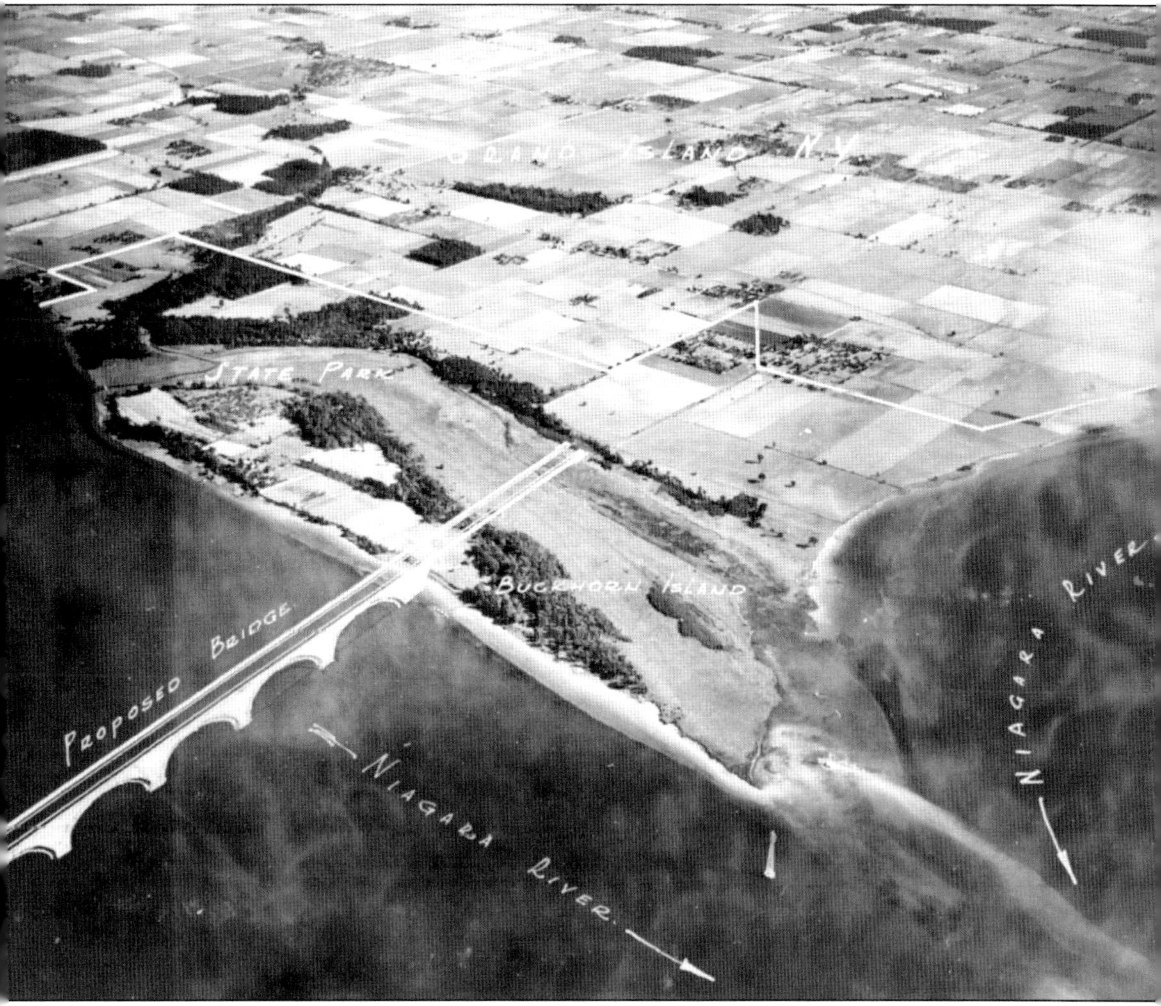

Over a century passed between an 1819 call for a bridge to the mainland in the Albany *Argus* and the beginning of construction. In 1872, the first definitive action took place with a charter to the New York and Canada Bridge and Tunnel Company. Nothing happened. In the 1890s, with the Pan American Exposition drawing near, islanders approached the federal government. The House Committee on Interstate and Foreign Commerce visited the island. A law was passed, but no bridge was built. After failed attempts at state action in 1904 and 1907, activity increased in the 1920s. Projects to make Grand Island the link for railroad bridges to Canada failed, but the creation of the Niagara Frontier Planning Board in 1925 led to this 1926 vision of the site.

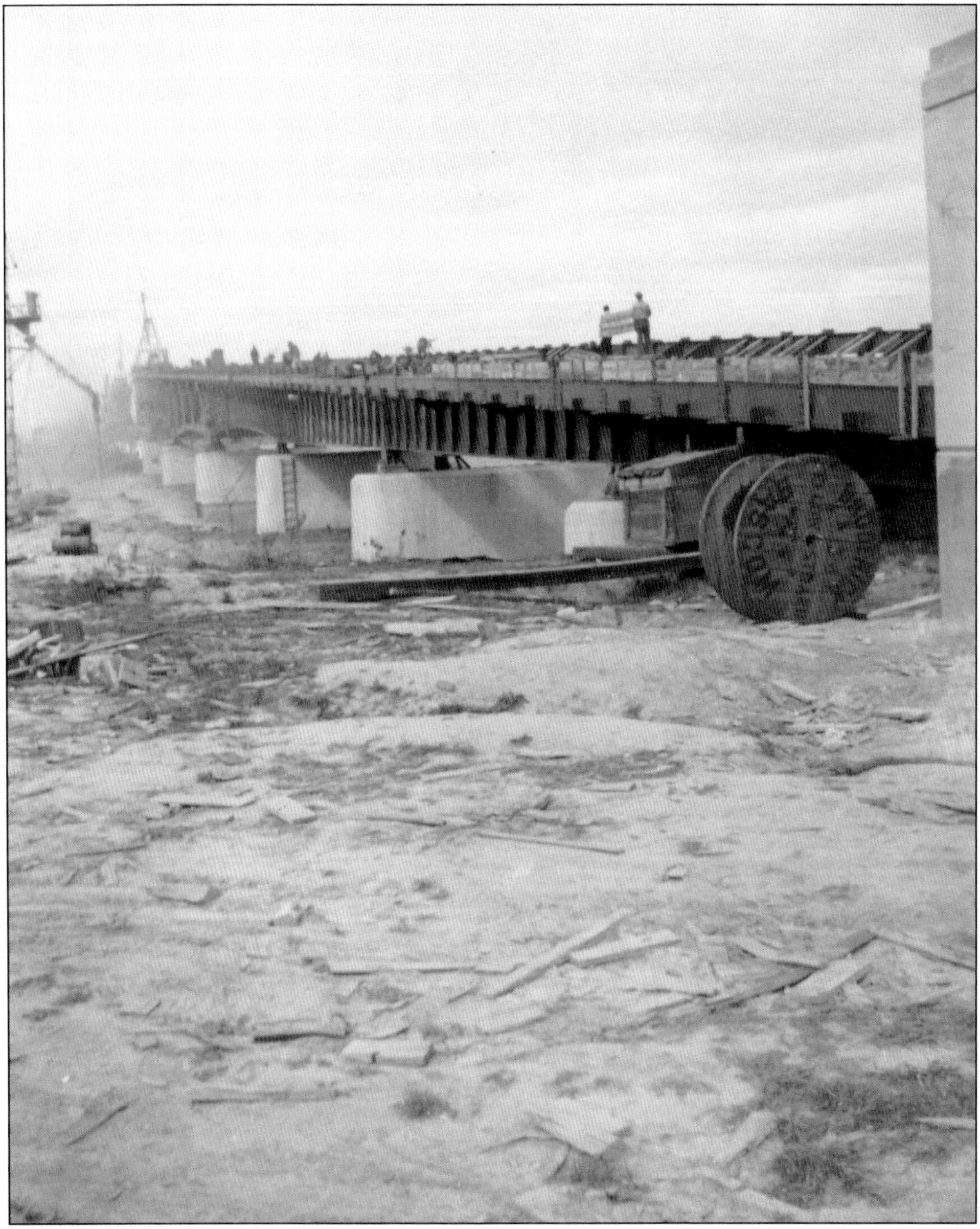

Construction of the first bridge, the south bridge to Buffalo, began in October 1933, largely due to political changes in New York. The creation of the Niagara Frontier Planning Board in 1925 brought the issue to state senator Charles A. Freiberg's attention. With his support, the Buffalo and Niagara Port Authority recommended building bridges to Grand Island. Gov. Al Smith had twice vetoed bridge bills, but in 1929 the legislature finally created the Niagara Frontier Bridge Commission thanks to support from Freiberg and Gov. Franklin D. Roosevelt. The support of Commissioner Robert Moses was also essential to moving the project forward. He was a powerful figure in New York government because of his personal control of the system of public-benefit corporations that built and maintained much of the state's infrastructure. Pictured here are the early stages of the giant construction project.

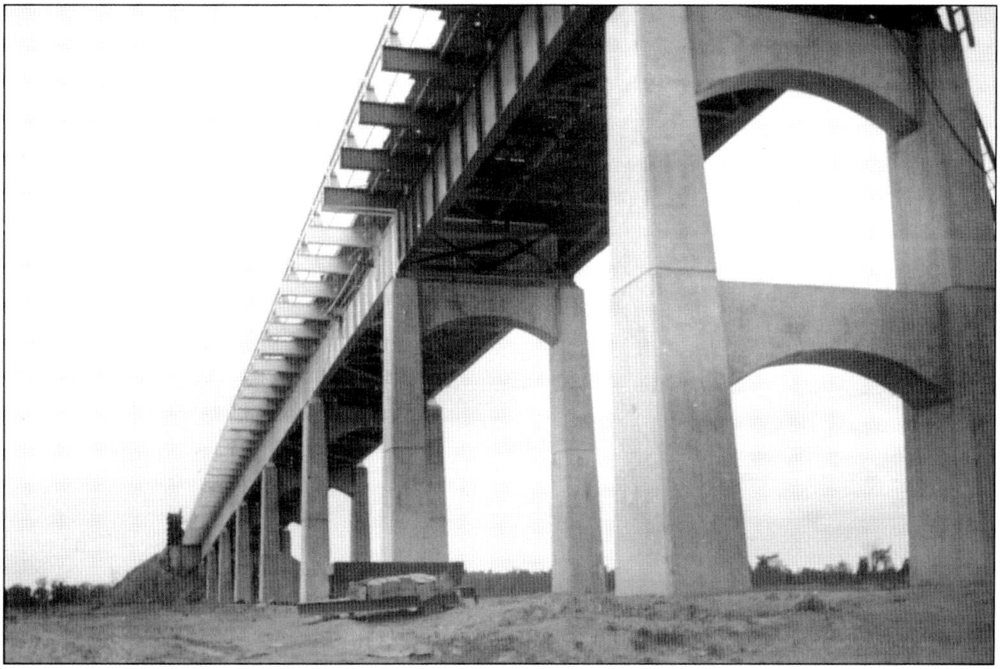

These photographs capture the first Grand Island bridges under construction. Islanders had never seen a project of this magnitude, and they could not have been happier. After such a long wait and so many disappointing outcomes to promising initiatives, they were finally moving closer to what had been increasingly seen as the main barrier to economic progress. The project created many jobs during the depth of the Great Depression, for approval of the project preceded the downturn. The Reconstruction Finance Corporation, launched by Pres. Herbert Hoover, provided necessary loans and probably sped up the start of work.

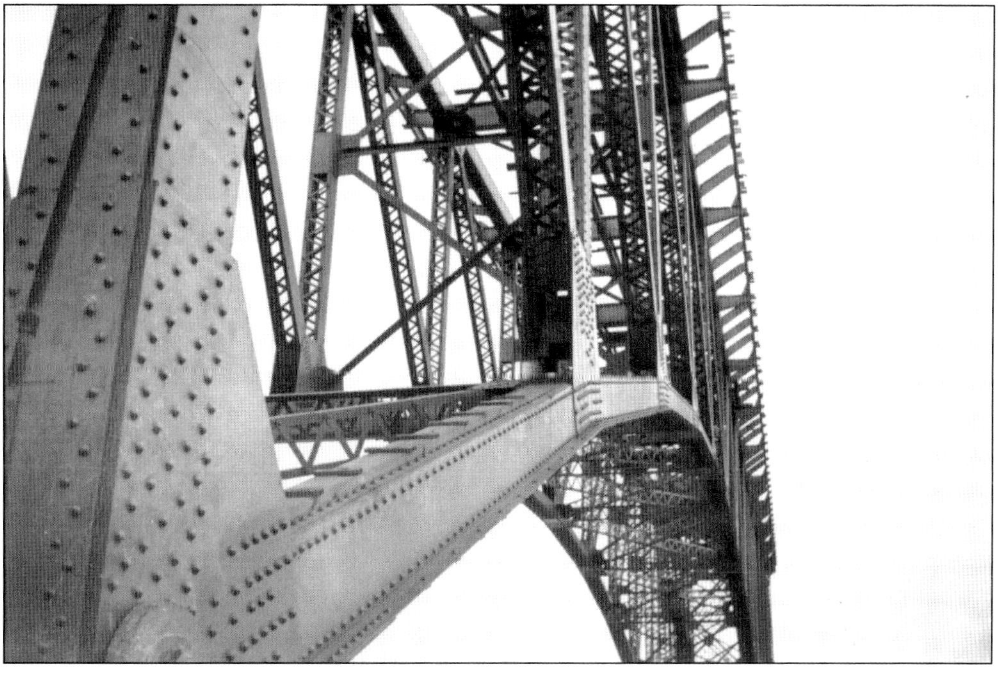

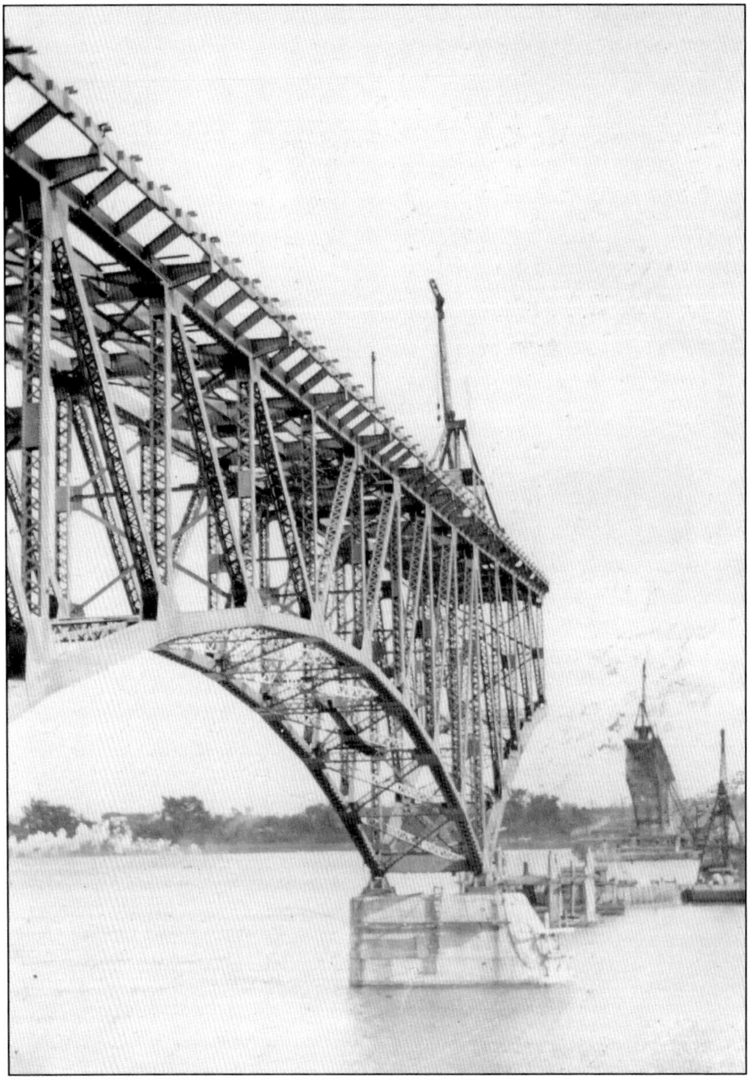

It took almost two years, but by the summer of 1935 the two bridges neared completion. The arches reaching into the river from the mainland and those built out from the island's shores grew closer together every day. The town had endured repeated frustration at the county, state, and national levels. At last, it was time to celebrate. The list of determined leaders included old island families and multiple generations: DeGlopper, Nice, Bedell, Wende, Huling, Long, Van Son, Grehlinger, Dinsmore, and Conboy. Finally, their work had paid off.

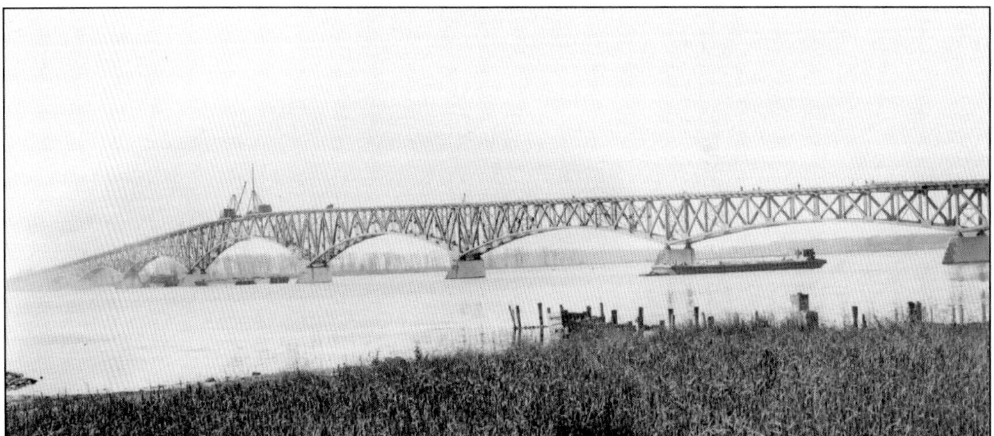

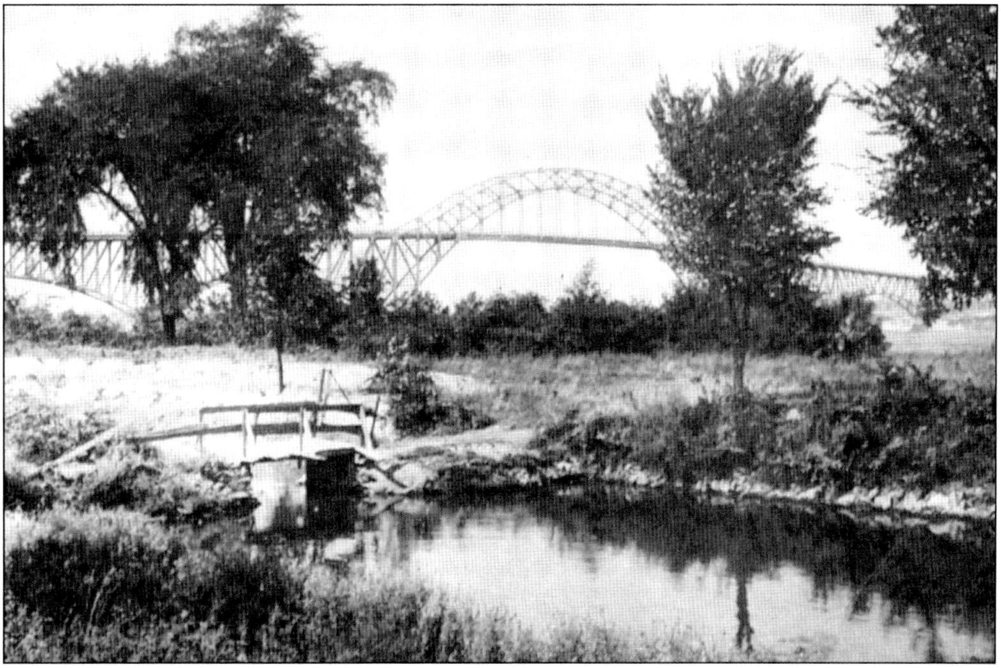

Few of the island's citizens were able to see those aerial views of their new bridges. The southern bridge seems so idealized that one has to look twice to make sure it is a real photograph and not an artist's rendering. It seems to combine the best of both worlds: the island's natural beauty and the modern technology that would shape its future. The addition of massive bridges over the years created other dramatic scenes. Was the sun rising or setting in the scene below? With the completion of the bridges, it seemed to be doing both at the same time. As the island transitioned from rural to suburban, one of the challenges was to maintain the right balance between the old and the new.

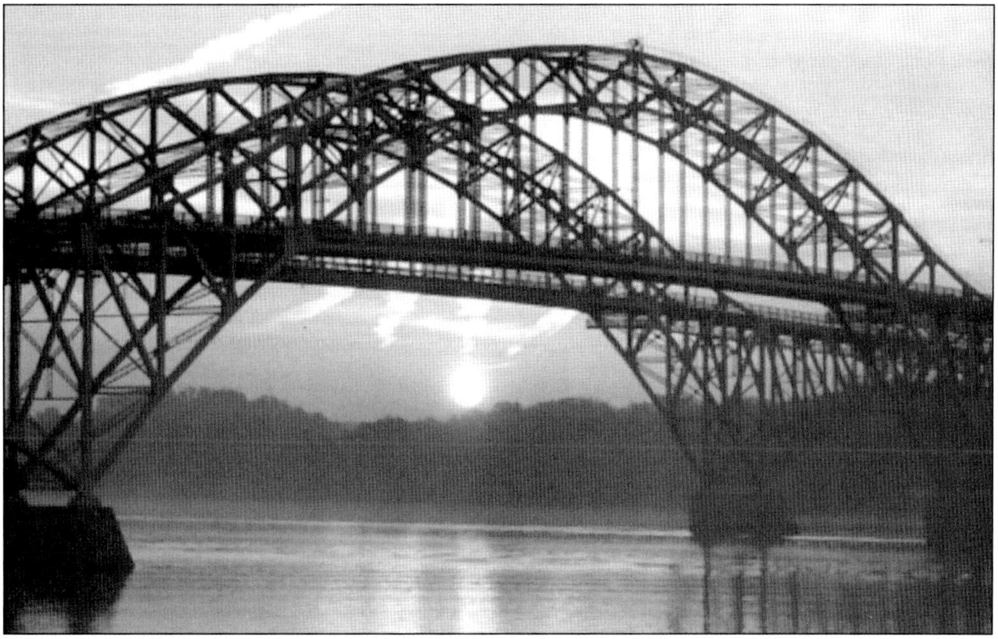

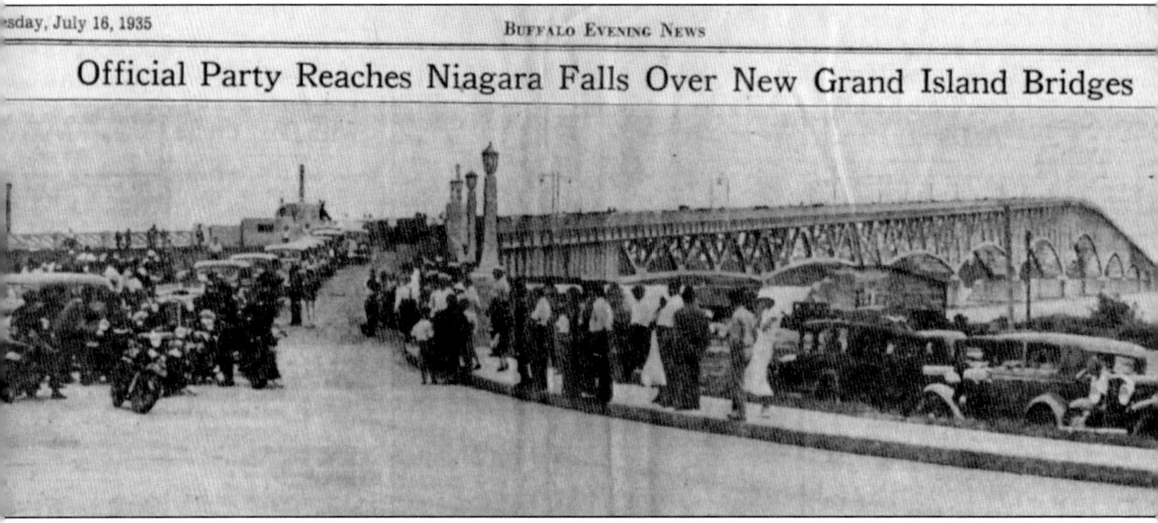
sday, July 16, 1935 BUFFALO EVENING NEWS

Official Party Reaches Niagara Falls Over New Grand Island Bridges

The grand opening ceremonies for the bridges drew almost everyone to the festivities. Islanders had already had their own celebration two days earlier, parading their cars over the south bridge through the Tonawandas to Niagara Falls and back across the north bridge to a party at the town commons. For the official celebration, a dinner was attended by 2,000 people. Special tribute was paid to former supervisor William H. Conboy, who had worked for the bridges for over almost four decades but was unable to attend the party.

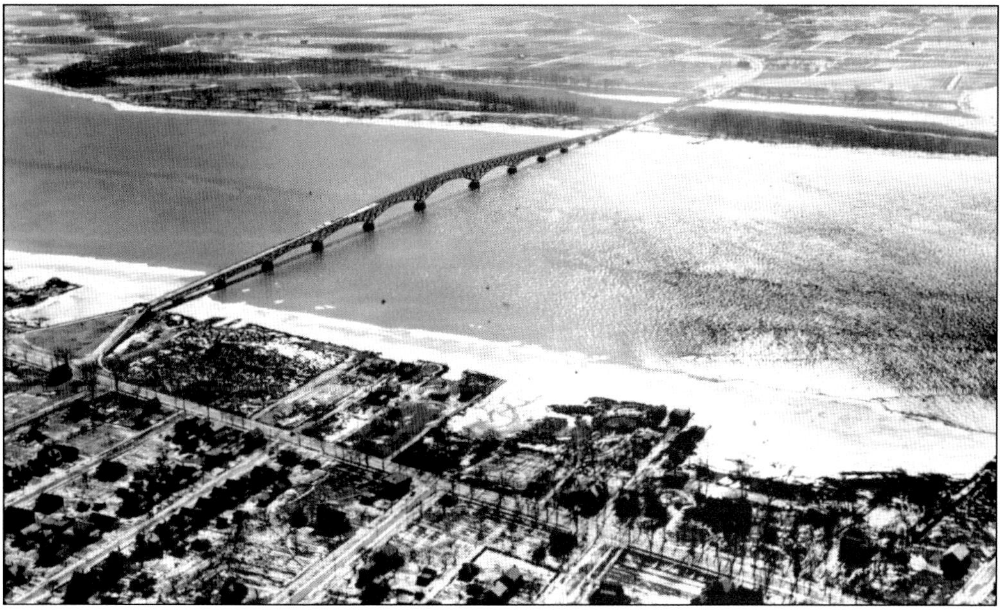

After a century of waiting for secure and easy connections to the mainland and to the cities to the north and south, Grand Islanders finally saw their dream fulfilled. They anticipated new opportunities—and faced new challenges. At the same time, they had suddenly lost forever the most distinguishing characteristic of their hometown. For better or for worse, things would never be the same. Almost overnight, Grand Island became the tourists' shortcut to Niagara Falls and the newest area for Buffalo's expanding suburbs. Depression and then war would delay the full impact, but some changes began immediately

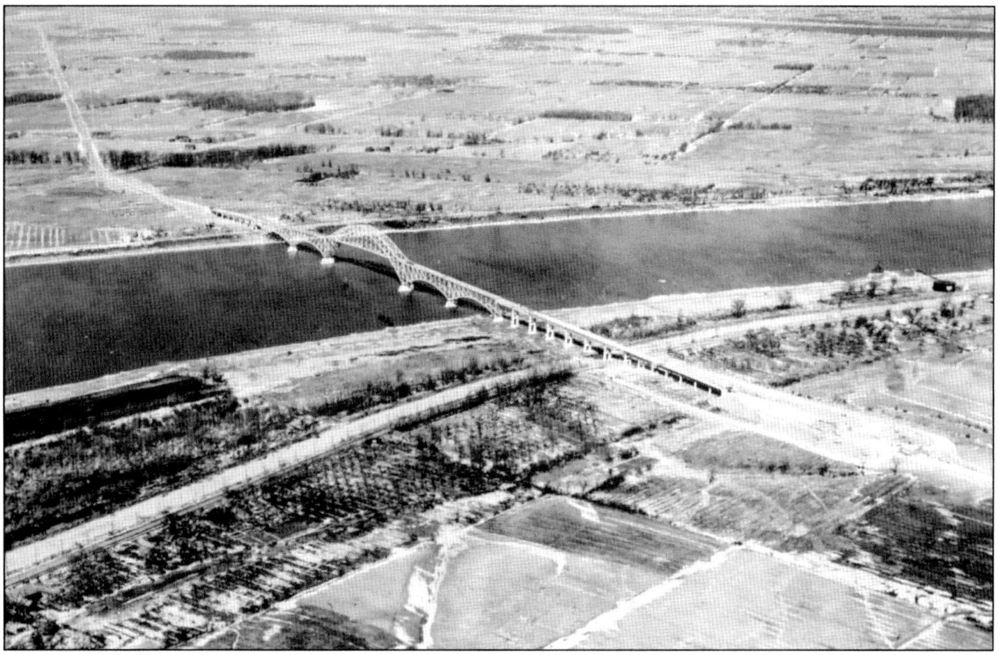

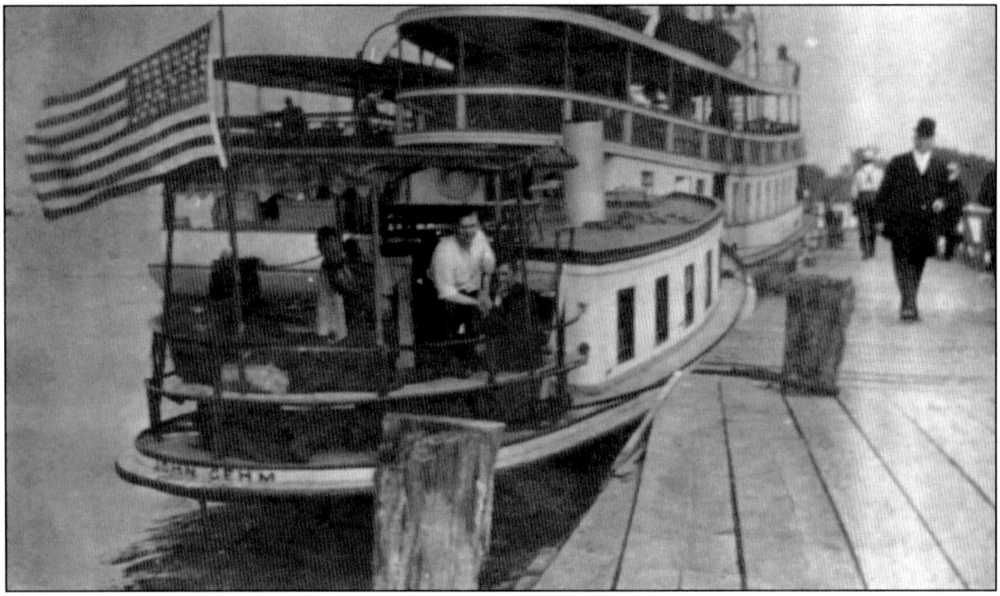

Grand Island's first ferries were chartered in 1825 and remained the island's only connection to the mainland except for a few individuals who had their own boats. The ferries often towed scows to increase their capacity, particularly after the automobile became commonplace. One of the ferries pictured here has such a scow. As the completion of the bridges approached in 1935, ferry operators planned their final trips. The effect was almost instantaneous. Some ferries quit by opening day. The others were gone in a few weeks. A few of the boats remained occasionally active for tours around the island, but the age of the ferries had ended at last.

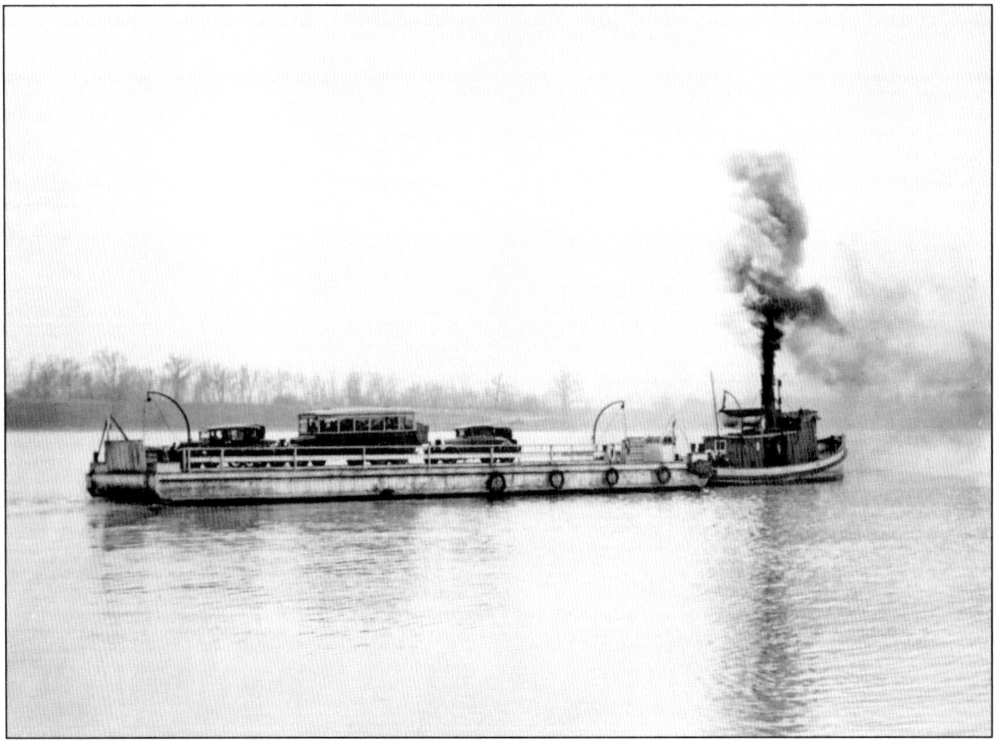

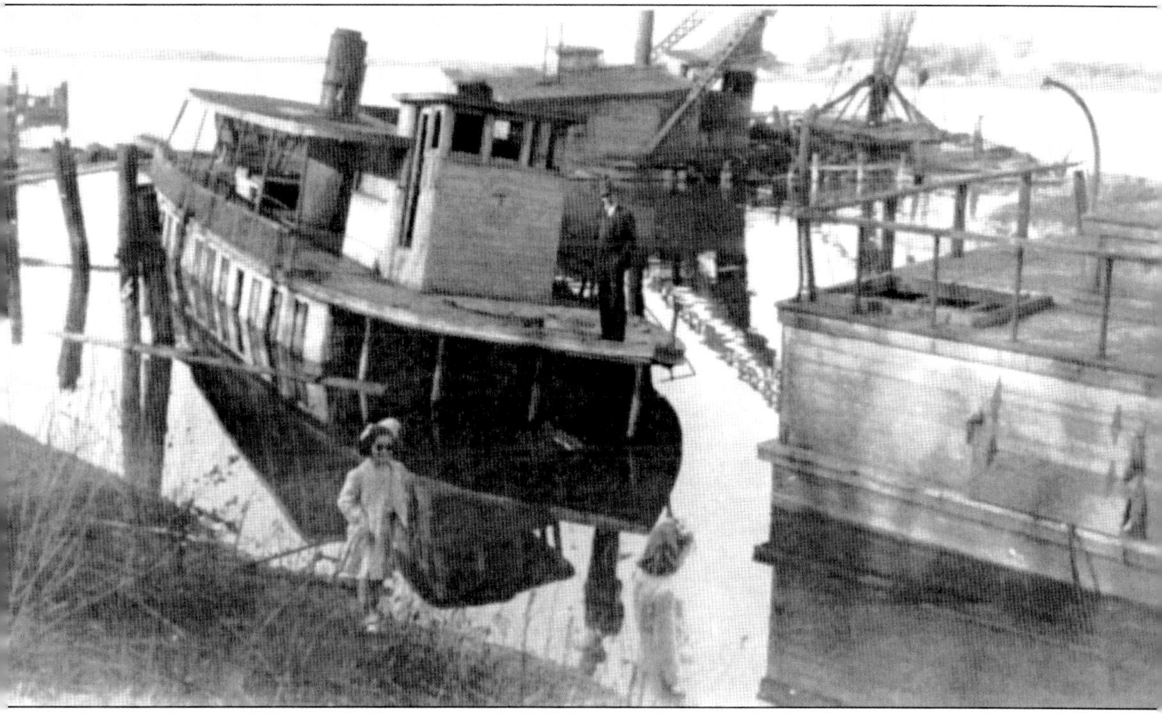

The completion of the two bridges quickly killed the ferry business that had served the island since the first permanent settlements. A few of the boats still cruised around the island with tourists; most of the island's service boats fell into disuse. Some were scrapped, and others were allowed to die a natural death. In 1945, Hugo and Catherine Diringer took their daughters, Mary (left) and Dottie (right), on a Sunday drive from Buffalo to a favorite fishing spot on Grand Island. The girls and Hugo are looking over a half-submerged boat. In 1950, the Diringer family joined the thousands of others moving to Grand Island in the postwar era.

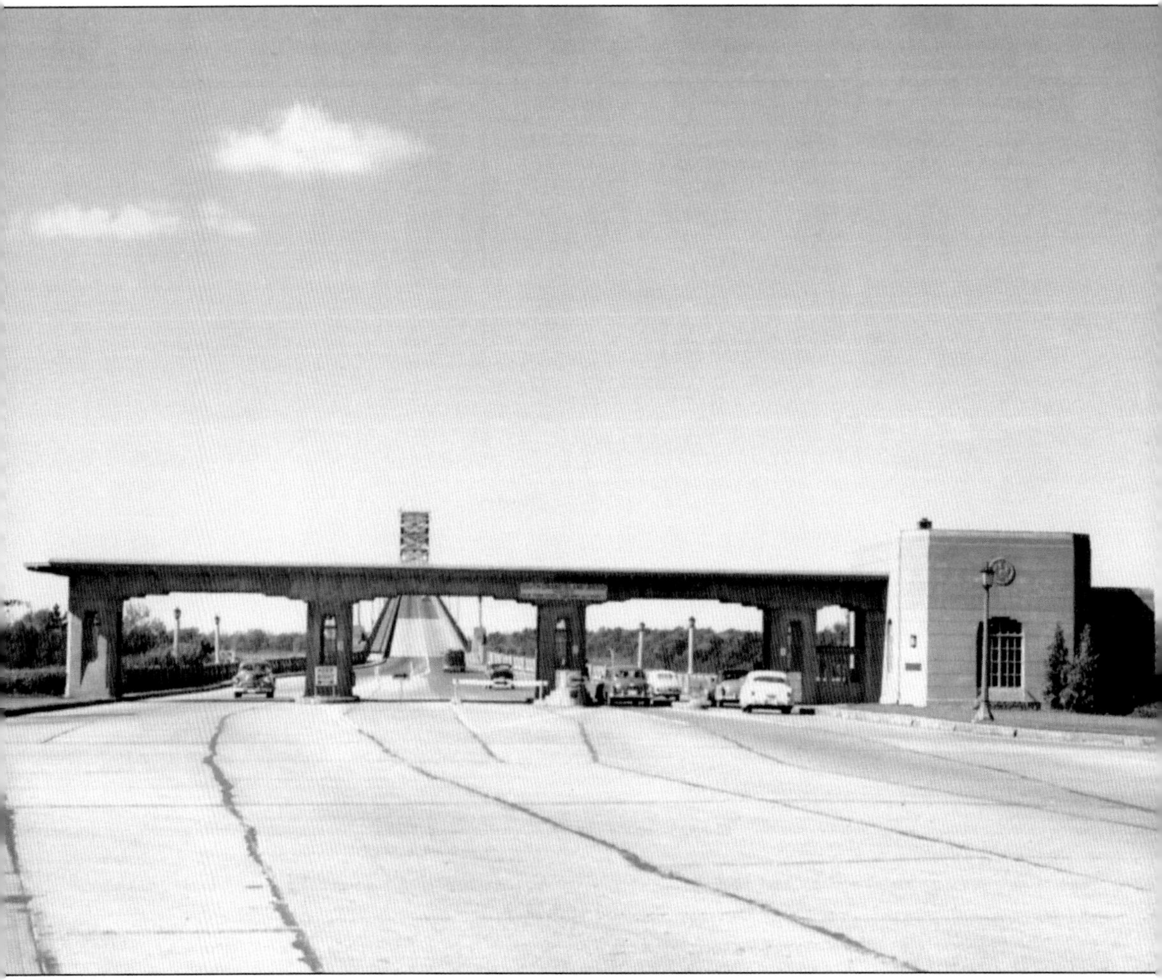

The bridges made life easier for Grand Island residents. Residents no longer had to pay or wait for ferries, but the bridges charged entrance tolls at both ends of the island. Many residents opposed this because they objected to the continued collection of tolls after the bridge construction costs were paid. In 1950, the state announced that the New York State Thruway Authority would be collecting tolls for two years. Of course the tolls have still not gone away, and islanders have to pay to go home.

Nine

The First 100 Years Are the Hardest

As the 1950s began, the people of Grand Island prepared to celebrate the centennial of their community's existence as a distinct town with its own local government, but Grand Island had always been distinct and unique. It had always been set apart in ways that shaped its destiny. Now in the midst of the postwar economic boom, the 1935 bridges were having their full effect. The town was becoming more like the rest of the region, but it was still shaped by its unique history. The decade was stereotyped as the time of the suburbanization of America. With its connection to the mainland, Grand Island's population nearly tripled in the 1940s, had even more growth in the 1950s, and ended the 1960s with 9,607 residents. Between 1940 and 1960 the population increased by 811 percent compared to a 36 percent gain for the Buffalo-Niagara Falls Metropolitan Statistical Area as a whole.

As impressive as the numbers are, they do not do justice to the scope of the changes. From a farming community of small villages operating under fundamental limitations and dependent on its boats, Grand Island was quickly transformed into a prosperous suburban town. The process began with developments like Sandy Beach and Grandyle Village, which produced greater demand for goods, services, and new businesses to provide for and employ the island's residents. In a generation Grand Island was transformed, but it still retained much of the natural beauty that had always been central to its charm.

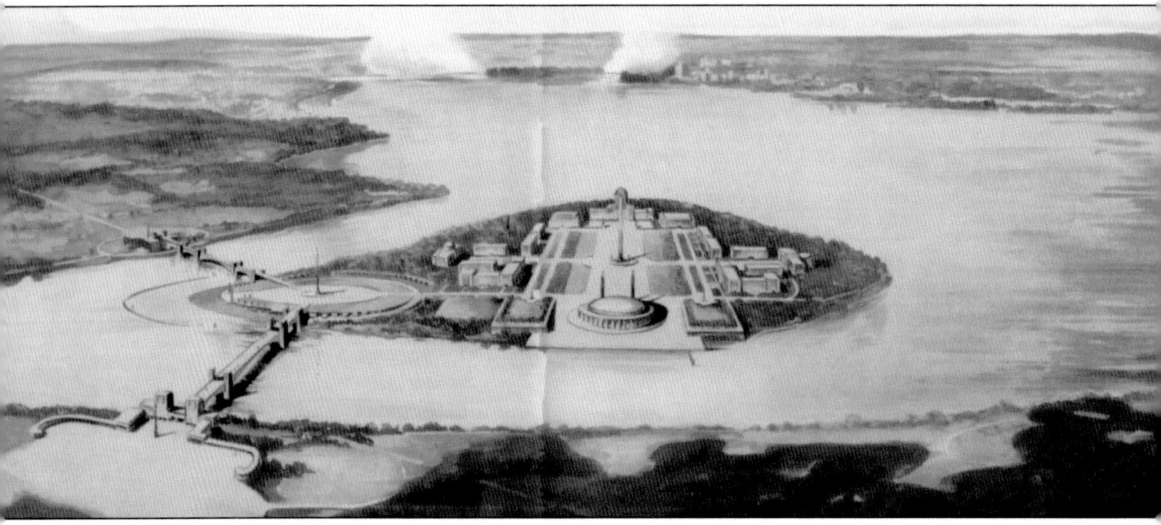

Grand Island's penchant for inspiring dreams was not limited to the 19th century. Just after World War II, Grand Island was mentioned as a potential site for the United Nations by an international committee that had originally been arguing for Canada's Navy Island in the West River. The commissioners pointed out Grand Island's advantages after the UNO Preparatory Commission decided the location should be inside the United States. The island would have given the United Nations a distinctly international location and symbolized the organization's goal of peaceful relationships among nations. It would also have radically changed Grand Island's destiny. This is a rendering of the proposed Navy Island installation with bridges to Grand Island and the Canadian mainland and the mist from Niagara Falls in the background.

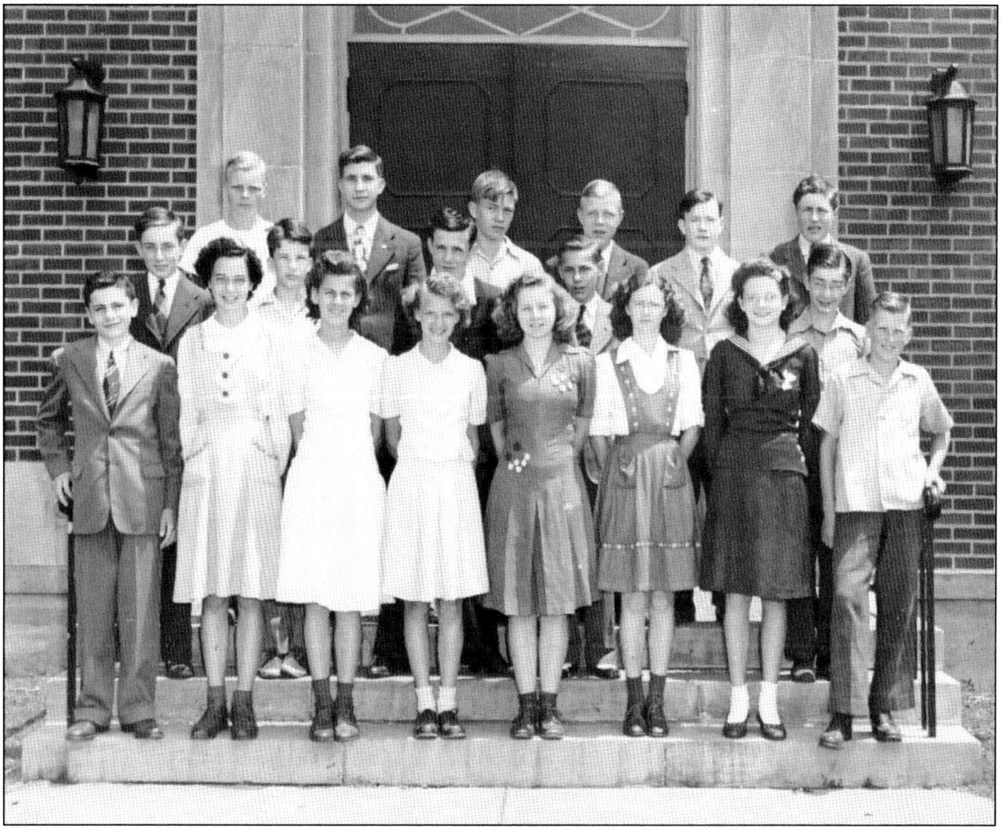

The conclusion of World War II marked the beginning of not only a baby boom, but also a housing boom in America. Little private housing had been built since 1929. This was the first time the full effect of Grand Island's bridges could be felt. Families poured in. It was really just the beginning, but the direction was clear. The 1944 graduating class at the Sidway School had 19 members. Five years later, the class of 1949 included 34 students. Total enrollment at Sidway in October 1949 was 493. Two years later it was 723.

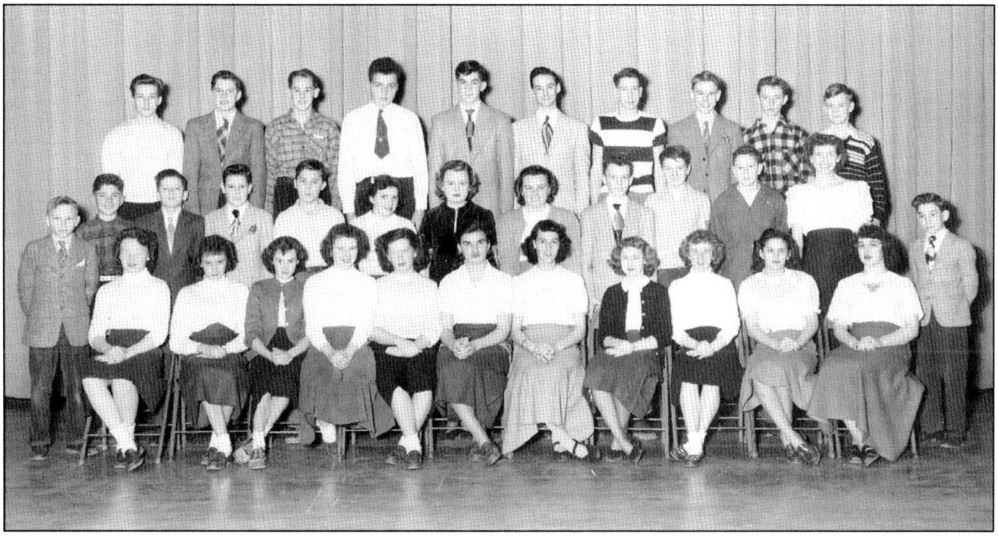

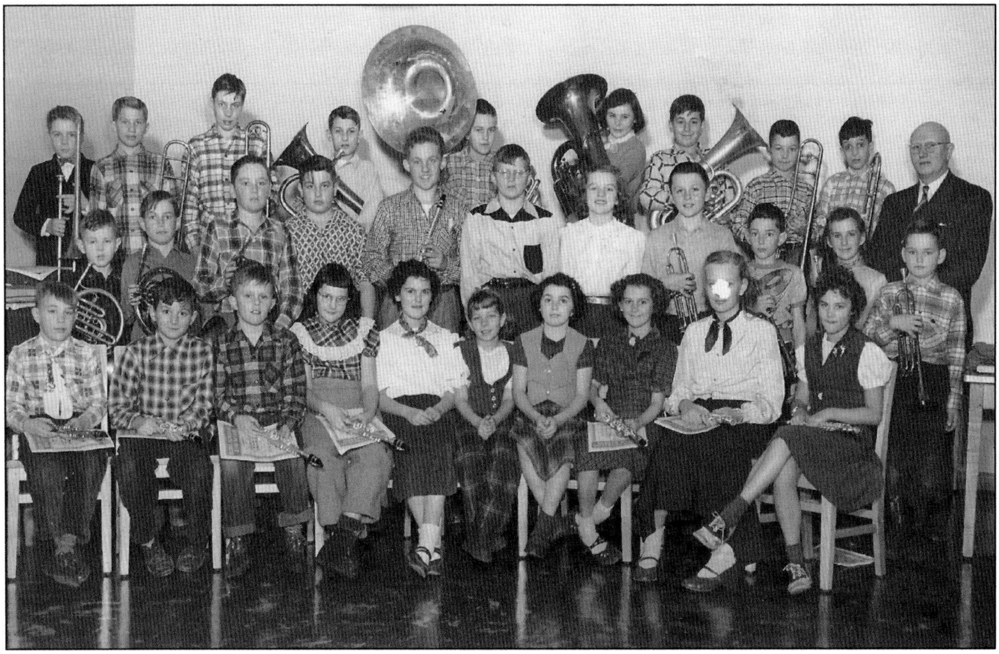

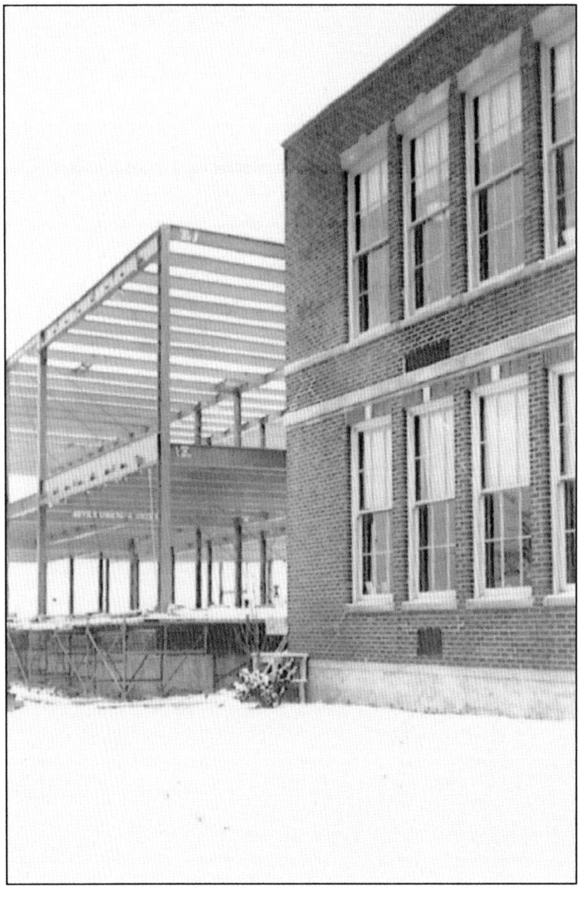

By 1950, four times as many people lived on the island as had been there before the bridges. Sidway School was feeling the effects. The 1951 school band, shown above with director William Pinkow (third row, far right), looks a little crowded.

With Grand Island's population tripling during the 1940s and then tripling again in the 1950s, the school district spent the first postwar decades racing to keep up, first by expanding the capacity of the Charlotte Sidway School. A second floor was added between 1946 and 1947, and a new wing was under construction by 1950. Additional schools would be needed soon.

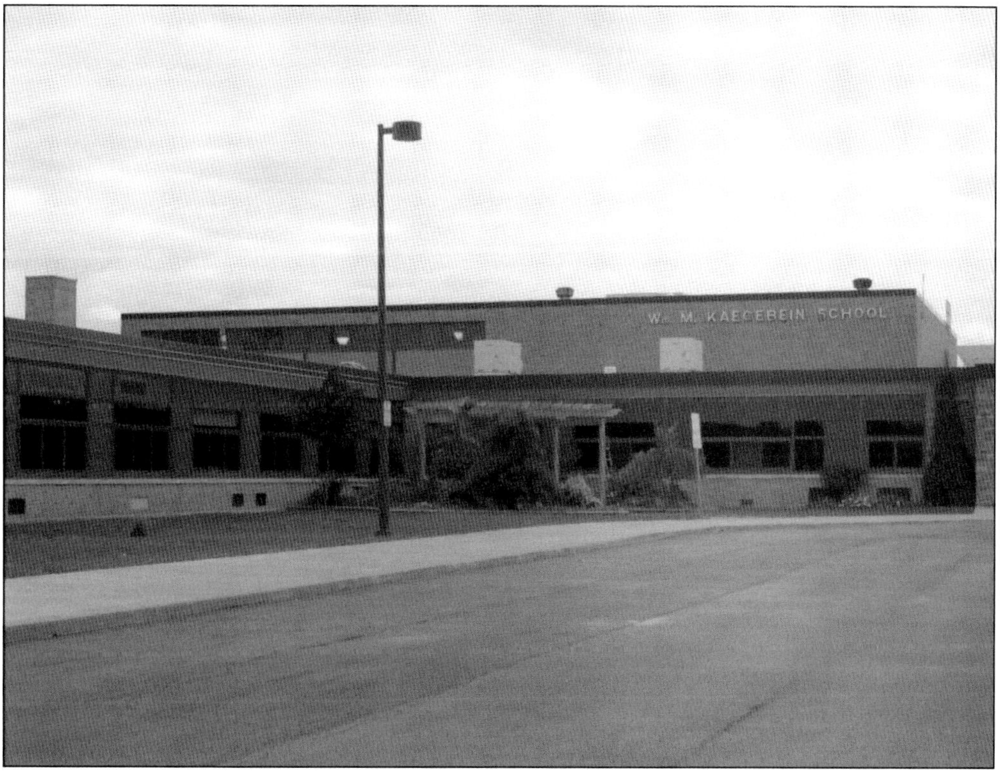

In 1953, a second large school opened and was named for William M. Kaegebein. In anticipation of additional room, Sidway School added a ninth grade class in 1950–1951, but older students still had to attend mainland high schools. It took a century to get from the first one-room schools to the consolidated Charlotte Sidway School in 1937. Nearly 20 years later, with the expanded version of that building bursting at the seams, Kaegebein School was a temporary solution. Construction continued, and a new high school was added in 1961.

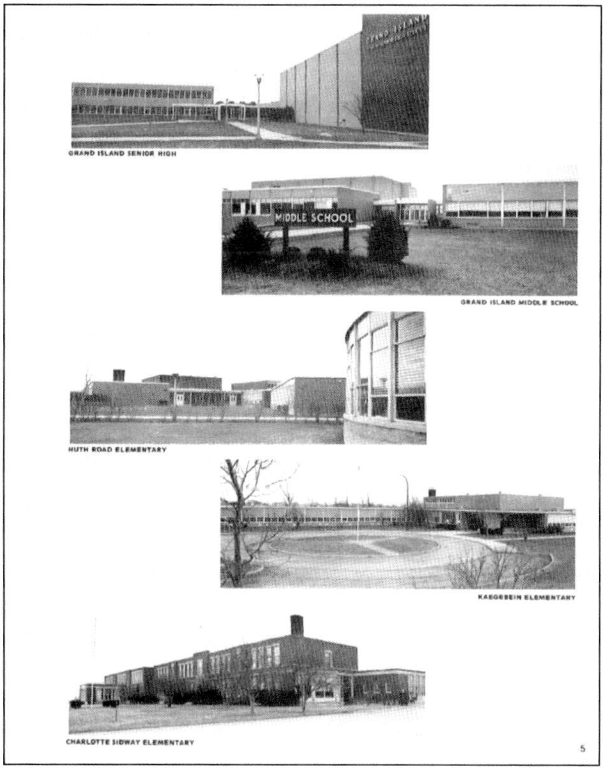

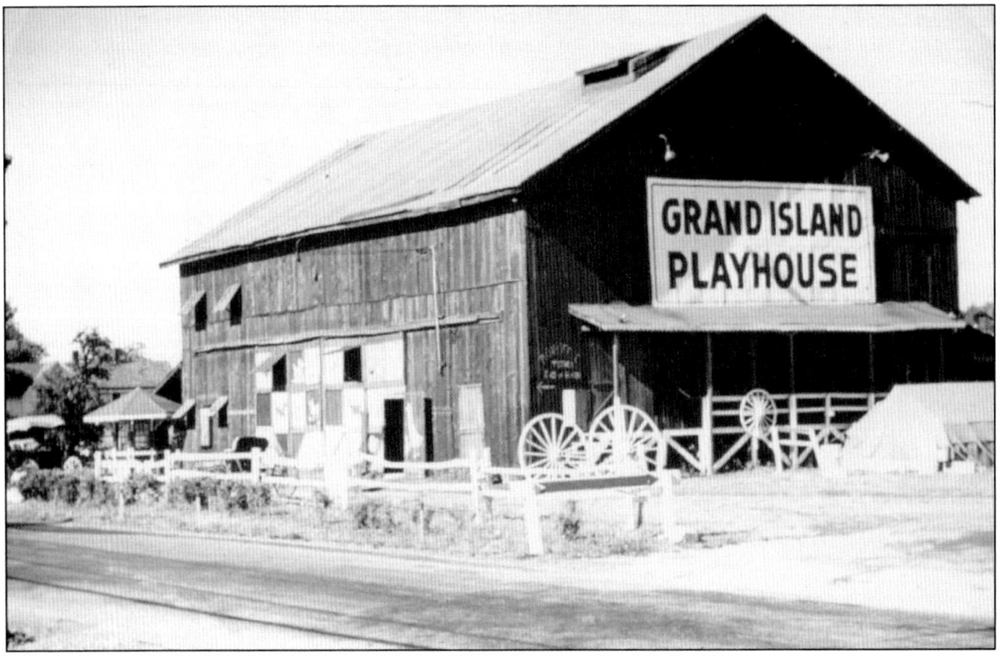

All this serious business did not mean that people on the island lacked a sense of humor. In 1948, an old barn on property belonging to the Long family at the corner of Baseline and Bedell Roads was converted into the Grand Island Playhouse. It became a big drawing card to the island with professional and semiprofessional players from the surrounding area bringing crowds several nights a week in the summers from 1948 through 1960. The building burned to the ground in 1969.

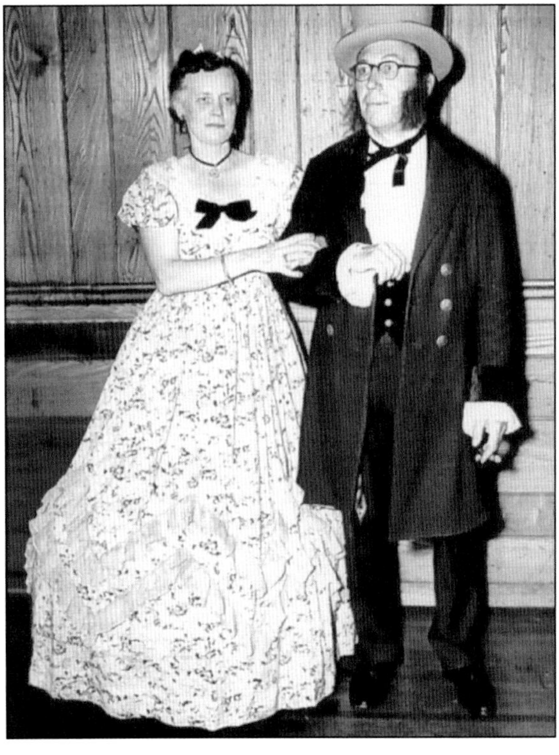

The Centennial Costume Ball kicked off a celebration of the town's 100th birthday. Peg and Roz Pfohl won the prize for the best costumes at the gala at the Beaver Island Casino. The next five days were filled with activities. A midway with carnival rides was open from early afternoon until midnight. Square dancing and fireworks competed with presentations of a historical pageant. Baseball games, wrestling matches, a greased pig catch, a Sadie Hawkins Race, and a pet show were offered. TB X-ray screening was offered as was an art, antique, and historical exhibition.

The highlight of the 1952 centennial celebration was the Grand Prix race sponsored by the Sports Car Club of America and the local Red Jacket Motor Club. The all-day event included races for different classes of cars as well as qualifying heats for the grand prix. The course included Whitehaven Road, East River Road, and Harvey Road before returning to Whitehaven. The big winner was Bill Spear of Connecticut, who finished just 30 feet in front of his nearest competitor. The event was a huge success, drawing a crowd of 100,000 at a time when the population of the island was just over 4,500.

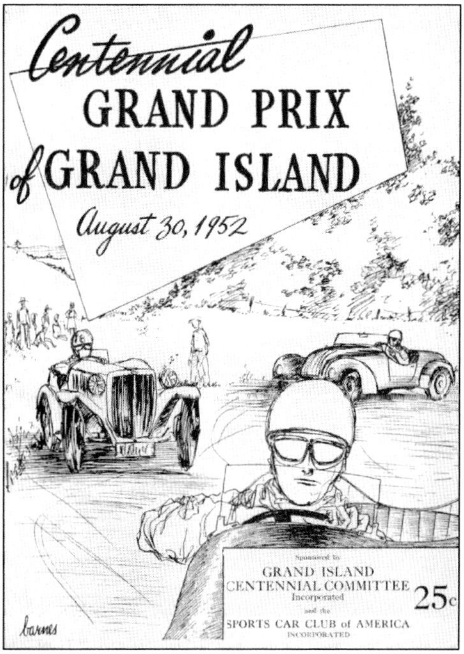

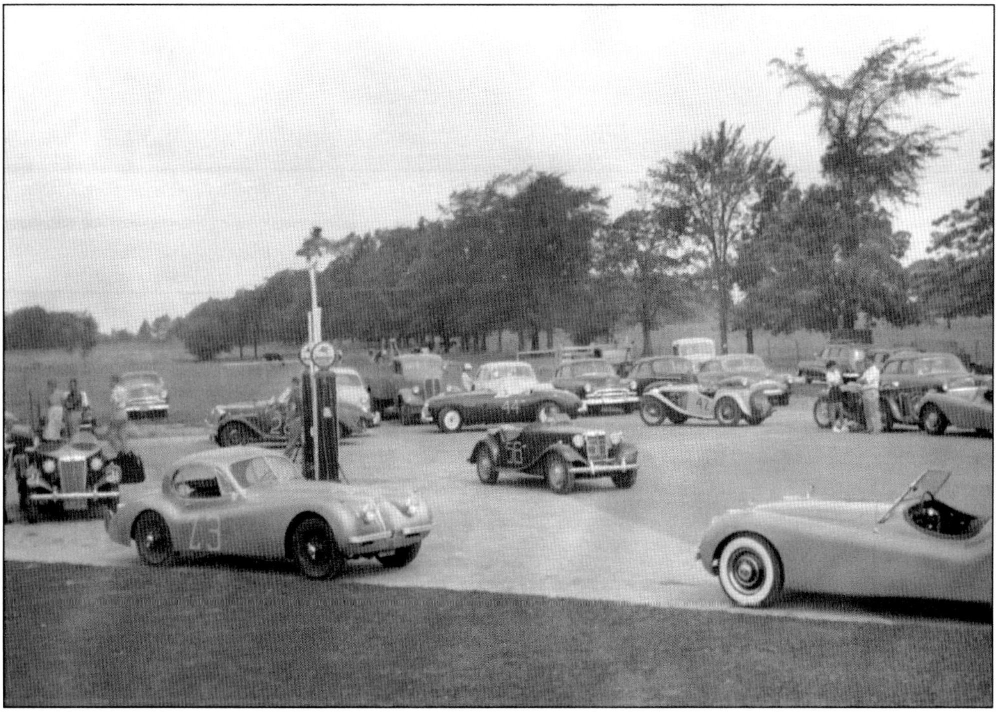

The drivers gathered at the Alt Chevrolet lot. The final race had an exciting finish, but the greatest excitement occurred in the second qualifying race. Richard Thierry of Norwich, Connecticut, driving the only Porsche in the race, hit a dip on Whitehaven Road just as he was preparing to pass the leader. At an estimated 110 miles per hour, the car veered into a ditch, launching it into the air. Somersaulting over the crowd, it crashed upside down on a car in a parking lot. Thierry survived. One spectator was injured by a piece of flying debris; amazingly no one died.

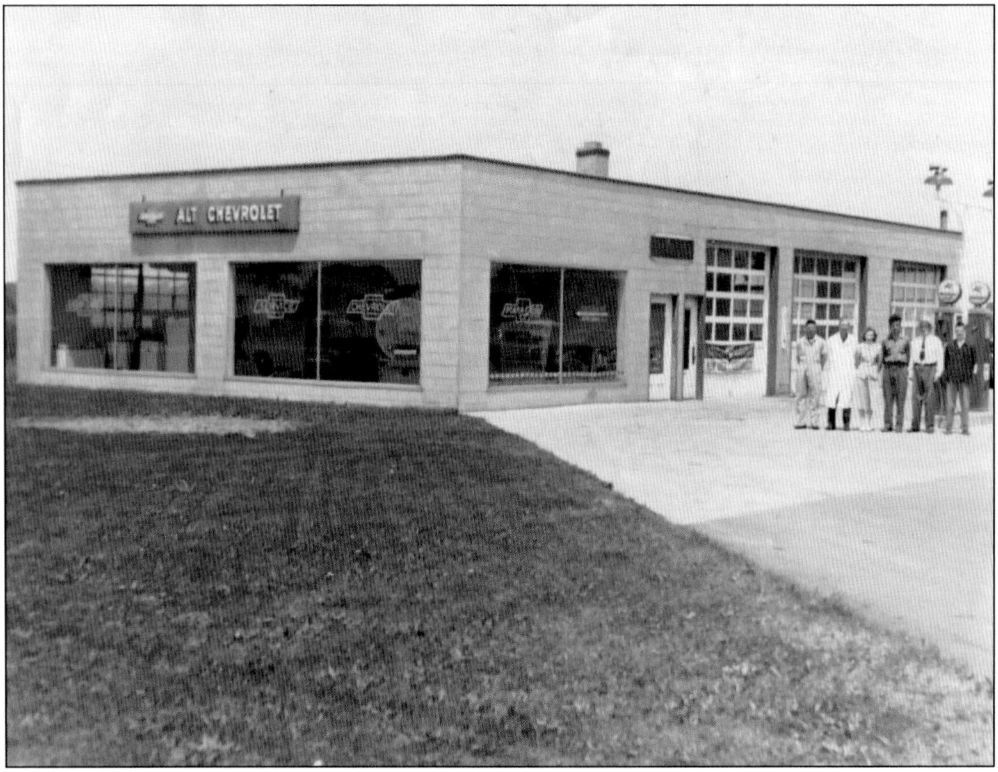

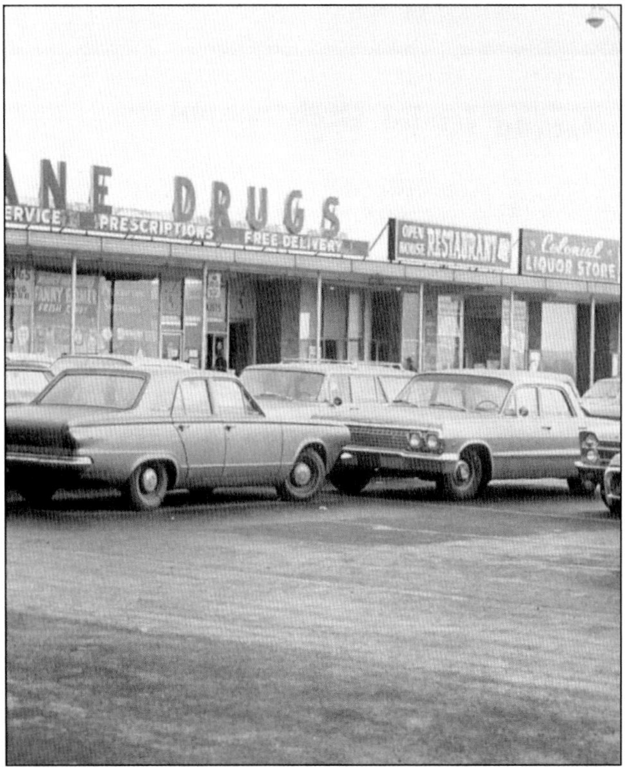

With a connection to the mainland available, Grand Islanders needed cars and everything that went with them. The Alt family, operators of a garage on the island since 1915, launched Alt Chevrolet on February 7, 1948. In 1952, Carl Weinheimer built Grandyle Plaza on Love Road. Grand Island Plaza opened in 1957, and the first tenant was Mancuso Brothers Barber Shop, followed by M&T Trust Bank. Next came Cataract Cleaners, Isle Hardware Corp., the Debbie Shop, Colony Men's & Boys Store, Lane Drug Store, NuWay, Richard Rays, Highland Boot Shop, and Island Radio & TV Service.

An early business was Gibco (Grand Island Biological Company). This led to the establishment of several other headquarters and production facilities for major pharmaceutical companies. Grand Island's locality makes it an ideal spot for trade in both the United States and Canada and ensures a supply of well-prepared professionals and staffers for the companies that locate here.

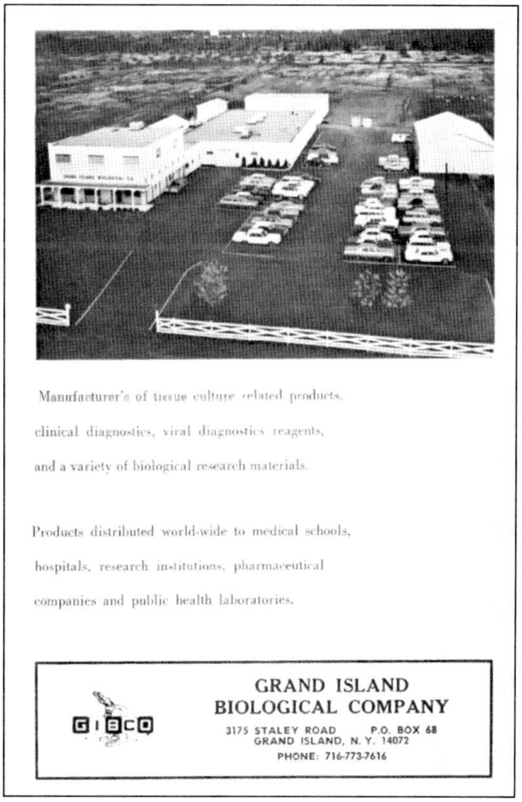

Another type of new business was radio station WBEN's transmission tower on the island. The town adopted a strategy of keeping commercial and government development closer to the interior, if possible, along the thruway connecting the two bridges.

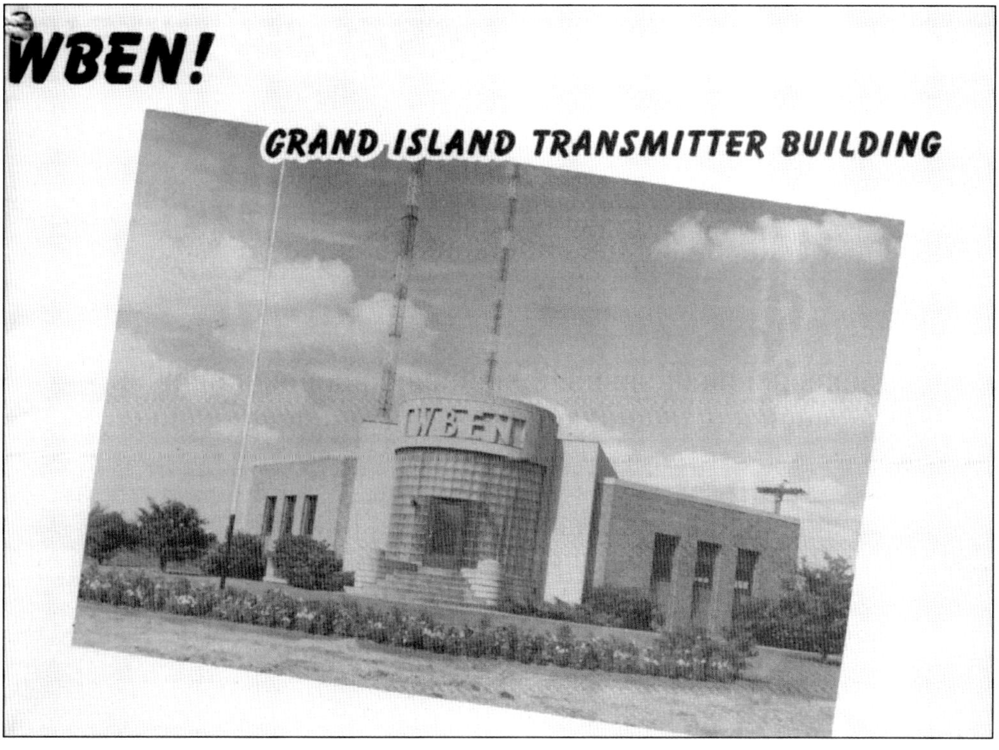

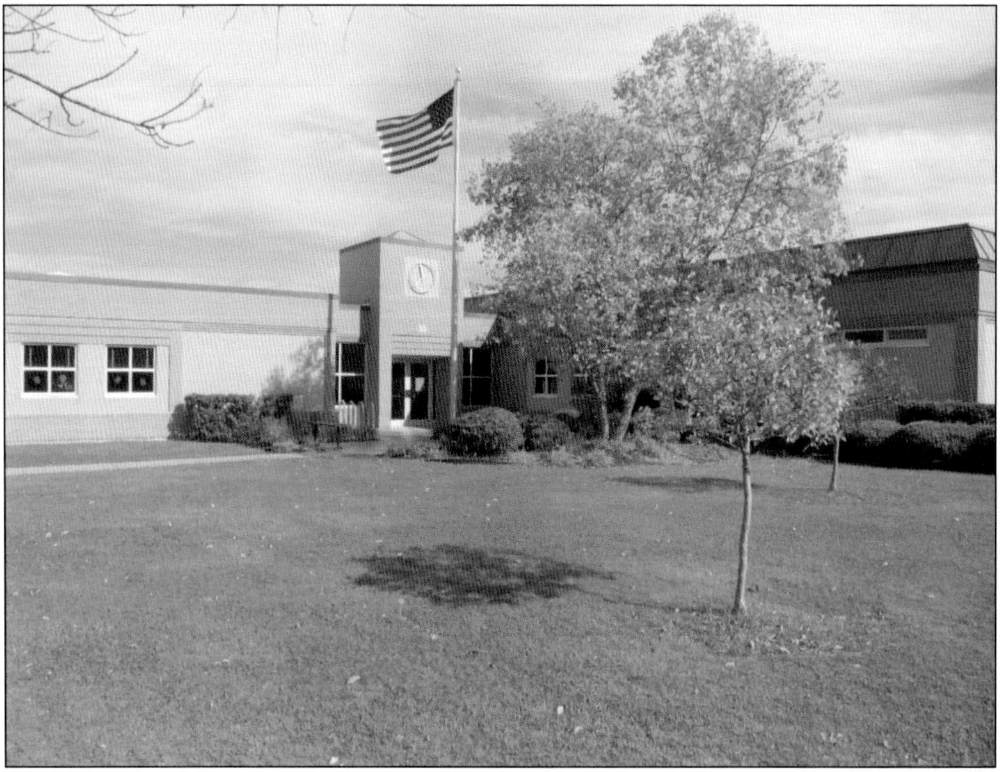

In 1945, Grand Island opened Memorial Library to honor those who served in World War II. The library was located in the basement of the town hall. Books were donated by residents, and in 1949, it became affiliated with the Erie County Library System. By 1968, a new library was opened on Ransom Road. The space that was vacated was soon put to use by town government in the modern town hall that provides all necessary services, including a courtroom.

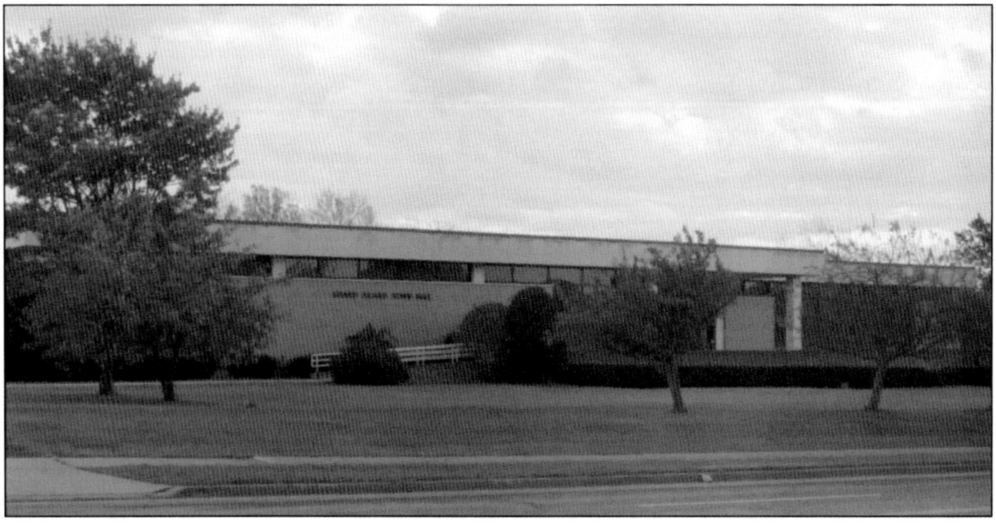

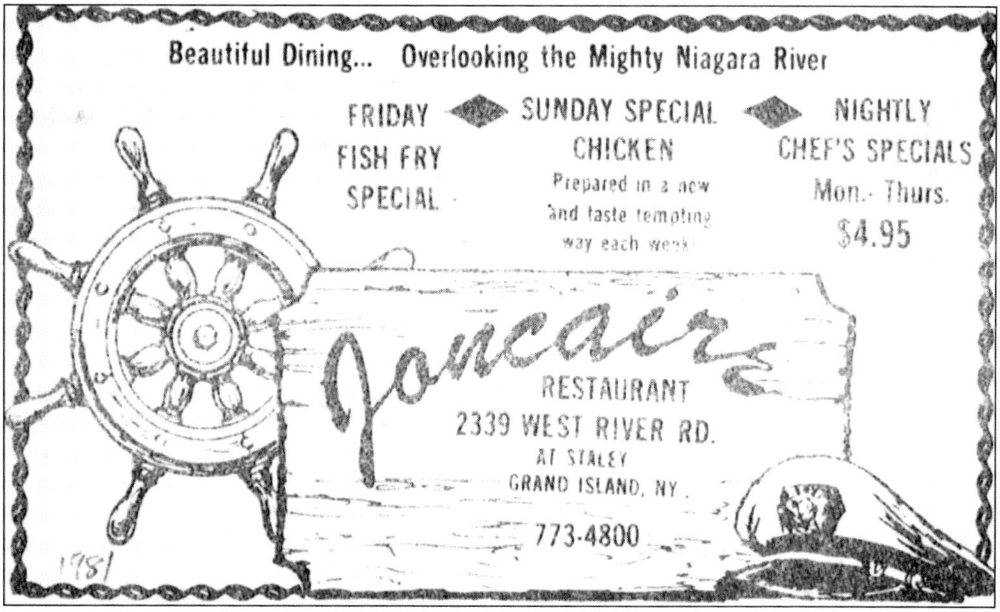

Bridges made it possible for more people to visit the island. Restaurants with a water view were especially popular. Joncaire, an old building that had once housed a delicatessen, was located on the corner of Staley Road and the West River, and the views from its windows were spectacular. Still standing is the Village Inn in Ferry Village. Always a great spot to spend an evening, it is located near the East River where the ferryboats docked in the original Ferry Village settlement.

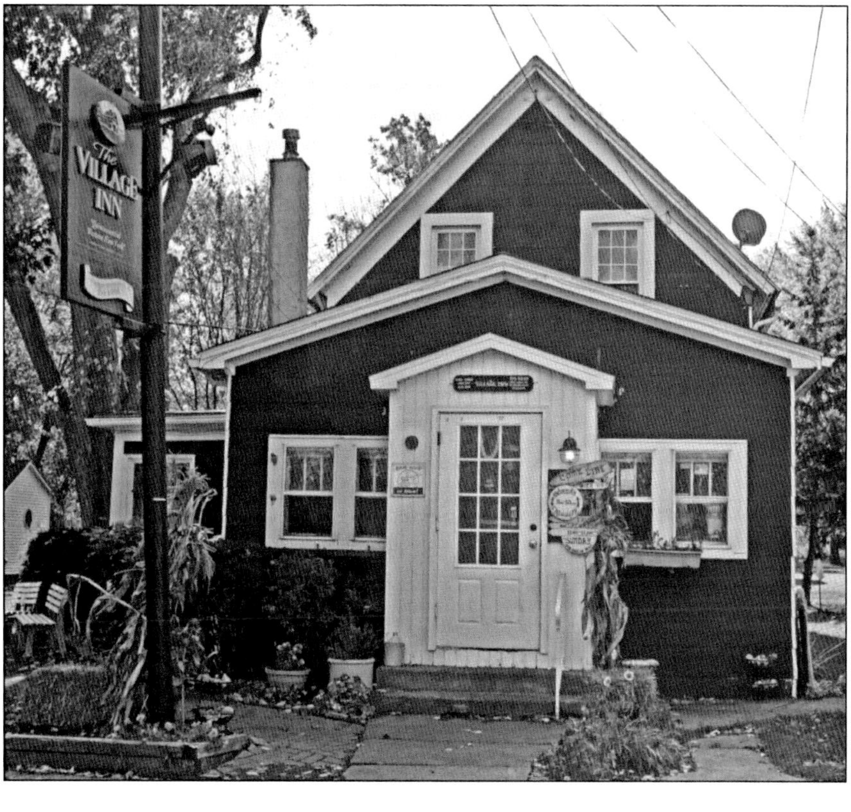

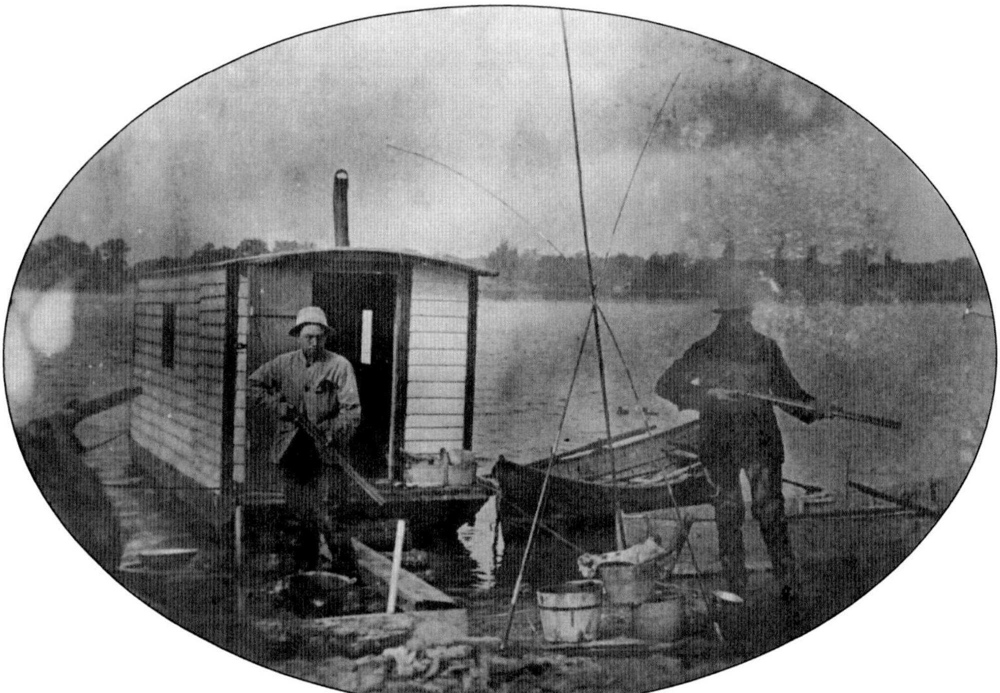

Grand Island has always been a great place to get away for some hunting and fishing or just to get back to nature. Distance from the mainland helped sustain the natural beauty of the island and psychologically magnified that sense of returning to an earlier time. G. Hilstrom and C. Medlecoth are pictured here camping at Burnt Ship Creek on the north end of the island. That was near Buckhorn Island State Park, begun in the 1930s and expanded in 1952 to preserve the natural state of its almost 900 acres of marsh and forest.

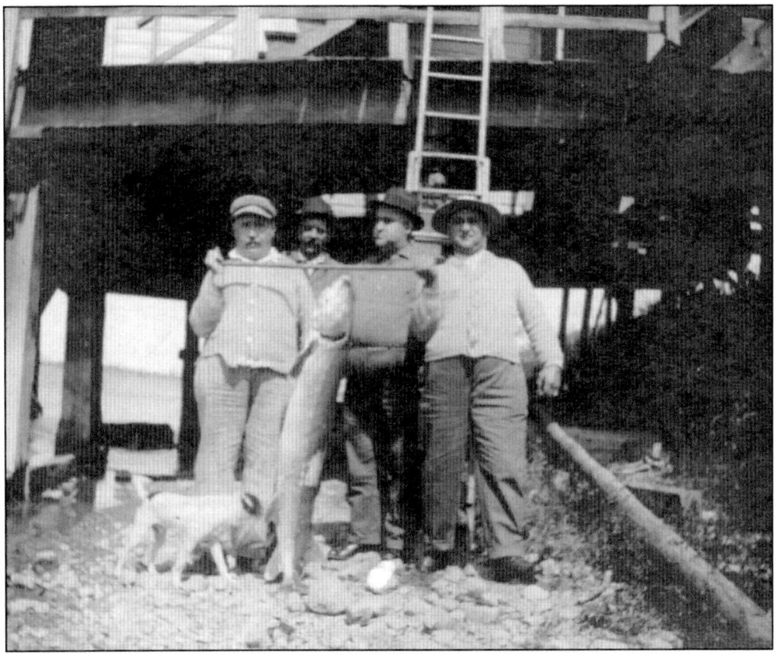

The park is not the only place to camp or fish. Two fishermen display their impressive catch years ago, but today's sportsmen still fish, hunt for fowl, practice at the gun club, ride snowmobiles, sail, kayak, motor in the river, and use the biking and hiking paths.

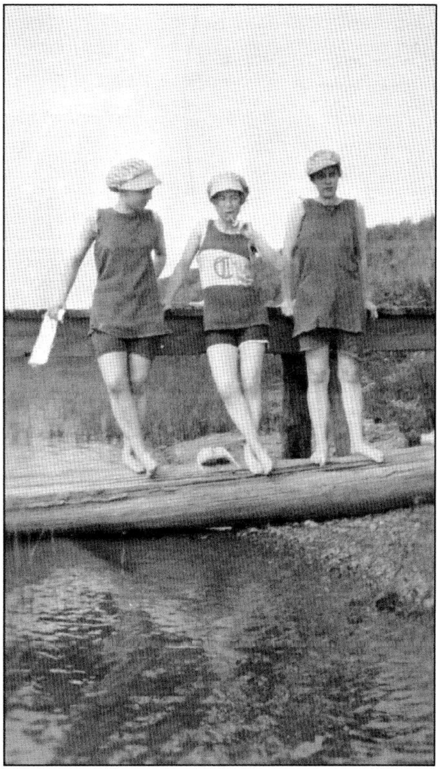

Swimming in the river has been the favorite pastime of islanders since the first settlers came here. From early groups enjoying themselves near the dock of the old Bedell House to today's visitors to Beaver Island State Park beach, the fun continues. On many evenings in the warm weather, divers can be seen prowling the waters of the mighty Niagara to see if they can find old coins, bottles, or other treasure left behind when ships sank in this area.

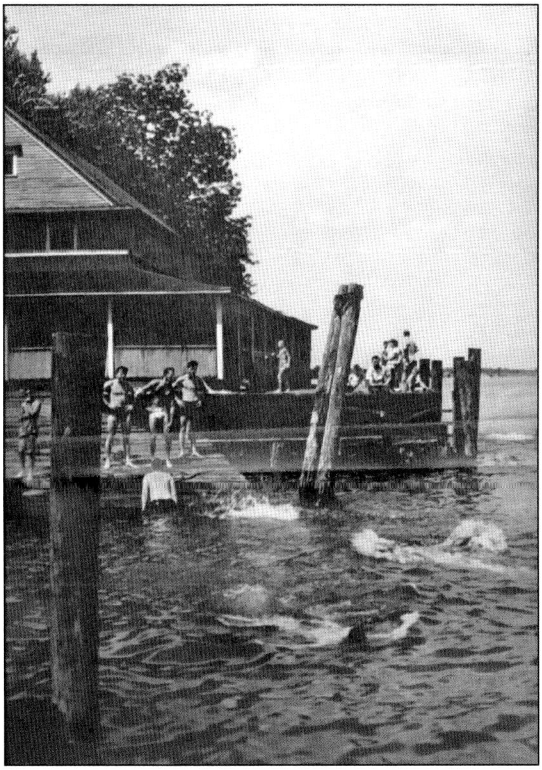

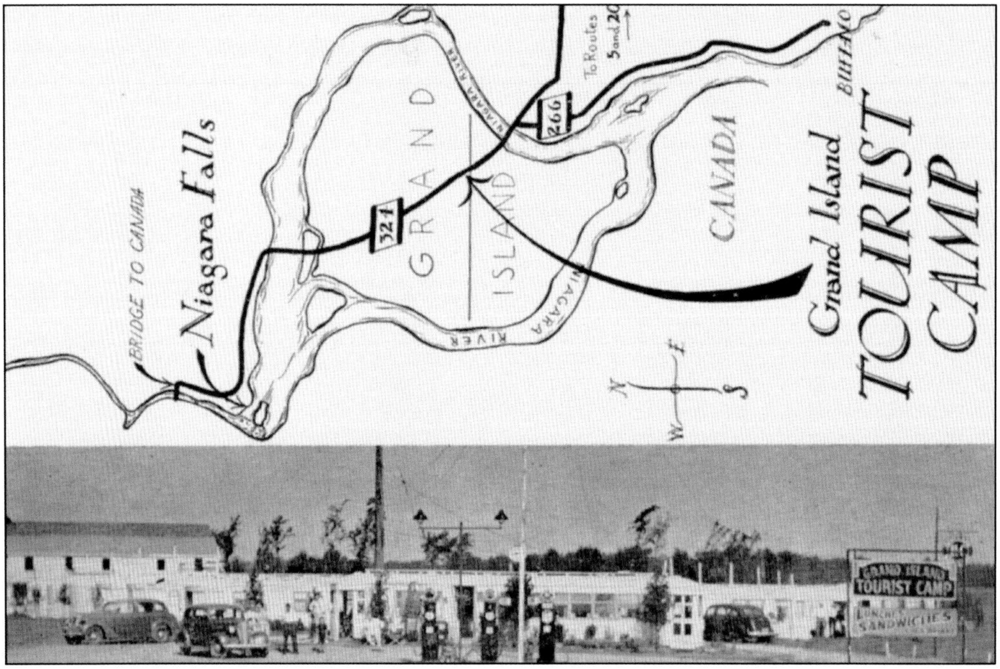

Grand Island is just a few minutes from a world wonder at Niagara Falls on the north, and Buffalo, the home of a treasure of historical buildings and other attractions, on the south. Tourist homes and hotels have attracted visitors for centuries. An early example was the Grand Island Tourist Camp, which featured "Simmons innerspring mattresses, modern toilets and showers, hot and cold running water in each room, and home cooking" in trailers that people could rent. The Cinderella Motel offers both rooms and campsites now and has been on the island for many years, but they no longer feature live peacocks as entertainment.

From the 1957 Grand Island Chamber of Commerce Directory:

...cnoski, Arthur S., 1157 East Park Rd. ....BRidge 49..
Cinderella Motel, 2797 Grand Island Blvd. ....BRidge 4095
..zek, Frank E., 2166 Long Rd. ....BRidge ...

From the 1969-70 Grand Island Chamber of Commerce Directory:

CINDERELLA MOTEL
and
MODERN CAMPSITE
Live Peacock Paradise
SWIMMING POOL
T.V. • RADIO • BATH • SHOWER
2797 GRAND ISLAND BOULEVARD
773-4095

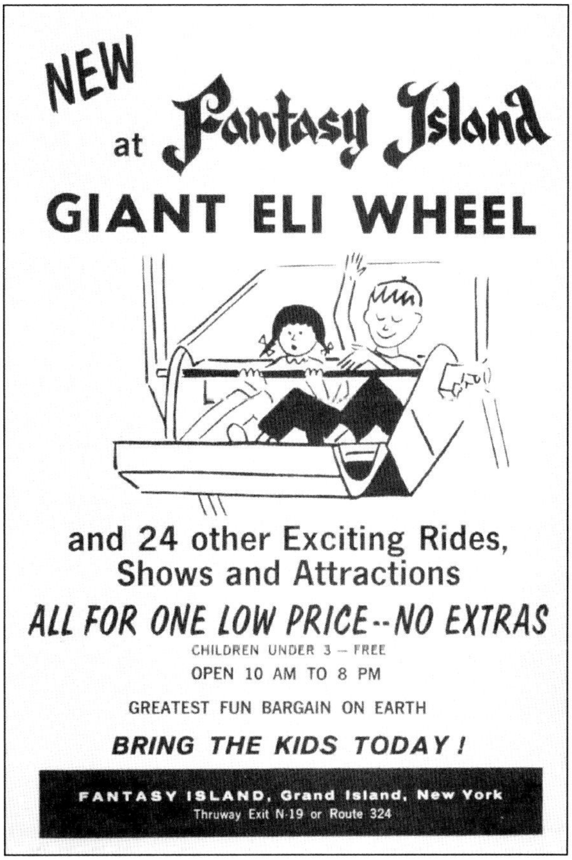

Some things never change, and one of those is the idea of Grand Island as a place for fun at amusement parks. Fantasy Island opened its gates on Grand Island Boulevard in 1961. There were financial problems, but in 1994 local businessman Martin Dipietro restored the original name, while adding his own. The souvenir photograph booklet celebrated the original opening. For Grand Islanders, Fantasy Island is not a postponed dream. The island lifestyle includes the amusement park, the wonders of nature, the joy of living near water, and the opportunity to share in a rich history.

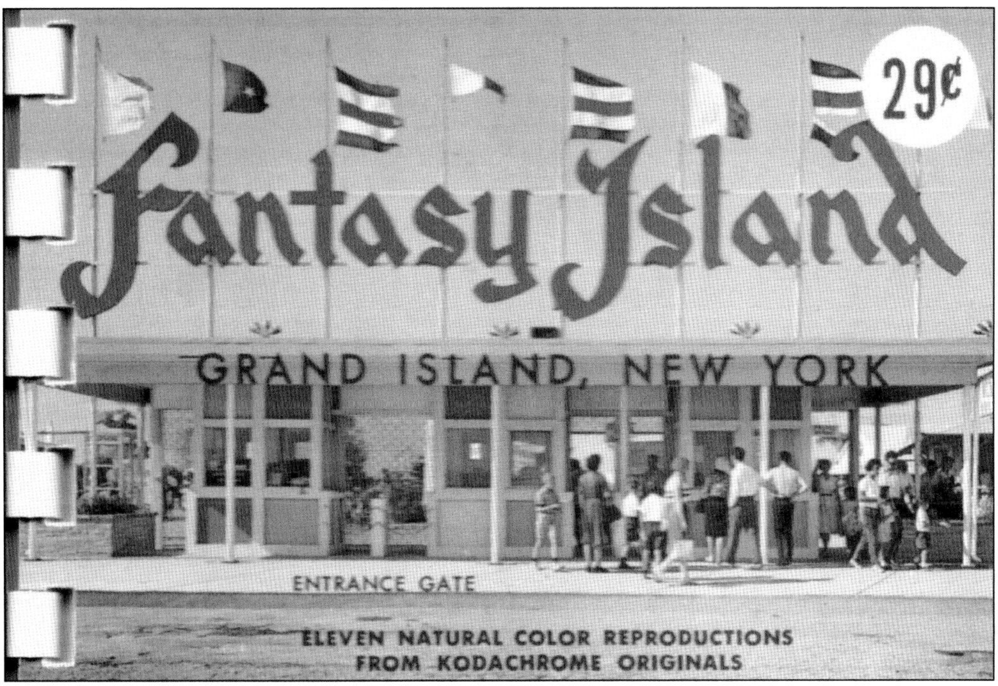